PREVENTING VIOLENCE, CARING FOR SURVIVORS

PREVENTING VIOLENCE, CARING FOR SURVIVORS

Role of Health Profession and Services in Violence

Editors

Amar Jesani

Padma Deosthali

Neha Madhiwalla

Publications

KALPAZ PUBLICATIONS

NEW DELHI - 110052

Preventing Violence, Caring for Servivors
Role of Health Profession and Services in Violence

Rs. 750

ISBN : 81-7835-296-6

Published in 2004 in India by

Kalpaz Publications,

C-30, Satyawati Nagar,

New Delhi-110 052

Email : kalpaz@hotmail.com

Lasertype Setting by: *Tact Computer Graphics*, Delhi

Printed at: Mehra Offset Press, Delhi

Contents

Preface

It is with great pleasure that we release this book based on the deliberations of the international conference on the role of doctors in caring for survivors of torture. The conference, organised by CEHAT in December 1998, raised crucial issues pertaining to the social responsibilities of the medical profession. Important presentations in the form of papers, posters, training workshops, exhibitions, audio-visuals and cultural events, all added up to pointing towards the malady that affects health professionals and the innovative ways in which campaigns and struggles have been conducted by people all over the world for a just, diverse and non-violent society.

Many new developments have taken place in India and around the world during the past five years. Unfortunately, the gains have been fewer than the losses. Health sector reforms and privatisation of health services has adversely affected the well-being of millions of people in India. The regulation of the private sector in India is long overdue. Irrational and unduly expensive treatment in the form of unnecessary injections and intravenous saline drips is extremely common in private hospitals. With private medical insurance covering hospital bills, over-medicalisation and over-charging of patients with paying capacity increases evermore. People, especially the poorest get into severe debt when a family member falls ill. We have witnessed numerous instances, when patients have been retained in private hospitals until they have spent their last rupee and then are sent off to public hospitals, so that the death gets registered in a government set up. This creates further mistrust for the crumbling public health services in the minds of the poor and allows the private sector to go unquestioned.

On the one hand poor women do not have adequate access to Caesarean sections during childbirth, whereas on the other hand, the rate of C-sections in private hospitals is on an alarmingly high rise. Equally disturbing is the rising rate of hysterectomies in the private sector. Younger and younger women are counselled to have their uterii removed, especially after they have been tubectomised. The attitude of rendering certain organs useless has also resulted in routine hysterectomies of mentally challenged girls in State run homes in India. This risky intervention has been carried out in the name of better management and good of the young wards. Simultaneously, doctors have also been involved in surreptitiously removing saleable organs such as kidneys of poor patients who have little recourse to legal redress.

The regulation of the medical profession is crucial in the absence of internal controls within the profession. Doctors desist from displeasing each other and defend their colleagues for various reasons, in spite of known instances of ethical violations or medical malpractice. Irrational medical practice, such as the routine usage of electro convulsive therapy, for example is rarely questioned. Not a single doctor was booked under the Pre-Natal Diagnostic Techniques (PNDT) Act, 1994 even though the identity of doctors performing foetal sex-determination is generally known within the profession. This unholy solidarity, combined with the apathy of State prompted some of us (CEHAT, MASUM and Dr. Sabu George) to file a public interest litigation in the Supreme Court of India in 2000. Similarly, the reluctance of the Medical Council of India to take timely action on the petition of the Medico Friend Circle against the virulent Hindu right-wing spokesperson (international secretary of the Vishwa Hindu Parishad – World Hindu Forum) and cancer specialist, Dr. Pravin Togadia, has led the MFC to approach the National Human Rights Commission (NHRC) as well.

This brings us to the issue of understanding the role of doctors in perpetuating dominant ideologies. The class and caste background of the medical profession manifests itself in the form of numerous biases against the poor, the minorities and women. For long, doctors in India have been active participants and proponents in population control activities of the State. The abysmal condition of the sterilisation camps for poor women has not deterred doctors from performing dozens (even hundreds) of tubectomies per day. Abortions in the public sector are often linked to tubal ligations or long-acting provider controlled contraceptives, reducing women's access to safe and inexpensive abortions, forcing them to use the private sector instead. The patriarchal bias is also revealed when the husband's signature is asked for (contrary to the law) at the time of abortion. The curious mix of modern technology and son-preference has resulted in doctors using amniocentesis and ultra-sonography for pre-natal sex-determination in India. The tragico-comic involvement of some surgeons in hymenoplasty (repairing the torn hymen) came into the public eye in the

1980s in Bombay, bringing to the fore the ingenuity of the medical profession in "creating virgins" for the marriage market.

The role of doctors in 'fixing deviants' is evident in the case of homosexuality, where aversion therapy and psychotherapy are used to browbeat people into heterosexual behaviour. With repressive laws related to homosexuality being operational in many countries, including in India, this inhuman and irrational medical intervention gets further legitimised. Similarly surgeons intervene at the time of birth to decide the sex of intersexual babies so that every individual fits into the straitjacket of the highly gendered two-sex norm. Later on, geneticists and endocrinologists "determine" the sex of biologically diverse people on the basis of chromosomes and hormone levels, placing them into firm male or female categories. The tyranny of biology is also evident in the fact that transsexuals such as hijras are registered as female in a hospital setting (since they are castrated males who opt to live a woman's life), but often get placed in male in-patient wards because of resistance from other women patients !

Historically, the medical profession has contributed both to progressive struggles as well as to reactionary ideology. The willing participation in and the active contribution of doctors to Nazi ideology has been well documented. During the carnage of Muslims in Gujarat in 2002, atleast three medical doctors participated in instigating and leading raging mobs into minority dominated neighbourhoods. Even public hospitals had become 'communalised', reducing people's access to life-saving interventions, fairly conducted autopsies and medico-legal documentation of physical and sexual assaults. Doctors who cared for victims from the minority community, were often threatened by Hindu right wing forces. There have been documented cases of patients being attacked by mobs inside hospitals and in one case, even in an operation theatre. Reports by the Medico Friend Circle and many other progressive organisations pointed towards a public health crisis, following the large-scale violence in Gujarat.

This State-sponsored pogrom made it impossible for victims and survivors to seek humane treatment, let alone legal redress and social justice. The fact that women can be specially targeted during mass ethnic violence and in conflict situations was neither understood nor addressed. Doctors also actively participated in the torture of those who were arrested for having allegedly set on fire a compartment of the train carrying Hindu right-wing followers. Sodium pantethenol (the so-called truth serum) was administered to some of the accused in order to gain "true confessions", inspite of the fact that this is a potentially life-threatening drug and its scientific applicability in extracting truth highly suspect.

With the Indian State increasingly becoming more draconian, the medical profession will have to take a clear position that is consistent with the Hippocratic Oath. The legitimisation of torture and killings of political opponents as well as the desensitisation of civil society on the treatment meted out to alleged terrorists (whether through 'encounter' deaths or through torture), or force-feeding of hunger strikers cannot be allowed to be conducted with the involvement of doctors.

The present government has been pressing for capital punishment for rape (women's groups, along with civil liberties groups have actively opposed this move), but not a single person has even been booked (let alone tried) for rape in the Gujarat carnage. Ironically, the Indian State, as it gets more repressive and intrusive in the name of law and order, has withdrawn from its social welfare commitment (in the name of health sector reforms) by introducing user fees in public hospitals, reducing budgetary allocations to health and education and by privatising government hospitals. Thus, paying for health care at one end and exorbitantly high tuition fees for medical education at the other end has accelerated the commercialisation of health care delivery. Furthermore, private medical insurance is gaining considerable ground in India, resulting in increased utilisation of the private sector, leaving the poor and destitute to fend for themselves in the resource-starved public hospitals. This is a clear violation of people's right to life and dignity. It is commendable that doctors and medical students in Tamil Nadu went on a strike in early 2003 (which the state government crushed) against the privatisation of medical colleges.

The repression of NGOs working on issues of HIV-AIDS and sexuality needs mention here. Internationally, India has shown its commitment to working on AIDS-related work, whereas internally it has arrested, humiliated and harassed organisations involved in condom distribution, research and empowerment of dalits and women in prostitution.

The denial of basic needs and political rights to people based on the number of children is also an alarming trend. The access of the third child (and subsequent children) to the subsidised foodgrains through the Public Distribution System has been curtailed. There is a clear inclination on the part of the government to deny maternity benefits to women from the third child onwards. When a miniscule number of women in India have access to maternity benefits in the first place, the State is expected to universalise this right, rather than withdraw it. Rights once given, cannot be taken away; they can only be further expanded. The fact that people's right to contest political elections is being taken away, based on the number of children they have, is even more disturbing. Not surprisingly, this move has affected people (especially women) from oppressed class and caste groups the most. In spite of its progressive commitment towards reproductive rights (during the ICPD conference in Cairo in 1994), India still maintains the incentive-disincentive based target approach in family planning.

The ideology of population control has now in fact become a killing machine. The eugenic, ethnic and religious biases play out during riots and hate-speeches, wherein the majority religion is warned about the minority taking over the country numerically. Unfortunately, most professionals, including doctors believe this too.

Violence as a public health and human rights issue is still not addressed within the clinic setting. Doctors are reluctant to take on the responsibility of attending court sessions or taking a stand against locally powerful groups (or families); thus the medico-legal documentation of rapes, suicides, homicide, deaths in police custody, caste or communal violence is not undertaken with the seriousness it deserves. A doctor's studied evidence in any of the above instances can make a crucial difference to the lives and dignity of the community. Women from marginalised sections, such as those living in poverty and destitution, in prisons, in an asylum, on the streets, in prostitution, in state run homes as well as women who do not conform to social norms, marriage or heterosexuality are at a greater risk of family and societal violence. These are the very groups that are rendered invisible, who face discrimination and who are further neglected or abused in clinic settings. Since doctors are usually the first contact persons after an episode of violence, their timely and sensitive intervention can make life bearable for the victim / survivor as well as increase her or his chances of demanding justice. Often health professional are neither sensitised nor trained to deal with conflict situations (war, military occupation, racial or ethnic violence etc.), leaving victimised sections of society completely bereft of humane treatment and medico-legal documentation.

The two-fold connection between health and violence also needs to be addressed by health professionals. Violence resulting in physical injury, emotional and psychological trauma and sexual assault – the unspeakable crime, need sensitive interventions from the medical profession. On the other hand, ill-health is known to precipitate violence. Pregnancy and disclosure of illness can make a person more vulnerable to beatings, desertion and severe harm, including suicide and homicide. Routine HIV testing done on pregnant women during their ANC visits (often without the knowledge and consent of the woman) predictably precipitates an unexpected and overwhelming crisis in the woman's life. Feelings of betrayal, denial, confusion, anger, suicidal feelings, ambiguity about continuing the pregnancy, having to confront the husband or partner, fear of having to deal with the family and so on are only to be expected after the HIV positive status is declared. Pre and post-test counselling for the woman and her partner are conspicuous by their absence in the clinic setting, at least in the public hospitals. The medical profession also needs to be sensitive to the fact that mental illness (real or alleged) can be used against a woman when the custody of children is being argued out in court. Confidentiality thus becomes crucial in such cases.

At the same time, gendered roles within the health care delivery system also need to be addressed squarely. The position of nurses (especially ANMs) is rather precarious within the system, in the community as well as in her own home. Sexual harassment within the set up cannot be ignored any more and a credible grievance redressal system needs to be placed in order.

During the past few years, there have been several attempts to influence providers of health care. Nation-wide trainings to sensitise public health professionals on the issue of gender have been undertaken with great commitment and rigour. This input is bound to have a positive impact sooner or later. Similarly, the experience of CEHAT's one stop crisis centre, Dilaasa, located in a municipal hospital in Mumbai has shown that change is possible once the active participation of all the hospital staff on the issue of violence against women is sought. Regular training on perspective, information and skills on how to get the various departments (casualty and emergency, obstetrics and gynaecology, psychiatry, burns, orthopaedics, paediatrics and so on) to work together results not only in quick treatment, but also in being sensitive about issues such as confidentiality, medico-legal documentaion and family dynamics.

The campaign to the right to health care has been taken up in India since 2000. Auditing the public health services, raising public pressure on making comprehensive health services available, accessible, answerable and affordable universally as well as monitoring the private sector for irrational and unduly expensive treatment are some of the strategies utilised by the campaign. With the campaign gaining momentum, public hearings (Jan Sunwai) of denial of health care resulting in death, permament disability, chronic health problems, financial distress and or psychological trauma have been organised. One such hearing took place before the National Human Rights Commission (NHRC) in September 2003. District and state wide public hearings are due to take place in the first quarter of 2004 as well. The contemptuous behaviour of doctors and other health staff towards poor patients, refusing to take in women for delivery, refusing emergency care (burns, accidents, suicidal or homicidal attempts, snake and dog bites etc), verbal and physical violence towards women in childbirth as well as getting women to sign up for tubectomy during labour pains are some of the depressing issues one has to contend with during these hearings.

The Indian government has ratified international treaties that concern civil, political, economic, social and cultural rights. In this background, the right to health care is thus a plausible and legitimate demand to make. In fact, the denial of the right to quality health care needs to be constructed as a violation of people's right to life and dignity. Poverty, the greatest structural violence of all, needs to be challenged and governments made answerable for what they do as well as for what they do not do.

While the struggle is certainly not over, the march has definitely begun. We have moved a long way from the traditional understanding of torture in the human rights framework. Non state actors are being made accountable for violations of human rights and affirmative expectations from the State are being articulated. People's right to health care (and to health) have now become commonplace words, thanks to the tireless campaigns around these issues. The medical profession needs to join hands in this struggle, especially in the era of globalisation and privatisation at one end and the resurgence of obscurantist science and medicine (in the name of reviving ancient cultural practices) on the other hand.

We hope that the dialogue that began in 1998 continues during the years to come. It is with this hope and assurance that we present to you some of the papers presented in the international conference on the role of doctors in caring for survivors of torture and violence.

Manisha Gupte

Trustee, Anusandhan Trust

Acknowledgements

The CEHAT had undertaken the task of organising an international conference on "Preventing Violence, Caring for Survivors" from November 28-30, 1998 with trepidation. At that time, CEHAT was only three-and-a-half years old, was struggling to survive, and its staff was young and inexperienced. In fact, much before its establishment in April 1994, some of its staff members and trustees were active participants in people's and human rights movements, and they have brought this sense of deep commitment to health and human rights to CEHAT. The staff and trustees tirelessly worked together to make the conference memorable.

The participants at the conference showed that there was a great wealth of experiential and theoretical understanding in India about health, health care, violence and human rights. They responded to the conference call with overwhelming enthusiasm. We, at CEHAT, had planned the conference for only 100 participants, but at the end, we had over 225 of them. They brought over 90 papers and extracts, and made presentations in various sessions of the conference. They also brought a lot of invaluable literature for the participants. They indeed gave content and meaning to the conference. We thank all of them. We also thank those participants who volunteered to chair the sessions, did reporting, and assisted in various other works. All the organisations—be they from India or abroad—participated in a true spirit of solidarity and shared their experiences. They too deserve our thanks.

We were especially supported in our work by Honourable Justice V.S. Malimath, the then member of the National Human Rights Commission (New Delhi), Honourable Justice B.N. Srikrishna, Judge of the Bombay High Court, Dr. Adriaan van Es, Secretary General of International Federation of Health and Human Rights Organisation (IFHHRO) (Netherlands), Ms Bonoo Sen, member secretary, National Commission for Women (New Delhi), Mr Jaap Walkate, Chairperson, United Nation's Fund for Victims of Torture (Geneva), Ms Ann Sommeville, British Medical Association (London), Dr James Welsh, Amnesty International (London),

Ms Sussannah Sirkin, Physicians for Human Rights (USA), Dr Iris Tetford, World Health Organisation (Geneva). We thank them for their constant support and for their presence and contributions to the conference. There were many others who were prevented from participating in the conference as they were denied visas. They include representatives of Treatment and Rehabilitation Centre for Torture Victims (RCT), (Denmark), International Council of Red Cross (Geneva), Amnesty International (London), Physicians for Human Rights (London), and many more. We regret that we could not help them enough to be with us, and thank their supportive messages to the conference. A special mention must be made of Mr Joep Toebosch (Commonwealth Human Rights Initiative) who encouraged us in the preparation of the conference, and assisted us whenever we needed support.

Lastly, the conference would not have been possible without the financial assistance of Actionaid (Bangalore), Ford Foundation (New Delhi), MacArthur Foundation (New Delhi), Swissaid (Mumbai) and IFHHRO (Netherlands). We thank them all.

List of Contributors

1. **A. K. Jayasree**
   FIRM (Foundation for Integrated Research in Mental Health), Kannammoola, Medical College PO, Thiruvananthapuram 695011, Kerala, India.

2. **Achala S. Daga, Shireen J. Jejeebhoy, Shantha Rajgopal**
   Contact: Dr. Achla Daga, Dept of Preventive and Social Medicine, Grant Medical College, Mumbai 400008, Maharashtra, India.

3. **Alex George**
   CHAI (Catholic Health Association of India), P.Box 2126, Gunrock Enclave, Secundrabad 500003, Andhra Pradesh, India.

4. **Ali Asghar**
   COVA (Confederation of Voluntary Agencies), 20-4-10, Near Bus Stand, Charminar, Hyderabad 500002, Andhra Pradesh, India.

5. **Amar Jesani**
   Coordinator, CEHAT, Mumbai, India.

6. **Ann Sommerville**
   Head, Medical Ethics, British Medical Association, BMA House, Tavistock Square, London WC 1H, 9JP, UK.

7. **Binoo Sen**
   Member Secretary, National Commission for Women, 4, Deen Dayal Upadhyaya Marg, New Delhi 110 002, India.

8. **Françoise Sironi**
   Dircctor, Centre George Devereux, University Paris 8, 2 rue de la Liberte, 93256 - Saint Devis, France.

9. **H. S. Dhavale, Leena Damani, Jhanavi Kedare, Shanu Jethani**
   Contact– Dr H.S. Dhavale: Department of Psychiatry, T.N. Medical College, Nair Hospital, Mumbai 400034, Maharashtra, India.

10. **Helen Sheehan**
    Department of Sociology & Anthropology, St. John's University, 8000, Utopia Parkway, Jamaica, NY 11439, USA.

11. **Herat R. Parmar**

    4/34, Ramgiri, 7th Road, Opp. Sindhuwadi, Ghatkopar East, Mumbai 400077, Maharashtra, India.

12. **Jaap A. Walkate**

    Chairperson, The Board of Trustees, UN Voluntary Fund for Victims of Torture, Geneva, Switzerland.

13. **John Chisholm**

    British Medical Association, BMA House, Tavistock Square, London WC 1H, 9JP, UK.

14. **Kamala Ganesh**

    SACH (Society for Action in Community Health), D-1, Gulmohar Park, New Delhi 110049, Delhi, India.

15. **Kishwar Ahmed-Shirali**

    ASK (Atma Swasthya Kendra), 208 Rakkad Road, V.P.O. Sidhbari (Kangra), Dharmashala Tehsil 176057, Himachal Pradesh, India.

16. **Malini Karkal**

    Forum for Women's Health, 4, Dhake Colony, Andheri West, Mumbai 400053, Maharashtra, India.

17. **Mani Mistry, Lalitha D'Souza**

    CEHAT, Mumbai, India.

18. **Martin Macwan**

    NAVSARJAN, 2, Ruciht Apartments, B/H Dharnidhar, Vasna, Ahmedabad 380007, Gujarat, India.

19. **Meena Sheshu**

    General Secretary, SANGRAM, B-11, Akshay Apartments, Chintamani Nagar, Sangli 416416, Maharashtra, India.

20. **Monica Sakhrani**

    R.No.8, 2nd Floor (Mezz), 7/10 Botawala Building, Horniman Circle, Mumbai 400023, Maharashtra, India.

21. **Nasreen Contractor**

    YUVA, Nare-Park Municipal School, Parel, Mumbai 400012, Maharashtra, India.

22. **Nilanjan Datta**

CCTV (Centre for Care of Torture Victims), 9F, Naba Kailash, 55/4 Ballygunge Road, Calcutta 700019, West Bengal, India

23. **Rajendra S. Bangal**

Department of Forensic Medicine, B. J. Medical College, Opp Zilla Parishad, Pune 411011, Maharashtra, India

24. **Renu Khanna, Korrie de Koning, Swati Pongurlekar, Usha Ubale, Manjiri S.**

Contact: Dr Usha Ubale, Brihanmumbai Municipal Corporation, (Women Centred Health Project), BMC Office, Nehru Road, Vile Parle East, Mumbai 400057, Maharashtra, India

25. **Shalini**

TARSHI, 49, Golf Links, 2nd Floor, New Delhi 110003, India

26. **Sherry Joseph**

Department of Social Work, Visva Bharati University, Sriniketan 731236, West Bengal, India

27. **Smarajit Jana, Suparna Ghosh**

Contact–Dr Smarajit Jana, Director, STD/HIV Intervention Programme, 8/2, Bhawani Dutta Lane, Calcutta 700073, West Bengal, India.

28. **Thelma Narayan**

Coordinator, CHC (Community Health Cell), 367 Srinivas Nilaya, Jakkasandra, I Main, I Block, Koramangala, Bangalore 560034, Karnataka, India

29. **V. Suresh**

Advocate, Chennai High Court, 32, Kachaleeshwaran Agraharan Street, Off Armenian Street, Chennai 600001, Tamil Nadu, India

Part-I
Introduction

1

Violence and Health Care Profession in India: Towards a Campaign for Medical Neutrality

Amar Jesani, Neha Madhiwalla

In the health discourse in India, the concern for violence has been conspicuous by its virtual absence. In much of the medical research, discussion, and publications, the mention of the victims and survivors of violence, their special medical needs and rehabilitation is rare. This is despite the fact that violence invariably inflicts physical or psychological trauma. The role of the health professionals is important in the treatment of the health effects of violence as well as its prevention through the process of securing justice for the survivors and victims. In any form of violence, the victims and many survivors come in contact with health care workers. Survivors themselves approach or are taken to health care services for the treatment of their physical injuries and psychosocial trauma suffered. After the death of victim, the doctor conducts autopsy. In fact, the medical record of violence on the survivors and victims constitutes one of the important evidences for police investigation and the legal process for punishing the offenders and compensating victims and survivors. The apathy of the medical profession could result in delayed or denied justice to many victims of violence.

Violence as a Public Health Issue

The figures quoted by the media and social science researchers from the various sources on the incidences of all types of violence and the estimated numbers of victims are indeed shocking. Besides, there is hardly any mention in our scientific journals and health policy documents about the implication of such a phenomenon for the health care services. While one does not want to sensationalise and exaggerate the phenomenon of increasing violence in our society, one also cannot desist from saying that for the health care services it is a big-but ignored, epidemic of the present time.

The science of medicine incorporates a sociological and epidemiological understanding. Medicine, and for that matter, any science not geared to the real social and epidemiological issues often loses its humanitarianism. Violence does not leave the health professionals completely unaffected. After all, doctors also come from a social milieu, which has varied and conflicting positions on violence. To what extent is the attitude of doctors to violence inflicted on certain groups shaped by their social positions and ideological orientation in our country? Finding answer to this question is not easy. For there has been very little empirical research conducted to find out health care providers' attitude on the subject and the extent to which individual biases get reflected in the medical practice.

The number of health care professionals in our country is staggering. We have 1.2 million properly qualified doctors (1 doctor for less than 900 persons) who are legally registered with three Medical Councils. In addition, we have about 0.3-0.5 million non-qualified and non-registered doctors practising in the country. We have nearly 0.6 million Nurses of various categories and also have a large cadre of other paramedical workers. In all, we have over two million professional and para-professional health workers who need to be educated to take cognisance of the violence as a public health issue and undertake advocacy to ensure that they play a positive, constructive and ethical role in caring for the survivors of violence.

This volume contains papers presented at the International Conference. They are organised in six sections, (1) An overview of the issues and concepts in Human rights and the specific responsibilities of the health sector (2)Violence by State Agencies (3) Communal and Caste Violence (4) Violence against Women;domestic violence and sexual assault. (5) Violence against women in prostitution and (6) Human rights issues involved in helath service delivery. There is very little written documentation available on the human rights issues involved in health care and is often only considered as part of individual doctor or hospital's philanthropic zeal. In any case, it is still not so much a concern for the profession and the system at large. While Indian Medical Association has begun discussing about and started some educational campaign among its members, they leave out 60% of doctors in our country who are non-allopathic doctors, and it is restricted to torture. Besides, it hasn't shown real commitment to the cause by taking action or campaigning for action against those doctors who have been named as collaborators in human rights violations.

Violence Against Women

The great surge of the women's movement in the 1980s brought the issue of violence against women on the political agenda of the country. Yet, a survey of violence against women in the less developed countries has shown that it is a grossly neglected public health issue (Heise, Raike et al, 1994). Violence against women and children is the most common form of family violence and it has social, cultural and religious sanction. The studies done by Flavia Agnes in the 1980s in Bombay and other studies have shown that it cuts across the class and class barriers. These social variables only change the form of violence, not its high prevalence. In India, more often than not, the women's movement and the health system have stood in opposition to each other. Most of the campaigns undertaken by women's groups and other human rights' groups on women's issues have highlighted the lack of gender sensitivity and neglect of women's rights by the medical profession. The retrogressive role played by doctors and other health professionals has been highlighted in the context of various human rights violations, including rape and domestic violence. Doctors have by omission or commission obscured women's voices, by neglecting to record the woman's own testimony, by not recording that the injuries or death has occurred due to violence or even by raising doubts about the woman's sexual history and character, which have no bearing with the crime. From this emerged a critique of sexism within medicine itself, especially on the manner in which doctors treated victims of violence (rape, battering) and enabled the perpetrators to escape punishment. It was noted that doctors invariably commented on the state of the hymen, made comments about the women's virginity status and made statements that threw suspicion on the woman's character, (e.g., habituated to sexual intercourse). On the other hand, while recording history, they paid no attention to the woman's appearance, injuries to other parts of the body, her mental state or her own reporting of history. Inspite of the fact that human rights issues in women's health have been widely discussed and debated, the health profession has failed to take much notice of it. There have been very few attempts from within the profession to critique and question the health systems treatment of women. Presented here are few of the attempts to examine biases within the system by health professionals themselves.

The role of the health profession is examined here from two different perspectives. Firstly, health professionals are witness to the consequences of violence. Battered women come into casualty wards of hospitals and are treated by doctors for injuries. When deaths occur from violence, health professionals are called in to ascertain and certify the cause. Doctors are called upon to investigate women who have been raped. Often, the point of contact is only the voice and story of an abused woman who calls up on the helpline. In all these situations the health professionals have an important role to play. They are in a position to enable women to reveal the existence of violence and encourage women to seek help. They are also in a position to play an important role in bringing perpetrators to justice by systematic and objective documentation of medical evidence, whether it is in the examination of rape victims, or the recording of medico-legal cases and certification of deaths. The need for them to be sensitive to the suffering of the victims and proactive in their care is highlighted in all the papers included in this section. In contrast, each paper points to the glaring gaps in information on all aspects whether it is casualty records, death certifications or reports of medical investigation of sexual assault.

The other set of papers looks at the specific problems of women in prostitution, especially in the context of the AIDS Control Programme. Women in prostitution are regarded as a 'high risk' group and, hence, there is a tendency to lower the standards of human rights or democracy where they are concerned. Summary arrests, forced testing and intrusive surveillance of their actions are some of the human rights violations that they are vulnerable to. Aprt from that, the AIDS epidemic itself poses other problems. They are denied access to care or treated badly by health care workers. The peculiar problems of commercial sex workers are important as they are a pointer to manner in which the social status of the group seeking services influences the responses of the health care providers. Dominant biases are reflected in the actions of the professionals who provide services, demonstrating the extreme vulnerability of groups who are in other ways marginalised and oppressed. It also points to the absence of neutrality and the precarious practice of ethics within the profession. The papers in this volume present the problems faced by them and also some attempts to organise and mobilise them have been examined in the section.

Communal and Caste Violence

Most of the sociological studies have shown that the doctors hail from upper caste and class strata of the society (Ommen T. K., 1978, Venkatratnam R., 1979). With the phenomenal increase in the number of private medical colleges, the dominance of these strata in the profession is on the increase. This social background of doctors provides a fertile ground for the social forces using caste (castism) and religion (communalism) for political mobilisation and capture of power. It is, therefore, not surprising that in communal and caste mobilisations, significant support has come from the professional classes, which include doctors. Our personal experiences with doctors at a professional level and in our interaction with them in several health service studies in urban and rural Maharashtra, we have found health professionals' views highly coloured by caste and communal ideologies. Very few studies and personal experiences of doctors are available on this subject. However, the available material does make one concerned about their role and attitude.

In the recent violence that was witnessed in Gujarat, it was evident that doctors, among other highly qualified professionals, took an active role in the carnage. Some of the most prominent leaders of the Hindu right wing groups, which actively incited mobs and organised the attacks on the Muslim community were doctors. The investigation carried out by the Medico Friend Circle in May, 2002, revealed that there was considerable polarisation within the medical profession along communal lines. The medical associations representing them did not condemn attacks on doctors belonging to the minority community. On the other hand, there was absolutely no condemnation of the doctors who were known to have participated in the violence. Some doctors also gave evidence of the fact that right wing groups were actively enlisting doctors into their cadres and trying to gain control of the profession.

The doctors as a profession were also conspicuous by their absence in the relief efforts following the violence in Gujarat. The state-run medical services in the relief camps were grossly inadequate and largely they not supplemented by any voluntary efforts from the profession. Laypersons with some knowledge of medicine were the primary providers of care for a long period of time after the camps came into being. The abysmal conditions in the camps were testimony to the fact that the medical profession reacted with the same sense of apathy and resignation to the situation as the rest of civil society.

While a big section of doctors worked tirelessly in providing medical relief to victims during communal riots in Mumbai in 1984 and in 1992-3, some doctors in personal conversations confessed that some of them were as much involved in believing and spreading wild rumours as the general public. During the 1984 anti Sikh riots , some social workers who took survivors to the city hospitals had complained apathy and indifference, particularly by the Class IV support staff, towards survivors from a particular community. An eyewitness testimony by a doctor (Sharma, 1991, pg. 9) on the behaviour of doctors at the M. G. M. Medical College and the M. Y. Hospital, Indore, during communal violence in October 1989 (the well-known rathyatra violence) is revealing. He and his colleagues from the Socially Active Medicos found that, the "doctors themselves harbour anti-minority sentiments and contribute to the harassment both by spreading rumours and by blatant discrimination in health care provision". According to this eyewitness account, the doctors contributed to communal tension by "increasing the death figures for the majority caste, thus making it appear that they were the ones victimised." He also describes an observation by his colleague on the medical care provided to minorities: "Far from stopping at manipulation of death figures, doctors were also seen to deny proper medical care. Dr. ..... , a member of Socially Active Medicos, while working in casualty ward witnessed blatant discrimination of patients according to caste; at times, he even saw a proper line of treatment suddenly changed when it became apparent that a patient was circumcised".

On the positive side, Dr. Sharma also describes the case of Dr. Ariwala, who during those violent days continued work at the hospital for long hours, thus leaving his house unprotected. The rioters indeed looted his house while he was caring for survivors at the hospital.

Caste and Communal Divide— While this negative role played by some doctors in events of violence must worry the health care professionals, they should also recognise that indifference to and approval of communalism and castism in the society could only divide them. In the worst cases, such a division could also fuel caste and communal conflicts. For instance, in the early 1980s, when the middle classes of our country raised the issue of abolishing reservations in higher education for lower castes (the Schedules Castes and Scheduled Tribes), the doctors were very much part of the campaign. Indeed, in Gujarat in mid-1980s, the medical students supported by doctors and organisations of their parents played a very prominent role in the anti-reservation agitation. Medical professionals publicly castigated the reservation policy and asserted that the ill-equipped and less-intelligent tribal doctors and those from lower castes were primarily responsible for declining medical standards and so on. It is also significant to note that, the anti-reservation campaign and the social atmosphere created by such powerful forces was used, at that time, in Gujarat by vested interests to inflict violence against lower caste individuals and groups.

Similarly, communal riots are accompanied by rumours against the minority, and such rumours could also include vicious hate-propaganda against doctors from the minority. This situation does not allow minority-victims to reach hospitals (because of the tense environment outside the hospital) and also make out the majority community to be victims in the hands of minority-doctors. Such atmosphere leads to communalisation of the provision of immediate medical care to the survivors of violence. For instance, in mid-December 1990, Aligarh, a town in Uttar Pradesh was rocked by communal violence. A local Hindi daily newspaper made allegations that "patients and their relatives had been deliberately killed on communal lines by the doctors on duty at the Jawaharlal Nehru Medical College, Aligarh Muslim University". Implying that the Muslim doctors at this hospital systematically killed the Hindu patients. It was also alleged that one of the reasons for the communal violence in Aligarh was such killing in the hospital. Indeed, these reports alleged that the neutrality of medicine was seriously compromised in the hospital.

While there was no investigation of the allegations of violence of medical neutrality in Lucknow hospital described above by Dr. Sharma, a medical group in New Delhi, called Delhi Medicos' Front sent a team of doctors to investigate the allegations in Aligarh. The team interviewed all individuals who were supposed to be eyewitness to the massacre of Hindu patients. Both Hindu and Muslim doctors were interviewed. The team ultimately came to the conclusion that: (1) No incident took place between December 7-10, 1991 inside the hospital building as alleged by the Hindi newspapers of the Uttar Pradesh. (2) There was no discrimination against patients on communal lines. (3) There were three stabbing incidents outside the casualty on the 8th and 9th December 1991 by some masked men. (4) Press reports in the Hindi newspapers of UP are totally false and baseless (Sofat, Saxena, Siddiqi, 1991).

Psychosocial Trauma Due to Communal Violence— Communal violence produces serious psychosocial trauma among survivors, the victimised community and among the witnesses. Following riots in Mumbai, there were numerous reports in the media describing the kind of psychosocial trauma suffered by survivors. Departments of psychiatry in various public hospitals provided information on the kind of symptoms suffered by survivors, particularly children. (see various press reports documented in Jesani, D'Sa, Alphonse, 1993, pp. 74-120).

Caste and communal violence is typically mass violence, which affects the whole community and leaves behind badly scarred the survivors The community loses its capacity to cope with the basic requirements for survival, both because their homes, property, assets and other resources have been deliberately and systematically destroyed and also because they find their fundamental rights as citizens under threat. Violence against minorities and scheduled castes, rarely occurs without large scale mobilisation and without the tacit sympathy of certain elements in the government machinery. Thus, for survivors to seek justice becomes an uphill task combating resistance and discrimination at various levels, apart from coping with their loss of their own loved ones and their homes and incomes.

Survivors are also witness and often victims of brutal attacks, which inflict physical and psychological scars and permanent disability. In such a situation, medical services are required not merely in the short term, but also as part of the long term rehabilitation process. Professionals have to be trained to address the physical and psychological needs of the survivors. Health services, in general, have to make additional efforts to reach out to the affected communities, rather than wait for them to access services. Concepts of distance, mobility and time change in the tense environment of the aftermath of mass violence and people affected by mass violence may refuse to come to even seemingly accessible health institutions. We observed this in Gujarat, where patients who were referred to higher facilities for investigations or surgery consistently refused to leave their homes or camps. A similar phenomenon was observed in Bombay after the 1993 riots, where survivors refused to go to hospitals for treatment, but willingly waited for medical teams to come to their homes.

Violence by State Agencies

Although an important element, violation of human rights by the state extend much beyond physical torture. Health professionals are invariably involved in the investigation of human rights violation through the conduct of autopsy. The abysmal condition autopsy rooms across the country, conduct of autopsies, quality of their reports and access to these reports etc. have been a matter of concern for long. There have been reports in the press about the pressure exerted by the police on doctors to give favourable findings. The famous case of police custody death of Dayal Singh made the Resident Doctors' Association of the AIIMS (New Delhi) protest against such pressure is mentioned in the Amnesty

International (AI, 1992) report titled "Torture, Rape and Deaths in Police Custody". Similarly, the autopsy reports of two nuns murdered in a Bombay suburb and the doctors' role in unscientific interpretation of its findings created a great furore (Solidarity for Justice, 1991). In addition to the autopsy reports of these nuns, we also had an opportunity to go through a sizeable number of autopsy reports of custody deaths and so called 'encounter deaths' in the last few years. In general we found that they usually have incomplete and often unscientific documentation. It is significant to note that the Supreme Court had to pass an order in 1989 that all post-mortem examinations held at the AIIMS be standardised.

The use of torture to extract information, confessions and obtain obedience is widespread within the criminal justice system. There have been instances of doctors participating in torture, although in India, there is little documentation of such involvement. Recently, this issue emerged again when those accused of setting the bogies of the Sabarmati Express on fire in Godhra were taken to the government hospital in Vadodara for interrogation after being administered with Sodium Pentothal. The response of the officials of the medical college and hospital that co-operation with the police was their 'duty' once again raised the concern about dual responsibility. Should doctors in government service maintain their loyalty to the employer (state), even when asked to participate in the violation of human rights?

Apart from the actual involvement of health professionals in human rights violations, when they witness the effects of torture, their failure to report such instances is another dimension of their involvement in human rights violations.

In one of the investigations (CPDR, 1990) of a police custody death in Bombay it was found that the young victim was brought to a public hospital in a serious health condition. The doctor took case history and gave routine medical care in the presence of a police officer that had accompanied the victim. As a consequence, the victim did not inform doctor about the torture. He was taken back to the custody where he was tortured more. He eventually died.

These examples only represent the tip of the iceberg. It is not that the doctors who often come into contact with the survivors and victims are always conscious accomplices in covering up cases. **A section of doctors involved are plainly ignorant about this aspect of medical work.**

Another section is indifferent to the plight of sufferer due to their own social biases against survivors and victims. Such indifference is also produced by social pressure to conform to the dominant belief. Besides, the **psychosocial trauma** inflicted by torture is completely ignored, often because there is no training imparted to them for managing such trauma and also due to the low economic value of such medical work. A third section simply believes that being in the employment of the government, the police department or the prison, they are bound by the orders of their superiors and the code of their service does not allow them to "blow the whistle". Another reason for doctors' apathy to these issues is that they consider themselves as mere technicians. Some doctors have often remarked, "we are doctors, we treat illness, we are not interested in torture or rape." They, therefore, do not make the necessary efforts to explore the causes and history. This is both inadequate science as well as inadequate understanding of medical ethics.

Doctor's Knowledge and Attitude—Recently, in a survey done amongst its members (743 doctors, 61.5 per cent of them General Practitioners, and 17.2 per cent of them in Govt. Service), the Indian Medical Association (1995) found that 71.1 per cent (or 533 out of 743) of doctors in India have come across a case of torture in their medical practice. Interestingly, of those who have seen a case of torture, only 23.8 per cent said that such case was brought to them by the police, thus indicating that the survivors of torture do directly approach the medical professionals. Further, 15.7 per cent of them said that they were witness to the infliction of torture, 18.2 per cent said that there are doctors in India who have knowingly participated in torture, but only 18.2 per cent knew where to report suspected cases of torture.

The most disturbing finding of this study is that 57.5 per cent believed that coercive techniques might be justified to elicit information from uncooperative suspects. 58.3 per cent thought that manhandling during interrogation was unavoidable. 36.7 per cent said that solitary confinement was not torture. 49.3 per cent justified forcible feeding of hunger strikers. And 49.7 per cent found nothing wrong or unethical in doctors remaining present during the process of execution by hanging.

The data of the IMA survey generally confirm what we have said earlier. They also emphasise that there is a great need to educate doctors in India to change their attitude in cases of human rights violation.

Human Rights and the State of the Health Sector

Traditionally, service provision in the health sector was viewed from a managerial perspective. The focus of analysis was to evaluate how optimally resources had been allocated, needs identified and personnel deployed. There was little, if any, space for recording people's perception of services and few attempts to understand the health care system within the larger context of their lives. Thus, the articulation of 'rights' to health care was unheard of. The 'right' to health care brings the focus on many different aspects of health care provision, quality of care, autonomy, ethics and right to information. It ensures that health care is not reduced to merely working out different combination of services and personnel, where the user has no choices. We examine here many such issues - quality of care, right to information and choice and protection from coercion in the context of intensive care units in Mumbai city, the tuberculosis control programme and the family planning programme.

The regulation of health care facilities is a core responsibility of the state. However, typically, the state has largely allowed the private sector to function without any restriction. Failure to protect the safety of patients by ensuring that minimum standards are met in health care facilities has a wide ranging impact on the people. Moreover, the absence of effective self-regulation within the medical profession points to the extent to which commercial interests have over-ridden ethics and concern for public good.

In the arena of public health, the state's omission is even more distinctly visible through the wide gaps in infra-structure and service provision. The illustration of the tuberculosis programme is used to demonstrate how the lapses of the health system has disastrous consequences for the poor. Rather than viewing public health merely as a technical exercise, when a 'rights' perspective is applied to the analysis, the actual concerns of the people emerge and are foregrounded.

Human Rights issues emerging from overtly violent situations involving women were at the focus of the campaign in the initial period. However, soon women's groups began to articulate and agitate against the violation of women's rights through the routine provision of health care services. The drive for population control, which was initiated in the late 1970s and has continued since has provided more evidence of the medical profession's disregard for women's rights. The use of coercive methods to promote family planning, using women as guinea pigs for untested and potentially hazardous contraceptives, blatant neglect of ethics in research related to women have been focal points of action for women's groups. This campaign, alongwith with developments in the international circle, e.g., Beijing Conference of 1995, has led to official denouncement of the policy of disincentives as well as targets (for government functionaries), who came under pressure to coerce women to accept family planning. Also India remains the only country in the South Asian region where long acting provider controlled hormonal contraceptives (injectibles and implants) are not part of the state family planning programme. However, there have been continued attempts to introduce these methods, inspite of the fact that no studies have been conducted (and completed) indigenously to test their safety and reliability. Another important and consistent argument that women's groups have been able to put forward is the lack of transparency and routine violation of medical ethics within the family planning programme. Instances of women being denied services (for delivery or abortion) unless they accept contraception are very common.

What Needs to be done?

Treatment and Rehabilitation of Survivors—All types of violence produce a traumatic effect on survivors. The trauma could be on the body or on the mind. In a famous case of mass torture of villagers by the security forces in Manipur, although there were official denials, a team of doctors which also included psychiatrists visited and examined 104 survivors in that area after 22 months of the incident. They found that a very high number of them were suffering from the post-torture traumatic stress. They found that 36.6 per cent were suffering from recurrent dreams of torture, 66.3 per cent of disturbed sleep, 54.4 per cent were not able to enjoy village festivals, food, sex and even friendship, 37.6 per cent showed loss of self confidence, developed a sense of foreshortened future, etc. (Biswas, Das et al, 1990).

There is extensive work done by doctors on the treatment and rehabilitation of survivors of violence in many countries, but in India the health professionals have not done much organised work. The survivors of violence are special types of patients, and they would be missed, and continue to suffer if not treated. While there is no doubt about their individual sufferings, they also add into the socio-political problem. The medical documentation and record generated in the process of treatment could be formidable evidence to get justice for them. Thus, an independent, conscious and trained health professional while treating cases of violence can also become a deterrent and a means prevention of violence.

For prevention of violence and rehabilitation of survivors, doctors need to work with other professionals, activists and officials. While doctors in India have gradually become used to working with hospital social workers (particularly in big hospitals), they still have not learnt to network with human rights lawyers, human rights organisations, anti-communal groups, women's organisations etc. to assist survivors in getting justice and for their rehabilitation. Rehabilitation of survivors of violence in our own society has many socio-political, cultural and economic dimensions. Often survivors need shelter homes, jobs and other support to start a new life or protection from offenders to go back to their homes in the locality where the violence had occurred. While doctors themselves are not in a position to undertake such social responsibilities, the success of treatment and rehabilitation normally depends upon getting such support for survivors. Such a medical goal can be achieved only in collaboration with other professionals and activists. Besides, despite democratic spaces available in our country, it is not uncommon for doctors actively trying to help victims to have to face threats and violence themselves, thus needing protection. This could be achieved only by having the support of strong and active professional organisations, as well as by having the support of human rights lawyers and activists.

Education and training of doctors—The educational and training intervention among health professionals (doctors, nurses and other paramedical) is at present a pressing need in India. Such an intervention must have three components:

(a) Effecting attitudinal changes and promoting professional ethics, (b) Education and training for providing ethical and rational treatment to survivors and for developing skills in investigation of human rights violation, and (c) Creating an environment and building an institutional support system for health professionals, including legal protection, to make it possible for them to play a positive and constructive role in both caring for survivors and preventing violence.

It must also be kept in mind that doctors and other health professionals are ultimately a part of society, and the code of ethics cannot completely insulate them from the societal influences in their ideology and practice. When a society condones violence against certain groups of people and when a section of it tends to participate in inflicting such violence from time to time, it cannot provide a correct and conducive environment for health professionals to be ethical in the event of violence.

Thus, it is equally, if not more, important to back up such intervention among health professionals with strong public advocacy and education on the subject.

Campaigns for medical neutrality—The long-term goal of all health activists is to make doctors real social reformers. They have often used the term social doctor to contrast the technician doctor. In the situation of violence, the first step for making the doctor socially oriented is to make him or her respect medical neutrality. The medical neutrality emphasises that in the situation of violence doctor's ethical obligation is to care for survivors and victims, never to side with offender and aid the pursuit of justice. At societal level the medical neutrality emphasises protection for doctors to discharge their ethical duties, protection for doctors who are "whistle blowers" (who make known the violation of human rights and unethical medical actions). To build such a campaign is the responsibility of health profession as well as the society at large.

Will health profession in India be able to ever build such a campaign? Given the rising curve of violence in India, the health profession is going to come under the greater medical, social and international scrutiny for its role in coming time. There is a need to make such a beginning. However, given the history and numerous reports of doctors' collusion in human rights violence in India, at the beginning of such campaign the professional associations and their councils will have to first take firm stand against medical collusion. They will have to make those who are guilty accountable and weed them out from their ranks. A casual admission that there are few black sheep within the profession would not have much credibility. It needs to be backed by concrete decisive actions. Such actions would greatly aid in building genuine campaign for medical neutrality in India.

Part-II
Human Rights and the Responsibility of the Health Sector

2

International Efforts for Prevention of Torture

Jaap A. Walkate

The subject you are about to discuss is of an actual and urgent nature and, moreover, a problem of enormous proportions. It is a problem, which is not confined to one country but is common to many countries in the world, albeit, in various degrees and forms. The programme of your conference is ambitious and well focussed on violence by state agencies, violence against women, and caste and communal violence. You will find that after the three days that you have set aside to discuss these topics you will leave with the idea that you have only touched upon these subjects and that you will need much more time to grasp the implications of the undisciplined use of force and to come to grips with the ramifications of each of these types of violence.

The use of force by state agents on citizens is, and should be, the subject of constitutional and statutory rules and regulations in every state. In addition to that, international law provides for a large number of rules which are contained in treaties, codes and resolutions drafted and adopted by the United Nations, the specialized agencies of the UN, the Council of Europe and other regional organizations. The best known of these texts is the Universal Declaration of Human Rights whose 50th Anniversary will be celebrated on the December 10th, only a fortnight from today (i.e. December 10, 1998). That Declaration has been the foundation of and inspiration for these international norms and rules of decent behaviour by state agents in relation to the citizens of that state. The drafters of that Declaration were driven by their zeal "to free mankind of barbarous acts which have outraged the conscience of mankind, and the advent of a world in which human beings shall enjoy freedom of speech and belief and freedom from fear and want" as the Preamble to the Declaration enumerates a variety of rights and freedoms which will enable the citizens of a state, the members of a society, to live peacefully together in a democratic constitutional framework in which the powers of the government are exercised only in accordance with the rule of law. The

Declaration's ultimate goal seems to be the creation of a sound, sane, and safe society. A society not subjected to the rule of law and is dominated by force and violence produces fear in its members and fear is crippling, paralysing and debilitating in its effects. In fact, it would constitute a negation of health as conceived by the World Health Organization (WHO).

The constitution of that specialized agency (WHO) of the UN defines "health" as "a state of complete physical, mental and social well being and not merely the absence of disease or infirmity". The absence of physical and/or of mental and social well being, therefore, would in itself constitute under the definition a lack of health. A fortiori, the occurrence of violence, the uncontrolled use of force or persecution on grounds of race, sex, religion, descent or class, causing fear in and damage to the individual constitutes a negation of "health" as defined by the WHO constitution. But at the same time it will constitute a violation of national and/or international law. Lawyers, human rights activists, physicians, health personnel and all of you present have the common duty to maintain and, wherever necessary and possible, to restore the physical and mental sanity of all members of the society to which they belong. They must do their utmost in the maintaining of the rule of law, in the administration of justice, on the execution of lawful punishment, in the safeguarding of the individual's dignity and integrity, and the guaranteeing of his/her human rights, including his/her right to, and I quote from one of those treaties, i.e., the UN Covenant on Economic Social and Cultural Rights: "The enjoyment of the highest attainable standard of physical and mental health." The protection of human integrity of each individual is his or her sacred duty.

The use of force by state agencies, such as the police, personnel of detention centres or, as the case may be, military units, not seldom involves such measures as torture or other cruel, inhuman or degrading treatment or, in some countries, corporal punishment. These (illegal) measures sometimes require the co-operation of health personnel: physicians or paramedical staff. According to reliable reports on the occurrence of torture, the perpetrators of such acts have used medical personnel. They contribute sometimes by devising methods of torture, which do not leave visible scars on the victim, sometimes by preventing torturers to go too far and to lose a valuable detainee who still should disclose more information, sometimes by reviving victims to prepare them for another round of beatings. In the past we have seen that medical staff of detention campous issued false certificates of mental illness, thereby subjecting their victims ("patients" is not the appropriate term) to a treatment with drugs that had bad effects on their psyche and body, thus constituting a form of torture. This conduct has been declared not only as illegal and punishable, but also as a "gross contravention of medical ethics" by the UN General Assembly in 1982 by the adoption of its Principles of Medical Ethics relevant to the Role of Health Personnel, particularly Physicians, in the Protection of Prisoners and Detainees against Torture and other Cruel, Inhuman or Degrading Treatment or Punishment.

These principles were drafted on the basis of preparatory work undertaken in the WHO and the World Medical Association, which adopted the Declaration of Tokyo in 1975—still the most comprehensive statement produced by the medical profession on torture. There are many more texts adopted by the medical and paramedical profession in relation to the treatment of detainees, such as national codes of medical ethics and statements on nurses in relation to detainees and violations of human rights, such as torture. However, what the UN Principles do is put the subject in a legal context and qualify violations as gross contravention of medical ethics, and as a criminal offence under international law. The same body of Principles declares inadmissible, and a contravention of medical ethics, the certifications or participation in the certification of the fitness of prisoners or detainees for any form of treatment or punishment that may adversely affect their physical or mental health, nor to participate in any way in the infliction of any such treatment or punishment. This is a clear reference to the participation of medical doctors in the application of - as is the practice in a few countries - corporal punishment, such as beatings or amputations, a participation, which should be avoided under any circumstance except in the cases where the physician is called upon to treat the person as a patient needing medical care.

Physicians, and more in general, health personnel, have, therefore, an important role to play in the prevention of violence, more in particular, of torture, and in the treatment of victims. First of all, in no case shall they participate in the infliction of torture, of cruel treatment, and/or corporal punishment. In cases where they are called upon to examine persons who declare to have been tortured, and to verify their statement, the physician's role may be crucial in saving the accused from detention and prosecution, and thus in abating mal-practices. Also, and more obviously, medical doctors will play a vital role in treating and curing victims of torture. It takes special skills to assess their statements and to treat the sequelae of torture. In the first place, often very refined means of torture have been used so as to leave no physical scars. But the deeper are the wounds of the mind and the soul. To ascertain a broken arm or leg is easier than to determine that the person has undergone electric shocks. Modern torture technology is developed with an eye on medical scientific publications on the subject, in the endeavour to make treatment of victims more difficult through lack of physical traces. In the second place, victims - or survivors as they are called by some centres - do not necessarily say they have been tortured, not seldom ashamed of what has happened to them (especially sexual torture can reach intimate places), or of the fact that they were forced to give up and "confess". A physician must have special experience, or get special training to find out what happened, and he must do so gently without scaring the patient who may be reminded of the past by the cell-like treatment room and the traditional white doctor's garb. It is a sad but inevitable conclusion that probably no victim of torture will ever recover completely from what he or she has suffered. In many cases the only thing we can hope for is that the victim will be able to live with his past and play a useful role again in society - and be a true survivor!

The systematic use of torture and maltreatment all over the world creates an impressive number of victims-and members of their families - who have been seriously traumatised and are in urgent need of psychological, medical and other assistance in order to overcome the sequelae of torture. We do not know the exact number of victims, but there must be hundreds of thousand; we do not know exactly the costs of treatment and assistance required, but it runs into tens of millions of dollars. Fortunately, there are all over the world small and medium sized centres for treatment of victims, staffed by physicians, psychologists, lawyers, social workers and, often, volunteers. What is needed is money to assist the survivors of torture and their families.

The UN General Assembly has assumed some form of "collective" responsibility for the rehabilitation of torture victims by establishing a Fund in 1981 to receive contributions for distribution, through established channels of assistance, as humanitarian, legal and financial aid. This Fund depends entirely on voluntary contributions from governments, private organizations, institutions and individuals. It is not financed through the regular UN budget. Over the past 16 years a group of donor states have contributed to the Fund on a yearly basis. This has enabled the Fund to set up a system for equitable distribution of the money to a great number of centres for treatment in a variety of countries. Many centres are in countries where victims have found refuge (that accounts for the number of centres in western countries), but at the same time many centres have been set up in countries where torture is practiced. This may pose specific problems. In one country, for instance, doctors who are treating victims are arrested by government agents and forced to give the names of their patients to the authorities so that they can take action against these people and their families.

3

Role of the Health Profession and Services in the Investigation of Violence Against Women and in the Treatment of Victims/Survivors

Binoo Sen

Violence against women is an extremely complex phenomenon, deeply rooted in gender-based power relations, sexuality, self-identity, and social institutions. Any strategy to eliminate gender violence therefore must confront the underlying cultural beliefs and social structures that perpetuate it. For decades, women's organizations around the world have worked against gender-based violence through advocacy, victim services, and consciousness-raising. However, in the light of growing violence against women, existing interventions need to be redefined.

Frequent incidents of violence restrict gender development. It limits the range of choices open to women and girls in almost every area of life, public and private - at home, in school, in the workplace and in most community spaces. It limits their choices directly by destroying their health, disrupting their lives, and narrowing the scope of their activity; and indirectly, by eroding their self-confidence and self-esteem. The wide range of discriminatory and criminal practices exact incalculable social costs as well.

While legislative and judicial activism have constituted the mainstay of the efforts to eliminate discriminatory behaviour, stereotyped roles and inequality of status, they can never be adequate. Laws alone, or judicial activism, cannot bring about enduring changes. The socialization process is too deep and too entrenched to be tackled through legislation alone. Very often, enforcement agencies and institutions remain steeped in gender biases. Further, the biases that restrict women's mobility and access to resources are deep-rooted in economic and social interests and unequal power relationships. Patriarchal controls redefine and re-assert themselves, cutting across barriers of caste and community, threatening the realization of a gender-just society, free from exploitation.

In this context, the role of the family is crucial. While respect for elders and strong family values are abiding features of diverse and pluralistic societies - cutting across religions, cultures, languages and castes - the family is also very often the site for discrimination and subordination. It is here that violence against girls and women reach alarming proportions. Female foeticide, infanticide, dowry violence, and torture, remain largely invisible, and often go unpunished in spite of Constitutional guarantees and the long arm of the law.

While preparing to come to Mumbai I came across a statement in an article which describes the helpless situation a woman invariably finds herself in times of crisis and oppression: "We have mouths but we use them only for crying." An average woman has no choice in relation to important events in her life, such as, marriage, parenthood, family planning, participation in community activities, and divorce. It is to these kinds of women that the medical profession has to provide relief from shock and pain.

The World Bank in 1994 came out with a discussion paper on "Violence Against Women - The Hidden Health Burden" (Heise, 1994). The study has given a cyclic description of violence perpetuated on women-right from the time of pre-birth till old age. The life cycle of women, and the kind of violence afflicted on her, shows that a woman is never free from the grip of oppression.

Phase-type of Violence: Pre-birth— sex-selective abortion, battering during pregnancy (emotional and physical effects on women, effects on birth outcome), coerced pregnancy (for example, mass rape in war); infancy: female infanticide, emotional and physical abuse, differential access to food and medical care for girl infants; girlhood: child marriage, genital mutilation, sexual abuse by family members and strangers, differentials access to food and medical care, child prostitution; adolescence: dating and courtship violence (for example, acid throwing in Bangladesh, date rape in the United States), economically coerced sex (African secondary school girls having to take up with "sugar daddies" to afford school fees), womanhood: sexual abuse in the workplace, rape, sexual harassment, forced prostitution, trafficking in women, reproductive abuse of women by intimate male partners, marital rape, dowry abuse and murders, partner homicide, psychological abuse, abuse of women with disabilities, elderly abuse of widows, elder abuse.

A life-cycle approach to gender-based victimization provides important insights into the immediate, as well as the cumulative effects of violence on the lives of women and girls. Violence can occur during any phase of a woman's life; many women experience multiple episodes of violence throughout their lives. A life-cycle perspective also reveals that violence experienced in one phase can have long-term effects that predispose the victim to severe secondary health risks, such as, suicide, depression, and substance abuse. Hence, the responsibility of the medical community is not limited to any particular stage of rehabilitation. It has to remain a continuous process.

Violence against women is also perpetuated because the development for women is not planned within a framework of equality. Equality is seen as a concern of the law, and does not consciously inform policy. Policy approaches target women as dependents rather than as individuals contributing equally to household survival and well being.

In understanding the role of health professionals and services in the investigation of violence against women and in the treatment of victims/ survivors, it is extremely necessary to understand the basic psychology of those who perpetuate these atrocities. Given below is an integrated model for 'Violence Against Women'. This model has been given in the chapter: "Motivations in Violence: Theoretical Explanations" written by Ram Ahuja in his book Violence Against Women. The integrated model takes into account the innate and acquired behaviour within human beings. The model concentrates on the psychological analysis of the socio-structural conditions in which human beings co-exist today. It also correlates with the social norms and socialisation process through which human beings co-exist, studies personal characteristics of offenders, their interpersonal trials, and evaluates the environmental factors; for it is within the ecological boundaries that personal dispositions to use violence or commit crime are developed, and crime-evoking situations arise.

In the investigation of violence against women, it is extremely necessary for health workers and service providers to concentrate on capacity building. A system, that creates conceptual clarity about the undermining of human violence in each act of gender violence. In order to successfully deal with the multifaceted dimensions of violence against women, networking at the grass roots, local, and national levels is a must. Vibhuti Patel in her article, "Campaigns Against Gender Violence" (1977-1993) in the book "Women Against Violence" edited by Shirin Kudchedkar and Sabina Alissa, states that in any cultural context, patriarchal control over women's sexuality, fertility and labour, manifests itself in physical and psychological violence against the relatively powerless sections, namely, children, women, ethnic minorities, oppressed castes and religious minorities. We need to contextualise gender violence within this ideological matrix so that we can identify the forces with whom we need to network.

The adjustment of victims to a new life after being stigmatised, (i.e., raped, molested, kidnapped, beaten, harassed), and their taking up new roles, involve several phases, although there is much intermeshing in them. Ram Ahuja in his book, "Violence Against Women", has identified the following four phases in a female victim's adjustments to life after stigmatisation, viz., (1) shock and pain, (ii) removing pain, (iii) avoidance and humiliation, and (iv) adaptation. Shock and pain depend on the nature of the crime committed against her, and on factors like age, education, employment and emotional attachment. Removing pain depends on support and security. Avoidance/humiliation depends on family members, kin, friends, and acquaintances. Adaptation depends on religious consolation, accepting social challenge, neutralization and attachment and identity change.

For health professionals and attached service providers it is important to be sensitised and be aware of the dynamics and impact of sexual abuse and violence. Awareness has also to be there in the political and social context of violence. On a number of occasions, the needs of women are misunderstood. As a result, they tend to be over medicated and over-psychiatrised during treatment. What is needed from health professionals is a proactive policy that responds to women in distress, takes care of their health needs, is able to link between emotional and physical well being and the deep impact of victimisation as a result of the violence being afflicted on them. Health professionals should understand that the first requirement of a woman in distress is emotional healing and social acceptance. This is the first step towards empowerment and the re-birth of self-esteem and skills within shattered human beings. Sexual harassment of patients, misdiagnosis and maltreatment of women should be avoided at all costs.

The National Commission for Women (NCW), recently conducted an investigation into the unfortunate rape of nuns at Jhabua, Madhya Pradesh. One of the recommendations to the state government concerns the role of doctors in facilitating such kinds of investigations. During the investigations, the Commission found the doctors who conducted the first medical examination lacking in both sensitivity and competency. The

Commission was concerned that their understanding of the meaning of "rape" was inconsistent with its medico-legal definition. Therefore, the Commission has proposed that doctors conducting medico legal cases (MLCs) be taught and sensitised on these aspects by forensic experts, legal practitioners, psychologists and gender specialists. The NCW proposes to write to the Indian Medial Association to incorporate a gender sensitisation module for doctors in their educational curriculum.

On a number of occasions, estimating the health burden of violence against women is hampered by the lack of data on the incidence and health impact of abuse. Crime statistics are of no use in estimating incidents of gender-based abuse because such crimes are not reported. As the stigma and ostracism associated with sexual violation is deep, data on rape and gender-based abuse is not easily available. The medical community should try to integrate questions on gender violence into national health surveys, and into ongoing research in such areas as AIDS, sexuality, and family planning. It should also try to introduce consciousness-raising material and training on the dynamics of abuse (including culture-bound practices that are harmful) into the curricula and professional licensing exams for such health care workers as doctors, psychologists, nurses, and midwives. Similar themes should also be included in the health department's collaboration with NGOs. The medical fraternity should also develop gender sensitivity training for forensic doctors on violence against women and upgrade skills as to how to collect and document evidence of assault, sexual abuse and rape.

As we are, day by day, being drawn in the whirlpool of consumerism, the mental-health consequences of violence are increasing in the form of anxiety, depression, suicide attempts, sexual dysfunction, and somatic health complaints. Very little awareness and information is available on the impact of domestic violence and sexual assault on birth outcomes, pregnancy complications, rates of miscarriage, and low birth weight. To counter such growing ills, professional counselling from the service providers in the medical profession would integrate the medical community with the community's social development.

It is also the responsibility of the medical community to undertake studies on issues concerning the community, such as, AIDS prevention, safe motherhood, and child survival, and mobilise support for target-free family planning. It is imperative for the health community to build linkages so that effective interventions can be made through self-help support groups and voluntary organisations.

One of the important recommendations for government action to combat violence against women in the World Bank discussion paper mentioned earlier, is providing financial and technical support to NGOs that provide services to and perform advocacy on behalf of victims of violence, especially those working from a feminist perspective. The study also recommended health professionals to work with women's NGOs to develop strategies to expand the availability of services for victims - from both governmental and non-governmental sources - including shelters, crisis centres, legal assistance, counselling, and support groups. The recommendation also suggested an action plan to activate health professionals. It called for establishing and implementing model protocols for the early identification and referral of abuse victims in health care settings, including emergency rooms and primary care facilities, such as, family planning and parental (or is it prenatal) clinics; train staff in counselling, examining victims, and collecting legal evidence for prosecution.

For the judicial department, the study recommended the amendment of laws and regulations to allow any licensed health care provider to examine and collect evidence of physical and sexual assault for legal purposes.

In countries where there has been some reporting of crimes against women, an increase in the incidents of domestic violence is also indicated. Domestic violence includes, rape, kidnapping and abduction, dowry deaths, torture, molestation, sexual harassment, importation of girls, sati, and other forms of violence. In 1996, the National Crimes Records Bureau, Government of India, stated that 1,09,259 cases of crimes against women were reported. The all-India crime rate, i.e., the number of crimes per lakh population, for crimes against women reported to the police was estimated at 12.4 at the national level. When put with reference to female population, the all-India crime rate doubled to nearly 25.7 per lakh female population. One must also recognise that a vast percentage of crimes against women go unreported due to the social stigma attached to them. Therefore, these statistics represent rates of reported crimes against women, while actual rates may be much higher.

Crimes against women in 1996 showed an overall increase of 5.9 per cent and 7.5 per cent over the respective previous years of 1995 and 1994. More specifically, the incidents of rape and dowry deaths in 1996 reported an increase of 7.9 per cent and 8.3 per cent respectively, over the previous year. The number of eve- teasing cases reported an increase of 17.7 per cent during the period.

The need to create awareness is immediate. The continuation of the violation of women's rights through the use of physical and non-physical violence prevents women from enjoying their fundamental freedoms and from participating as full members within their families and societies.

4

Domestic Violence : A Health Care Issue?

John Chisholm

Domestic violence is a major medical and social issue. However, few guidelines for health professionals have been produced on the topic. Earlier this year, the British Medical Association (BMA 1998), the professional organisation representing all United Kingdom doctors, therefore published a report entitled, "Domestic violence: A health care issue?" in response to a motion passed at the BMA's 1996 Annual Representative Meeting, so as to encourage all health professionals to raise their awareness of the problem, and to develop strategies to identify and reduce the injuries caused. The report concentrates on all types of abuse between sexual partners, and does not consider in detail other aspects of family violence, including child abuse. The BMA is thus acting in the spirit of the 1996 World Medical Association (WMA 1996) declaration on family violence, which recommended that national medical associations should encourage and facilitate research to understand the prevalence, risk factors, outcomes and optimal care for those who have experienced family violence, and identified doctor's important role in prevention and treatment.

The term domestic violence refers to physical, sexual or emotional violence by an adult perpetrator, directed towards an adult victim, within a close relationship. Most often, the violence will be by a man, on his wife, ex-wife, female partner or ex-partner. The term includes, criminal and non-criminal behaviour and the perpetrator uses that behaviour to maintain control and power over the other person (Dobash and Dobash 1979)

Domestic violence includes such examples of physical violence as sleep deprivation, starvation, biting, bruising, burning, choking, hitting, kicking, knifing, punching, scalding, scratching, slapping, strangling and even murder. Sexual abuse and assault includes forced vaginal, anal and oral sex, urination on the woman, sexual assault using objects, forced mimicking of or participation in pornography, forced tying up, and enforced prostitution. Psychological abuse includes verbal abuse, criticism, humiliation and degradation, threats, forcing the woman to undertake menial or trivial tasks, extreme jealousy and possessiveness, isolation from family, friends and work, financial deprivation, destruction of personal belongings, and making the woman think she is going mad.

Domestic violence affects a significant proportion of the population at some time in their lives. It accounts for a quarter of all violent crimes in England and Wales (Mayhew, Mirrless-Black, Percy 1996). It is a serious crime, which has a substantial impact upon the health and welfare of adults and children. Some one in four women experience domestic violence, yet only 25 per cent of all incidents are reported to the police (Mayhew, Aye Maung, Mirrless-Black, 1993). Domestic violence is the least likely violent crime to come to the attention of the police or the criminal justice system (Mayhew, Mirrless-Black, Percy 1996). Sixty-nine per cent of domestic violence incidents result in injury - more than for any other violent crime (Mayhew, Mirrless-Black, Percy 1996). It is usually repeated, and often escalates, over many years (Dobash, Dobash 1992). Only some 30 per cent of women seek help soon after an attack (Bewley, Friend, Mezey 1997). Women are often at a greater risk of violence on separation (Wilson, Daly 1988) and a father's continued contact with children after separation or divorce may provide a particular flash point for further violence (Hester, Radford 1996).

Many reasons have been identified for why individuals experiencing domestic violence find this difficult to report to the police and other agencies, including:

- The emotional relationship between victim and perpetrator
- The perpetrator's behaviour fluctuating between extremes
- Fear of reprisals
- Tendencies to minimise rather than exaggerate the violence, and hide it from family and friends.
- Pressure from the family or local community to remain in the relationship
- Worry about the effect on their children, whether they stay or leave
- Financial dependence on one's partner
- Not knowing a safe place to go or the sources of help and advice available
- A less than helpful response from agencies from which help has been sought

- Undermining through repeated abuse of a woman's confidence in her ability to take decisions and act (Home Office, 1995).

It has been argued that domestic violence to men by women occurs as frequently as violence to women by men, and it may be that men are even more likely to conceal domestic violence against them than are women, but evidence is lacking and more research is needed. Currently available data show a clear gender pattern, with the majority of domestic violence perpetrators being adult males, and most victims female (Mayhew, Mirrless-Black, Percy 1996, Gelles, Pedrick-Cornell, 1990).

Various research reports by psychologists have identified common characteristics in the perpetrators of domestic violence, including holding traditional views about men's position in the family, pathological jealousy, hostility to women but dependence on the partner, and low self-esteem (Schornstein 1997). However, no studies attempt to compare the behaviour, attitudes and psychological profiles of abusive and non-abusive men, and it is not possible to identify character traits, which could predict the likelihood of someone becoming an abuser.

The Domestic Abuse Intervention Project in Duluth, Minnesota, USA, manages one of the longest running projects working to change the behaviour of perpetrators, and has developed training materials for use in reductive group work. Duluth battered women devised the 'Power and Control' and 'Equality' wheels to help perpetrators recognize the difference between controlling violent behaviour and more egalitarian behaviour. The model of violent behaviour includes physical and sexual violence, coercion and threats, intimidation, emotional abuse, isolation, economic abuse, using children, using male privilege, and minimising or denying the abuse or shifting blame. The model of non-violent behaviour includes showing respect and trust, giving support, being honest and accountable, negotiating fairly, taking shared responsibility, having economic partnership and responsible parenting (DAIP, undated).

Getting perpetrators to accept their own responsibility is the first objective of most reductive anti-violence groups (Edleson, Tolman, 1992). Many perpetrators try to control the medical setting by talking to a partner, answering all questions directed at her, refusing to allow her to be seen on her own, and communicating directly with the medical staff about their partner's health care in her absence. Patient advocacy services are particularly important for women who lack language skills.

Some women stay with or return to abusive partners, for a variety of understandable reasons:

- The perpetrator not letting her go
- Fear for her life
- Feeling that it is all her fault
- Feeling that there is no way out
- Isolation from family and friends
- Feeling of inability to cope independently
- Concern for the welfare of children
- Denial of the impact of violence on her own or her children's welfare
- Stigma and an unsympathetic response from family, friends or service providers
- The impact of the violence on the woman's health, so that she is seen as the major problem and the effects of violence are misinterpreted as the cause
- Being in love with the perpetrator and hoping he will change
- The perpetrator's threats or attempts to commit suicide (Glass, 1997).

Battered Women Syndrome (Walker, 1979) is characterized by psychological, emotional and behavioural deficits arising from chronic, persistent violence. Its central features include learned helplessness, passivity, paralysis, and a cycle of violence with three phases: build up, impact, and contrition and remorse, before the cycle starts again. In its extreme form, a traumatic pathological attachment may develop between victim and perpetrator. Nonetheless, the majority of women in violent relationships do leave and separate permanently (Biennia, Harked, Nikon, 1981; Hoof, 1990; Pahl, 1985). It is perhaps more helpful to replace the question as to why battered women do not leave, with a question about who stops them leaving and why.

Women from minority ethnic groups, especially those for whom English is not their first language, may find difficulty in accessing refuges, legal and welfare services (Bhatti-Sinclair, 1994; Mama, 1989) may fear deportation if their immigration status is insecure (SBS, 1993), and may feel constrained from contacting the police or social services or separating from their partner by notions of family honour and shame (Hester, Radford, 1996). Access to translators and patient advocates can be particularly important.

Many women who experience domestic violence go undetected—partly because women do not report, and partly because doctors and other health professionals do not identify them. Many reasons for this failure on the part of doctors have been suggested, including:

- Doctors' fears or experiences of exploring the issues of domestic violence
- Lack of knowledge of community resources
- Fear of offending the woman and jeopardising the doctor—patient relationship
- Lack of time
- Lack of training
- Lack of control
- Infrequent patient visits
- Unresponsiveness of patients to questions
- Feelings of powerlessness, inability to remedy the situation

The consequences of domestic violence in terms of the effect on the mental and physical health of women and children, and the resultant health and social costs, are extensive. Domestic violence may present in a variety of ways:

- Physical injury
- Insomnia
- Anxiety
- Depression
- Drug and alcohol abuse
- Other mental health problems

Disclosures of violence require confidentiality, privacy, sensitive questioning and a non-judgmental attitude. Women may not disclose violence unless they are asked directly. Identification is the necessary prerequisite to ensuring appropriate care. The BMA has suggested an action list for health care professionals:

- Privacy and confidentiality

- Questioning
- Respect and validation
- Assessment and treatment
- Record keeping and concise documentation
- Information giving
- Support and follow up

The annual report for 1996 of the English Chief Medical Officer, which highlighted domestic violence as an area for special attention during 1998, states that effective implementation of the new legislation in part IV of the Family Law Act will require improved recognition of domestic violence, further facilities to help, advise and support women who experience domestic violence, and an effective interface with other agencies, especially social services and the criminal justice system (DoH, 1997). Current proposals for National Health Services (NHS) reform in each of the four countries of the United Kingdom afford additional opportunities for strategic planning of better integrated care for patients who experience domestic violence, through, for example, agreed health improvement programmes for local populations, long-term service agreements with explicit quality standards, and an emphasis on closer liaison between health and social services, and better inter-agency coordination (SSH, 1998a; SSS, 1998, SSW, 1998; DHSS, 1998; SSH, 1998b; SO, 1998; DHSS, 1997).

Health care professionals need to recognize their responsibilities for managing violence against women, and to realise that they can make a difference. However, these responsibilities are not those of individuals alone; health care professionals must work within a multidisciplinary and interagency approach. There is a pressing need too for more research into the effectiveness of interventions to deal with domestic violence.

Interventions include not only trying to stop the violence, but also validation of the violence, medical treatment, information giving and support, and facilitating referral. Treatment of the symptoms of domestic violence is unlikely to be more then palliative, however, so long as the patient remains in a high-risk situation.

The nature of domestic violence means that health professionals assist in a process of empowerment and self-management by the woman of her own situation. It may take time before she reaches the point where she is ready to take definitive action, and thus an apparently unsuccessful interaction with an abused patient may be more successful than initially supposed (Stevens, 1997).

The BMA's report concludes with 21 recommendations, in four broad areas: recommendations concerning national policies, health professionals, education and training, and research.

In the realm of national policy, the health departments are seen as having a role in connecting existing initiatives, informing health care professionals, coordinating the effective use of NHS resources, increasing the funding and resources devoted to domestic violence, and promoting inter-agency strategies at local level. The health authorities' health improvement programmes should contain inter-agency agreements to provide for the recognition and management of domestic violence, with continuous monitoring of the frequency of its occurrence and the effectiveness of solutions.

Social and legal services offering support and help need to be developed and provided and local government needs to assist in funding refuges, raising public awareness, assisting in help-line provision, improving access to safe housing and providing legal advice and protection. Those who provide services to the public need to understand the nature, context and pattern of domestic violence, so as to provide needs-led services which are more accountable to service users.

There needs to be a wider definition of domestic violence in police records, criminal statistics and government crime surveys, and the laws on violence and harassment need to be amended so as better to protect and support those who suffer non-physical domestic violence.

So far as health professionals are concerned, perhaps above all, greater awareness of domestic violence is required. Professional and representative organisations should develop policies and guidelines on the identification and management of domestic violence, and should disseminate guidance via conferences and the production of accessible materials such as briefing papers, contact lists, posters and booklets. There should be continuing commitment to the implementation of guidelines, staff training and regular audit of process, outcomes and rates of identification.

As doctors, we need to develop a safe and private environment for questioning, and a non-judgmental and supportive attitude. We also need information about local resources and initiatives, including refuges, the police domestic violence unit, children's organisations, legal advice organisations, and support and counselling groups.

An inter-agency approach is helpful, including liaison with voluntary sector agencies, which can themselves provide training, information on support groups, resources and referral agencies, and guidance on best policy and practice.

Health professionals also need to be supplied with basic information on the nature and prevalence of domestic violence and the steps to be taken following disclosure. Education and training about domestic violence need to be part of undergraduate and specialist training and continuing professional development. Medical professional bodies themselves need to produce educational programmes and guidelines, covering such matters as documentation of injuries and the production of evidence for the courts.

An extended and comprehensive research base is needed, and there needs to be much more research in a number of areas:

- The prevalence, identification and care of women experiencing domestic violence, and the benefit of screening
- The short and long-term physical, psychological and social implications of domestic violence for adults and children
- The prevalence of male-reported domestic violence and the circumstances in which it occurs
- Doctor's responses to domestic violence in black and ethnic minority families and lesbian and gays relationships
- The relationship between domestic violence and people with disabilities; and
- The role of the medical profession in civil and criminal legal proceedings

A central, accessible database of domestic violence research also needs to be established.

5

Medical Ethics and Human Rights: Perspective, Approach and Work of the British Medical Association

Ann Sommerville

The BMA's interest in medical ethics and human rights

For the past 150 years, the British Medical Association (BMA) has been debating and writing about issues of professional ethics. When it was established in 1832, it listed among its main objectives "the maintenance of honour and respectability of medicine by defining those elements, which ought ever to characterise a liberal profession" It saw medical ethics as representing the collective conscience of the profession and assumed that all doctors would agree to bind themselves to a set of shared values. When it actually came to trying to define those values, the BMA noted that within virtually every culture around the world, medical obligations were expressed in similar terms. Compassion and a duty to the needy continue to be recurrent themes in most medical ethical codes. As the Declaration of Kuwait states, doctors should focus on the sick and vulnerable whether they be "near or far, virtuous or sinner, friend or enemy"—thus neatly encapsulating many of the themes—medical neutrality in civil conflict, concern for populations overseas, and access to health care as a human right—that are pre-eminent in the BMA's current ethics work. From the outset, other common concepts of medical ethics included the duty to use medical skills wisely to benefit patients, to influence society in a way that promotes health, and above all, to avoid harm.

Over the years, BMA publications have reflected a strong and persistent concern for the welfare of vulnerable people. In the 1830s, when the BMA was established, there were calls within the medical profession for doctors to be the "natural defenders of the poor and needy". It must be said, however, that often the best way to get politicians interested was to appeal to their self-interest, rather than their altruism or morality. In 1850, the BMA President argued that "neglect of the poor was endangering the rich and that it was better, because it was cheaper, to preserve the poor man in health, than to maintain his widow and orphaned children". As soon as it was established, the BMA became involved in campaigns designed to protect public health. Later, the BMA's concern turned to reducing abuse within institutions of various types, including prisons. A core principle echoed in many BMA publications over the years is that the practice of medicine is a privilege which carries with it strong moral obligations. Just how those professional obligations tie in with concepts of human rights has become an increasing issue for consideration.

In this century, with the growth of research by human rights organisations like Amnesty International, it became evident that health professionals are usually among the first people in society to witness the effects of violence and human rights violations. Doctors are often the only professional group to have access to a very wide range of institutions—from orphanages to prisons, police stations to mental hospitals, rehabilitation centres to morgues—and may be in a unique position to see the violence hidden from wider society. Because they are among the first to see evidence of abuse, and because they have clear ethical obligations expressed in professional codes, the BMA believes that doctors and their professional organisations can and should be a powerful influence in campaigns to reduce violence. What we have been increasingly searching for, however, are very practical measures that will help doctors do that.

The BMA's strong interest in "human rights" began 20 years ago when it received reports about involvement of doctors in the torture and maltreatment of detainees in various countries. In some cases, doctors, not active in the maltreatment, were said to have collaborated by producing false medical reports and death certificates. The opportunity for the medical profession to play a key role in stopping torture was brought home to British doctors in the late 1970s, when forensic doctors in Northern Ireland tried to draw public attention to evidence of ill treatment of detainees there. Eventually, the effort to document abuse was successful and it was acknowledged that doctors had contributed to the exposure of maltreatment but it was also noted that some doctors had become victimised themselves in one or another way. Since then many doctors around the world, who take considerable risks to reveal instances of abuse and maltreatment, have contacted the BMA. A constant source of profound frustration, however, has been our inability to fulfil their expectations. Having raised their hopes that the profession will respond to their appeals, we still lack effective response strategies or measures for ensuring their safety and that of the victims they represent. Part of our current work is to liase with other medical associations, organisations of lawyers and human rights specialists, as well as international organisations, to try to establish more reliable monitoring of abuses and rapid response mechanisms. Increasingly, we see the solution as lying within strong networks of different professionals committed to similar aims and backed by influential voices - such as medical associations - ready to speak out within the international community.

Why and How Medical Bodies Should Protect Human Rights

"The physician's role is always a political one, whether physicians recognise it or not. Even a decision to try to be 'apolitical' is a political act; it permits others in society to make the decisions that profoundly affect the health of the society without appropriate physician input. Since the doctor cannot claim to be apolitical, the only question is what political role he or she will play. Will it be centred around short-run, self-serving demands or will it be a role centred around the health needs of people and efforts to move society and medicine in directions that will meet those needs?" (Sidel, 1986)

First, medical associations must be convinced of the relevance of human rights concerns to their own work. This can happen either as human rights being seen as part of medical ethics or as part of a public health concern. Medical organisations should have an interest in all of the factors, which affect the health of a population. Medical associations also have a duty to protect the independence and safety of doctors. The BMA regards these issues as "ethical" and as "health policies", although some policies, such as setting standards for HIV services, or for how doctors deal with evidence of violence against women, could also be subsumed under a human rights rubric. While preoccupied by such health issues in the UK, the BMA has also increasingly seen itself as having an ethical obligation to campaign actively on policies which harm the health of populations in other parts of the world. At present, we are involved, for example, in campaigns against the inclusion of medicine and basic foodstuffs in trade embargoes against Cuba and Iraq, campaigns against doctors participating in judicial punishments and female genital mutilation, campaigns against the manufacture and use of land mines, and the campaign to reduce the Third World Debt which has a disastrous health impact on poorer nations. In the wake of the hurricane in Central America, for example, the BMA issued a press statement calling on the UK government to take the lead in cancelling debt repayments from the countries worst affected. Such activities are a central part of the BMA's work and are seen as part of a medical association's obligations to promote public health in the widest sense.

A key factor in developing human rights strategies is the interest and political will of ordinary doctors. Like many medical associations, the BMA is a voluntary organisation representing the interests of the doctors. Its policies and priorities are determined each year by its members at an annual meeting. Since the early 1970s, many of the resolutions passed at these meetings indicate a continuing preoccupation with issues of human rights, social justice, the fate of patients and colleagues in repressive regimes, and the inability of marginalised populations to avail of quality health care. The BMA is committed to such issues because it believes that they form natural and correct areas of concern for the medical profession. The letters we receive from practising doctors reinforces this view. We see that education in medical ethics, and in concepts of human rights, are essential in helping to develop awareness among doctors.

"Concern for human rights should be an intrinsic part of the ethical responsibilities of the medical profession. For doctors, an individual's complete welfare is of paramount importance. So many factors contribute to a person's mental and physical well being. A doctor cannot work effectively if social and political factors are ignored. Where such factors are important, I believe a doctor has a duty to speak out ... I believe also that doctors should actively campaign to expose and eradicate human rights abuses, and that abuse should be defined in the widest sense. I would like to see the BMA take a much more prominent role concerning human rights abuses, both here and abroad. We must be seen to be confronting and condemning abuses at home if we are legitimately to criticise others elsewhere. As a group, doctors have the potential to be a very powerful influence but they will need to present a united front", an extract of a letter from a BMA member.

Medical associations can contribute to training in ethics and human rights in a variety of ways. The BMA, for example, makes available ethical guidelines and practical advice for people like police surgeons on the Internet or by mail. It runs an advisory help-line for doctors faced with difficult human rights dilemmas and doctors in many parts of the world have used this. Unfortunately there are seldom easy-answers to the questions they raise, but we try to put them in touch with others who may be able to help. Education in medical ethics and human rights can be conducted not just by guidelines or through discussion groups. We recently received, for example, the Indian Medical Association's report on 'Knowledge, Attitude and Practice of Physicians in India' concerning medical aspects of torture. The report was based on questionnaires distributed by the IMA as part of an action plan to mobilise Indian doctors on the issue of care and treatment of torture victims. Over 70 per cent of the doctors who replied said that they had come across cases of torture but only 18 per cent knew where to report it. We were very interested by the fact that over 90 per cent of the Indian doctors who replied thought that there was a need to define further medical ethics in India as part of the strategy to reduce abuses. The IMA is planning to develop continuing medical education programmes, but the effort of circulating the questionnaire widely may itself be useful in raising awareness among doctors.

Widespread surveys, such as the Indian one on doctors' knowledge about and attitudes to torture have been carried out in several parts of the world, including the Philippines. The BMA has also circulated questionnaires in parts of Latin America and Asia. Findings in the Philippines indicated that many doctors were unsure about what constitutes torture and showed "a significant degree of tolerance for violent and coercive behaviour against persons under detention". This indicates that an important aspect of training for prison doctors and police surgeons concerns awareness of international legal standards regarding treatment of detainees. Skill in recognising and documenting the clinical sequelae of maltreatment is also an obvious area to be included in training packages supported by medical organisations.

Professional bodies can also provide support to rehabilitation centres. The number of rehabilitation centres worldwide for torture victims, staffed by paid and volunteer health professionals, has increased substantially. In 1993, Amnesty International wrote to more than 100 groups reported to be working with victims of organised violence in more than 25 countries. It compiled a survey of the kinds of services on offer and, by way of practical assistance, disseminated information about how to apply for financial support from the UN Voluntary Fund for Victims of Torture. One of the consequences of the expansion of these centres is that the ongoing reality of torture is brought home to more, even if still a small minority, of practising health professionals and a specialised expertise in physical and psychological rehabilitation is rapidly developing in health care teams.

Medical associations can be influential because of the power they are able to exercise over ordinary members of the community. Another of the key BMA principles is that those who are in positions of power or influence have obligations to ensure that such influence is used well to benefit people. One way of doing this is by empowering patients by giving them information about their rights, and about international legal instruments that support those rights. Another way is to try to educate people about the pejorative effects of cultural practices, such as female genital mutilation or abortion of female foetuses. Campaigns such as these are immensely sensitive in that they involve concepts of cultural relativism or cultural imperialism, but nevertheless, the BMA's line has been that doctors have duties to try to explain to people why certain cultural practices need to change. Another highly controversial campaign has concerned the involvement of doctors in judicial punishments, such as floggings, hanging, branding or amputation. In its early publications, the BMA shied away from addressing such issues, which were seen as cultural matters to be resolved within each society. Increasingly, however, the BMA has adopted the position that an ethical obligation of all doctors is to try to reduce "harm" in its widest sense within the population. This means that doctors sometimes have to take an unpopular position with regard to cultural or judicial practices. The evidence that we have received in compiling our latest human rights report is that in many areas of Africa or Central Europe, doctors pay a high price in terms of suffering or assassination for trying to alter societal attitudes.

Medical associations can exercise political influence for change within countries with poor human rights records. They should also seek to co-ordinate the professional response to violence and abuse. Collaboration of doctors in human rights violations continues to be documented in countries like Turkey, but it is too simplistic to condemn those involved without acknowledging the danger and threats that confront them. What they really need are practical solutions, which allow them to fulfil their ethical obligations without necessarily risking the lives of themselves, their patients, or their families. Thus the BMA has become increasingly preoccupied with the question of how human rights violations can be documented by doctors in a way that does not put either the victim or the doctor at risk but allows the international community to understand and react to the reality of hidden violence. We want safe reporting mechanisms and easy access by doctors to information about how to identify signs of abuse. We have supported, for example, a new UN post of Rapporteur on the Integrity of the Medical Profession, whose duties would parallel those of the rapporteur on the independence of the judiciary, and who would monitor cases where doctors were under threat to conceal evidence. We are examining how abuses reported in one country, can be tried by courts in other jurisdictions, and the BMA has campaigned for the establishment of the International Criminal Court to deal with abuses of human rights. We are working with networks of doctors who are interested in sharing survival strategies, and campaigning on behalf of colleagues under threat. We are examining international linkages so that, for example, Turkish doctors can smuggle out factual data about evidence of violence, and forensic specialists outside the country can interpret this. We are compiling a database of the human rights activities of all medical associations around the world. By combining different elements of expertise across international borders we believe that ways can be found of both exposing the violations while still protecting the victims and their doctors.

In addition to major initiatives, medical bodies can also carry out simply baseline activities. For 15 years, for example, the BMA has implemented a letter writing campaign in response to evidence of abuses of human rights anywhere in the world, which involved doctors either as victims or collaborators.

How the BMA's Perspective and Approach Changed

In the past, BMA publications on human rights concentrated on a narrow, traditional interpretation of human rights. That is to say they focussed primarily on the evidence of medical involvement in torture or extra-judicial executions. As we approach the 21st century, however, the BMA has looked back at the wide range of issues—social and cultural as well as civil and political—that are encompassed within the UN instruments. We are increasingly examining how doctors can be effective in promoting civil and political rights, such as a "right to health", as well as in preventing abuse of the traditional rights, such as freedom from torture and maltreatment. Thus as it has become more involved in human rights work, the BMA's perspective has changed. In 1984, the BMA's annual meeting called for a working party to be set up to investigate allegations that doctors in some countries were co-operating in state torture. Two years later, the BMA published a booklet called The Torture Report. As its title suggests, this brief report was concerned primarily in the role of doctors as collaborators in the violation of civil and political rights. It ignored matters such as the growing role played by doctors in some countries in carrying out or supervising judicial punishments.

The BMA's 1986 Torture Report found "incontrovertible evidence of doctors' involvement in planning and assisting in torture, not only under duress, but also voluntarily as an exercise of the doctor's free will". When the brief report was received at the annual meeting of 1986, members mandated the BMA, whenever possible, to help and support doctors anywhere in the world who are faced with evidence of torture.

As medical and humanitarian groups gradually learned of the BMA report, and its promise to try to provide help, a tide of appeals, evidence and testimonies flowed in. Often frustrated and desperate, doctors and medical students from many different countries reported the familiar indicators of routine or institutionalised abuse. Disappearances of colleagues or patients, unexplained deaths in custody, forensic evidence of beating or torture, the presence of mutilated corpses in police morgues, pressure on doctors to sign death certificates without examining the corpse, incommunicado detention, and denial of medical access to certain prisoners, or police refusal to allow a doctor to speak privately to patients hospitalised in suspicious circumstances. As an organisation without investigatory powers or experience, the BMA was unable to provide immediate and practical solutions. It could document and redirect the evidence to other agencies with more experience and influence. Lobbying and letter writing campaigns on human rights issues to heads of state, governments, medical organisations or international funding agencies, such as the European Parliament, also formed a continuing element of the BMA's work. It was evident that more effective and less piecemeal strategies were needed.

In 1989, another debate at the BMA's annual meeting drew attention to this growing body of material and asked for a new working party to review it and produce recommendations for action. This time a more substantial report, Medicine Betrayed, resulted in 1992. Unlike the earlier BMA document, it was not confined to examining medical involvement in torture but considered the role of doctors in a wide range of human rights violations and in judicially approved procedures such as execution and corporal punishment. Balancing the picture, it also drew attention to the way in which doctors who attempt to resist collaboration in abuse frequently fall victim themselves to harassment, torture or murder. Forty-five recommendations in the report set out a preliminary plan by which it was hoped that medical associations and individuals could begin to address abuses and, hopefully, to construct a framework of protection for victims. Education of the profession as to their ethical obligations was a key recommendation. Realistically, however, the BMA was well aware that recommendations alone would change nothing, and that by far the harder task lay in pressing for their implementation.

This is the focus of our current efforts in the third book we are now preparing, and for which CEHAT is among the many expert bodies that has provided advice. The BMA is anxious to move away from just documenting bad practice to providing concrete examples of good practice. We notice that in many areas of the world, lawyers' organisations have been more successful in protecting their own members and their clients. Awareness of international law and internationally endorsed standards of practice, as well as knowledge of how to use the UN instruments, has undoubtedly helped. We want doctors to understand how this knowledge may help to protect them and their vulnerable patients. We understand that education is not just something that happens in classrooms, but also by example and the proven experience of others.

We have been collecting evidence by way of interviews and questionnaires from doctors in a wide range of countries. We are also visiting detention centres and institutions in an effort to identify good models of practice. The BMA is also increasingly working on the issue of access to health care, and to a reasonable living environment, as a matter of human rights. The longest chapter in our new book focuses on "health as a human rights objective" and aims to show how health professionals and human rights workers often have shared concerns and common goals. We recognise that there is still considerable debate about whether human rights language should be extended to encompass issues of poverty, justice, equity in regard to health. Nevertheless, since we believe that well organised networks of interest groups can exercise influence over national and international policies on health issues, we support the use of any terminology, which furthers that aim. One of our priorities is to identify how organisations like ourselves, can work closely with other professionals and NGOs who have similar aims.

Some Suggestions for Future Development

Disseminating information and evidence about abuse is clearly not enough. Practical measures need to be found for moving the debate forward. Issues that we consider in our new book include ways in which alliances of disparate organisations can be formed to pressurise governments to act, and how regulations can be tightened to reduce opportunities for abuse. Global communications systems are facilitating the development of international networks of health professionals, lawyers, patient-advocates and human rights activists. More co-ordination is required, however, to minimise the duplication of effort, especially of evidence-gathering missions or trial observations. As a contribution, the BMA, like other organisations, is compiling databases of material about human rights. A number of international health bodies, such as the World Health Organisation (WHO) and Commonwealth Medical Association (CMA), have made good use of the convergence of health and human rights taxonomies by blending both elements into their plans and educational efforts. Some organisations, such as the BMA, are only just beginning to explore these possibilities. The late Dr Jonathan Mann saw this integration of the different spheres of expertise concerned with health and with rights issues as part of a "bridge to the future". He wrote that "lack of knowledge about human rights among health professionals, and about public health among human rights professionals, is the dominant problem" for the "nascent health and human rights movement" (Mann, Gruskin, 1997). He saw evidence, however, that this movement was growing rapidly and its development would inevitably accelerate once better methods of co-operation were established. We hope that the development of such co-operation through regional, national and international networks will be one of the key practical contributions of this conference organised by CEHAT.

Strategies for co-operation on human rights issues have been developing in a piecemeal fashion, involving health professionals, lawyers and human rights organisations. The IFHHRO network of organisations at this conference, among which CEHAT, is a valued member, has been very influential. It manages to work across national and cultural boundaries. Good models like this exist at national, regional and world level but it seems they sometimes work on parallel, rather than intersecting lines. Too often, it seems, individuals and organisations with an interest in these issues invest time and effort in reinventing action programmes that have already been tried out elsewhere. Where strategies have proved successful in one context, information about them needs to be shared with others facing similar human rights challenges. Knowledge about bad risks and failed missions also needs to be shared in a manner that would help others avoid the same mistakes.

We have spent a lot of time liasing with doctors around the world in order to find examples of good practice, workable models of what can be achieved, and measures, which we hope will protect doctors and vulnerable patients. Many of the recommendations we have made are already part of the work of CEHAT. That is to say that this organisation and this conference provide good models for other organisations and other countries. The BMA is grateful to be invited to this event in order to learn from—and hopefully to pass on to others—the collective experience and knowledge of those who are represented here during this conference. We recognise, however, that there are no easy answers to the dilemmas, which will be discussed here.

6

Characterstics of Violence Induced by Current Therapeutic Systems : Description, Analysis and Impact on Ethical Issue

Françoise Sironi

Who am I to talk to you about violence in France? I am a clinical psychologist and psychotherapist who could never separate clinical practice from ethical concerns. Therefore, it was natural for me to be a very active member of the medical group of the Amnesty International (French Section) for ten years. I did my Ph.D in clinical and pathological psychology on the treatment of torture victims. There I described how I had to change my psychotherapeutic practice, how I had to innovate techniques in order to efficiently treat torture victims and victims of collective violence. In my Ph.D I've also analysed the nature of human induced trauma, the methods of torture, the torture system, and the training of torturers. I strongly believe that one cannot treat a torture victim if one doesn't take into account the context of the torture, the methods of torture and the intentions of the torturer. I've written a book on all these issues. I am also one of the founders of the Paris-based Primo Levi Centre, which treats torture victims and is supported by Amnesty International French Section, Médecins du Monde (MDM), and some other NGOs in France. At present, I no longer work at the Primo Levi Centre because of the responsibilities I have at the University. I am actually a Master of Conferences in psychology and psychopathology at the University Paris 8, and I am also the director of the Centre Georges Devereux, a University treatment centre located inside the University of Paris 8. This centre is dedicated to migrant populations, and to cultural, social and sexual minority in France.

Violence must be contextualised in its cultural reality. The University of Paris 8, as well as the Centre Georges Devereux are located in Saint-Denis, the hottest suburb of Paris in terms of delinquency, violence, murder, and poverty. How is it to work while being constantly surrounded by violence? Although danger is permanent, the doors of our University remain open at all times. And I am proud to belong as a teacher to the only

University in France, which accepts students who have failed in their secondary school examinations but have cleared the University entrance qualification. The University Paris 8 in this way gives a second chance to those who want to study, taking into consideration the fact that failing such an important examination, like the secondary examination, is not a proof of lack of intelligence and interest in knowledge but can be the consequence of social and cultural discrimination. The Paris 8 University is also the most innovative university, because it is open to various kinds of experimentations - banking on the audacity of the teachers, of the students, and of the type and quality of research that is conducted under those conditions. Although May 1968 is far behind us, the subversive spirit of those who were teachers in our University, namely Michel Foucault, Gilles Deleuze, Félix Guattary, Noam Chomsky, Armando Verdiglione and many others, is still alive, and, who knows, possess us for the best.

If I had to describe the most visible aspects of violence in France I would say that violence in France looks like violence in any other western country: riots, unemployment, acceleration of the gap between the extremely rich and the extremely poor, the marginalised, the multiplication of neo-groups, and attacks and burnings of administrative buildings representing state power. Nevertheless, these last events are not brought out in public, the attacks and burnings are rather hidden, in order not to frighten the population. Besides the violence of the marginalised and the excluded in one of the richest countries in the world, that is France, there is an increasing amount of state violence there. This kind of violence, described in the 1998 report of the Amnesty International, is of the same nature as that of in any other western country: policemen who murder people, mainly "without having the intention to kill". The majority of those killed in this manner, are migrants, refugees, and people from non-western countries.

Now, if I were to describe the less visible aspects of violence in France, but which is actually central to the phenomenon of violence, I would say this: one of the most central, yet hidden causes of violence in France is the absolute pervasiveness and power of state culture. Institutions like public schools and the legal, social and health systems convey state culture.

One of the most prevalent types of violence occurs because health professionals refuse to take into account the culture of their patients. Disrespecting the culture of a person, discrediting him for belonging to a community, is a violation of human rights, and a disregard of ethics by health professionals. Health professionals totally discredit and deny the idea of cultural belonging when they are confronted with migrants and refugees coming from non-western countries. Culture is not just the colour of the skin, it is not added to the personality, it is an organic part of the personality.

The concept of human rights is considered to be universal and culture-free, and is above the complex matrix of identities of that individual. The individuals, who speak on behalf of human rights themselves form a group who think that they are singular individuals, free electrons - subjects, who can escape to any culture, and who refer to themselves as being universal. I can tell you that as a health professional, as a psychotherapist born on the French-German border from an Italian father and an Alsatian mother, a person working and teaching in the most violent suburb of Paris, I am not culture-free, my technique is totally underlined by culture, even if this culture comes from the accumulation of my singular experience. Those who believe that they are escaping from any cultural moorings, thereby, themselves constitute a group, is a delusion. We act as if there is a universal element in each individual, which can be separated from his personality, which we refer to as the "human psyche" or the "human suffering" but in reality we also deal with the presence of the group in the individual. That is to say that the concept of human rights is not culture-free, because the users of this concept are themselves constituted in a group, which interacts with other groups.

Now, what Analysis can we do as Regards Violence?

In France, the influence, weight and presence of the state is very important. In western countries, and particularly in France, our philosophy is an individualistic one. You can see it in the Laws, the Rights, through the theories that underlie the therapeutic systems as well as the social, educational and judicial systems. However, social exclusion is becoming more and more important. The scholastic difficulties of the pupils are becoming more and more disastrous; illiteracy is growing. Schools have failed in their attempt to integrate and affiliate individuals to a unique state culture. Neo-groups, with geographic or territorial boundaries inside some quarters of Paris or inside some streets of the suburbs, are appearing. Each group has a name, a specific culture, neo-rituals, initiation processes. The codes are very rigid. The more you deny the existence of groups and consider only the single individual isolated from his group, the more you will encourage the appearance of artificial groups (like neo-religious groups, sects, neo-political groups). We are witness to the revival of pre-existing groups (like religious ones for example) but the rules and practices of these pre-existing groups have become rigid. . We can therefore see the emergence of fundamentalism.

In our clinical practice at the Georges Devereux Centre, health professionals and social workers refer patients because their treatment is not progressing and the professionals feel the need to understand their patients' problem better. Most of the patients referred to the Centre were undergoing treatment for a long time, and were without results. The symptoms - psychological, social and educational - of the problems that they present appear to be without a solution. A symptom can be the expression of hidden logic, which is not only individual and intra-psychic, but finds coherence in the historical past. Those symptoms, whatever they may be, are a testimony to the underlying existence of other ways of thinking in an historical perspective. Those persons with their mysterious symptoms have lost a sense of their historical and cultural context because they are no longer familiar-with the culture of their origin.

What is even more interesting than looking at the causes of non-integration is looking at the function of non-integration. Non-integration is an active strategy of resistance against being subjugated by the various state institutions.

At that point, we can relate our analysis of violence in France to what Michel Foucault defined as the subjected or submitted knowledge. By subjected or submitted knowledge, Foucault refers to historical data and information that has been buried or hidden in functional coherence. This subjected knowledge is not sociology of life in a psychiatric hospital; or for example, sociology of delinquency. Subjected or submitted knowledge is in fact blocks of historical knowledge, which is always present, hidden inside functional and organised units. This knowledge re-emerges in critical research. This definition of subjected knowledge can be applied to ethno-psychiatry: to find what is behind, what was before and what reappears under the figure of psychopathology in western society.

Let us deliberate over the violence induced by therapeutic and social systems in a western country like France. "Although health professionals claim that they only work in order to relieve individual pain, we cannot ignore that therapeutic and social systems do actually constitute extremely powerful social and political forces" (Nathan, 1998).

Illustration 1: Mrs. B

Mrs B was treated with psychotherapy at the Georges Devereux Centre. She is a migrant, from Algeria. Her problems started about a year-and-a-half ago. Her husband left her alone with two little children and no money. Mrs B is unemployed. The mental health of Mrs B declined sharply. She was totally depressed and lost. She entrusted her two children temporarily to the state social services. Meanwhile, she went to a hospital for treatment. But three weeks later she could not regain custody of her children. A year later, she has still not got her children back.

The psychologist of the social care institution thinks that Mrs B is still too fragile to take care of her children. Yet, this decision of the psychologist induces iatrogenic suffering. In fact, Mrs B is depressed because she cannot get her children back. The social services also find Mrs B to be aggressive, and that she suffers from persecution complex. In fact, they are interpreting and pathologising a behaviour that is a natural response to her present situation. It reflects the anger, sadness and powerlessness of a mother who is longing for her children.

The second reason why she cannot get her children back is the enquiry that has been made by the social services. The French law stipulates that if your home is too small, i.e., if you don't have 8 square-metre per child, you cannot get your child back once it is entrusted to social institutions. This is why many poor people evade the state social services. Instead of being helpful they turn out to be repressive.

Illustration 2: Mr J

Mr J is a native of Nigeria. He is a Yoruba and got married to a Yoruba woman in France. They have two children. The couple divorced. As is usually the case, the court decreed that the children be entrusted to the mother. The Yorubas are patri-linear and therefore the children belong to the paternal lineage. The mother knew it, but did not do anything about it since the French law was on her side. The father disagreed, and a family council took place between the two families in Nigeria. Finally, the children were entrusted to the father. The girl was happy about this decision, knowing that anyway she would have regular contacts with her mother. However, the boy was unhappy since his relation with his father was strained He started stealing money from his father's wallet. The father was strict and couldn't bear this. When this initially happened, he slapped the boy and threatened him, "If you do it again, I will beat you again!" When the son stole again, he was too scared to return home from school. Therefore, he told the director of the school that his father ill-treated him. The director, without checking out the facts or questioning the boy, allowed him to stay at school for lunch. She did not call home to advise the father and his second wife. They were anxious about the boy's whereabouts and looked for him in the school. The director told them that the boy wouldn't go home that night. He'd be entrusted to an institution for children in order to protect him from his father.

Illustration 3: Cases of Ill Treatment and Victims of Incest

A young girl tells of her suffering to her schoolmates and teachers. The authorities arrest her father, and she is taken out of the family. She stays in a collective for some time, and is afterwards placed in another family. These girls undergo psychotherapy and most of the time one is working through the guilt of the child for having destroyed the family. Yet, very often, they are very ambiguous about their feelings towards their parents since they still love their father and do not want to see their mother crying. Suggestion: Why not to call a family counsellor for help?

The therapeutic systems subject the users to pressures, which lead to the formation of groups and associations of the users. Therefore, these groups or associations could be of AIDS patients, or people suffering from mucoviscidose, bulimia or mental disorders. These groups refuse to be analysed or defined in the conventional manner any longer. The power of such groups is best demonstrated in the case of homosexuality. Did you know that until 1985 homosexuality figured in the DSM (American classification system and diagnostic of mental illnesses) manual where it was considered a disorder? Thanks to the pressures brought on the establishment by homosexuals, that homosexuality has been struck off the DSM Manual.

At Georges Devereux Centre we take a positive clinical approach and a positive participatory treatment line with migrants, minorities and the marginalised. We are more on the side of the patients we treat than on the side of health professionals we are working with.

In the last five years the Georges Devereux Centre, attached to the department of psychology of the Paris 8 University, is an experimental place of mediation between scientific thinking and the beliefs brought back by the migrants and the marginalised. Mediation demands that one first recognises and describes the misunderstandings, oppositions and conflicts, and second, believes that an acceptable peace is possible, that learning the best way to live together is possible. Professor Tobie Nathan president and founder of the Georges Devereux Centre, heads the psychology department. He is a very popular, creative clinician and researcher who, has written many books and articles on psychology, psychopathology and ethno-psychiatry. If Georges Devereux (a French psychoanalyst and anthropologist who spent most of his life in the United States) founded ethno-psychiatry as a discipline almost 30 years ago, Tobie Nathan is the one who developed the discipline, both on the theoretical and clinical side.

Ethno-psychiatry is a discipline that brings about an understanding to the suffering of the patients by not cutting them from their various affiliations and cultural groups. For western health professionals, mainly as regards psychology and psychopathology, the solutions to such problems are final. They have the tendency to analyse cultural singularities as being signs of psychopathology. But psychopathology is a complex matrix constituted of the patients, the health professionals, and at least two theories about the patients' suffering: one pertaining to the patient, his surrounding, and his family, and the other that of the health professional. It is this intermeshing of the various strands that constitutes psychopathology. Therefore, whenever one practices psychotherapy, it is important to take into consideration all these elements.

Ethno-psychiatry as a discipline demands from the clinician and the researcher to re-think the pre-existing categories, which until now defined the object of his studies. The categories, for example, can be nosographical ones. A patient does not exist in nature all by himself but he is build-up according to categories and theories. What kind of patients are we producing with these categories? Which items are privileged, which of them are left in the dark? Who has interest in building this nosography: the chemical and pharmaceutical industry, or the patients? Or for that matter, when was the concept born? Who has interest in rigidifying the definition and use? Such rigorous analysis leads to either a validation or invalidation of pre-existing categories and concepts.

Another principle, which characterises ethno-psychiatry, is the analysis of therapeutic systems wherein all pre-existing hierarchies are ignored, and where none of the systems are excluded, be they modern, psychoanalytical, ethnical, religious, or social ones. In studying them one also brings out their underlying theories, the hypothesis they have about a human being, their coherence and efficiency, as well as their limits.

Ethno-psychiatry also juxtaposes the concepts of psychiatry, psychoanalysis and psychology with the theories and therapeutic systems of the ethnic and marginalized groups. The discipline does not take part in the quarrel between the defenders of universality and the defenders of cultural relativism, but is permanently inventing methods to confront theories with clinical and cultural realities.

The discipline submits our interventions to the analysis of the concerned persons and groups whom we 'pretend' to describe and treat. It also invites the clinician and researcher to acknowledge the methodological constraints in their own theories and practices and restrains them from pronouncing any judgement without participating in the patient-professional discourse.

Ethno-psychiatry is also a clinical methodology and a clinical setting, which, in fact, is a logical consequence of its theoretical stance. Many persons constitute an ethno-psychiatric therapeutic setting. We receive the patients in large groups composed of the patient, his family or friends, and the different people who are a part of the network around him (social workers, doctors, educational workers, and teachers if they are children). Though the main therapist directs the assembly it is the cultural mediator who plays an important role in the gathering. He is the one who speaks the language of the patient, and knows the culture and the therapeutic systems of the country to which the patient belongs. He, therefore, is able to delve deeply into the subtleties of the meanings that develop during the course of the discussions. Each one in the assembly presents his viewpoint to the patient and the main therapist organises the ways in which these elements of understanding can be presented and restored to the patient.

The word culture is, for Tobie Nathan, a way of legitimising the knowledge of others. It permits one to build an anthropology, which is really symmetrical, because it constrains the clinicians, health professionals and researchers to confront honestly the knowledge issued from heterogeneous worlds. "Rehabilitating the world culture", says Tobie Nathan, "means submitting the researchers in human sciences to the expertise of those you pretend to describe. This is really what constitutes, according to me, a fascinating programme, on a theoretical level, a programme that comprises new and major ethical stakes or goals."

These are then the conditions of a real ethical approach to the patients because it does not discredit them. The deontological consequences of such an approach are that the patients are no longer in the position of an object. It is no longer possible to interpret their psychological functioning from the standpoint of a theory, unless one clarifies the theory to the patient. The theory, then, also becomes an object of study. The patient thus becomes a real partner, an indispensable alter ego in this participatory effort to find a solution to his suffering. In ethno-psychiatry one re-thinks with the patient the causes of his suffering as well as the theories with which they have been constructed. This participatory approach definitely interests him. It has nothing to do with his educational level because it considers each one of us to be a thinking being. It demands of you to consider and handle the patient as a partner with equal knowledge. Equal must be understood in terms of the fact that the ideas and theories that the patient is building in his head about his suffering are as worthy as yours. The patient is invited to discuss the observations of his therapists, to argue their hypothesis, to share the responsibility of the treatment since he has been apprised of all the theories and stances that the people in the group have taken. Of course, the patients are not used to this. We are training him, in a certain sense, to become what we call a "patient-expert". The health professionals, who are part of the network, too, are being trained to handle such an approach.

Practiced this way, ethno-psychiatry creates, through a kind of natural process, an ethical rigour, because it does not subject itself to deontological principles. What could be considered as ethical principles, are in fact, its theoretical positions and its usual clinical practice.

At that point, what we said about our practices in ethno-psychiatry has to be related to a second definition, which Michel Foucault gave about subjected or submitted knowledge (the first definition has been stated above). By subjected or submitted knowledge he also means different knowledge that is disqualified because it is considered as being not elaborate enough; it is likened to what one calls naïve knowledge, the knowledge of the delinquent, the psychiatrised patient, or knowledge hierarchically inferior, and that is thought to be located beyond the required scientificity. This knowledge from below is non-qualified knowledge, yet, parallel and marginal according to medical knowledge. This knowledge Foucault qualified as being the knowledge of the people (which has nothing to do with common sense, on the contrary). It is a specific knowledge for Foucault, a differential knowledge, which is unable to build unanimity and draws its force from the fact that it opposes all others that surround it.

Michel Foucault thinks that it is the blending of this buried knowledge of erudition with the knowledge disqualified by the given hierarchy of knowledge, gives to the critique its essential force. Ethno-psychiatry too can be described in the same manner - as the blending of buried knowledge and disqualified knowledge. It is considered as being subversive.

We are criticised by, what I call the lifeless, flabby and weak Left, as well as by the Extreme right. The flabby Left defends the values of the republic, of secularism. Many health professionals are leftists, flabby socialists, because it is culturally correct to be a leftist. Nevertheless, they are as conservative as the rightists. They don't reconsider their theories, the way they treat patients, or the way they consider psychotherapy. They are scared to saw the foot of the chair they are sitting on. The critics from the Extreme right belive that our thought processes are closer to them since we don't discredit the theories of the migrants, and that we consider their therapeutic systems as worthy of being studied and taken into consideration.

Anyway, this way of practicing ethno-psychiatry is always considered to be subversive and many wish that we disappeared from the scene. For the moment, we are still here, because we too have a lot of support, and which is growing by the day in France, as well as all over the world. This way of practicing ethno-psychiatry gives us utmost freedom. It is the best way to work with violent patients, by totally inverting the previous logic of health care.

Let me conclude with this African proverb:

As long as the lions won't have their own historians

The hunting stories will continue to glorify the hunters.

Part-III
Violence by State Agencies

7

Violence by State Agencies: Two Case Reports

Rajendra S. Bangal

A medical professional often comes across victims of torture (either by state agencies or by other people). Therefore, he must be aware of the ethical aspects of torture with special reference to declarations, principles and guidelines applicable to medical professionals.

Torture and violence have been identified with the police in India ever since the Vedic Age (2000-1400 BC). Kautilya, Manu, Chandra Gupta speak about it. The Indian Penal Code (1860), the Indian Evidence Act (1872) and the Criminal Procedure Code (1898) include in them relevant sections on torture. But investigating officers due to their over-zealousness and ignorance of the recent methods of crime investigation resort to torture as a 'simple way' of crime detection.

A doctor can be involved in the acts of torture in many ways: as a humanist citizen, a participant in the process of torture, a victim of torture (e.g. in Chile, Turkey), etc. Various declarations and principles regarding the ethical aspects of torture are available. Doctors may face the dilemma on whether to adhere to ethics or obey the orders of superiors when such an order may not be illegal.

Two case reports are mentioned below in which I was involved in the capacity of a doctor conducting post-mortem examination. The names and dates in these case reports have been changed.

Case Report: 1

A 35-year-old male was in police custody for some petty offence. On January 1, 1996, at 3 p.m. he became comatose and drowsy. There was hallucinatory behaviour and disorientation to time, place and person, He was admitted to X jail dispensary. By 5 p.m. He was not responding to painful stimulus. His pulse was 64/min and blood pressure 86 mm Hg. (systolic). In the jail dispensary the diagnosis was: alcohol intoxication withdrawal symptoms.

At 6.25 p.m. he was then referred to Z hospital (a well established government. hospital with a medical college attached to it). When he was received in the casualty room of this hospital, he was unconscious, his pupils were dilated, sluggishly reacting to light, his blood pressure was 150 mm Hg. (systolic) and alcohol-like smell was present in his breath. In the casualty room he was again diagnosed as suffering from alcohol intoxication withdrawal symptoms and shifted to the ward. The examination in the ward revealed that he had a right black eye, and this was noted in the case paper. However, again a provisional diagnosis of alcohol consumption with sedative overdose was made. Therefore, a Ryle's tube aspiration was done. The sample was preserved and handed over to the police. By 8.35 p.m. his spontaneous respiration stopped. He was immediately shifted to the ICU and put on ventilatory support. On January 2 at 7.20 a.m. he went into deep coma. There was hypothermia, his pulse was not palpable and the blood pressure was not recordable. A diagnosis of unknown poisoning with cardio-respiratory arrest with anoxic brain damage was made. Throughout the day, his hypothermia continued (rectal temperature < 35°C). His condition did not improve and he expired the next day, i.e., on January 3 at 1.15 p.m.

A police inquest was made on January 3 in the evening and the department of forensic medicine of the same medical college received the body on January 4 at 12.15 a.m. His post-mortem was conducted on January 4, between 12.30 a.m. and 1.45 a.m.

Post-mortem findings: External: (1) abrasion 0.5x 0.3 cm. over inner aspect of left side of lower lip, near the region of lower left lateral incisor and the canine teeth, (2) contusion surrounding the lateral aspect of right eye. **Internal:** (1) below the scalp there was a haematoma of 4x2 cm. over the left temporal region, (2) haematoma was present in the whole left temporalis muscle, (3) a large 1 cm. thick layer of organised subdural haematoma was found covering the whole superior and lateral aspects of both the cerebral hemispheres, (4) haematoma was also present at the base of the brain and in the subarachnoid plane, (5) from the 2nd to the 7th rib on the left side were fractured, (6) the whole posterio-lateral surface of the left thoracic wall was contused internally, (7) the thoracic cavity contained 100 cc. of fluid blood, (8) gastric mucosa was normal, the stomach contained 30 cc. of yellowish sticky fluid without any specific smell, (9) liver showed fatty changes, (10) the age of the injuries was 4 to 6 days before death.

Viscera were preserved. The cause of death was given as "death due to shock following head injury". The chemical analysis report of the preserved viscera was received on January 8 (three months later). The findings stated that ethyl alcohol was detected in: stomach and intestines: 30 mg/100 ml; liver, spleen and kidneys: 13 mg/100 ml; and blood: 40 mg 100 ml.

The case was handed over to the state CID for investigation. Their queries and my conclusions during investigations were: (1) What was the age of the injuries? I concluded that it was approximately 4 to 6 days before death. (2) Whether the injuries were possible by falling on a stone? I concluded that they were not possible by a simple fall. (3) The provisional diagnosis of alcohol consumption and sedative overdose was made in this case, and at one place in the case notes it was mentioned as 'unknown poisoning'. What was my opinion regarding this? I concluded that the alcohol levels detected in the viscera were too less and nowhere near the fatal dose. Moreover, no sedative or any other drug or poison was detected. Thus, taking into consideration the indoor case paper, post-mortem findings, and the chemical-analysis report, I was of the opinion that the "death was due to shock following head injury."

Discussion: The present case throws light on two important topics. First and foremost is regarding the violence by state agencies. From the post-mortem findings it was clear that; the person was assaulted by hard and blunt objects, and the injuries were sustained when he was in police custody. After receiving the post-mortem report, the investigation was handed over to the state CID, and the National Human Rights Commission raised the matter. All the police personnel, who were responsible for the custody of the victim were immediately suspended and were booked under relevant sections of the Indian Penal Code.

Secondly, the diagnosis of the head injury was completely missed during the treatment! The patient was admitted at two places before his death. It is a well-known fact that the symptoms of alcohol overdose and head injury are similar. In fact, head injury is one of the differential diagnoses of alcohol intoxication. Therefore, when a diagnosis of alcohol intoxication was made at both the places, the concerned doctors did not bother to rule out the possibility of a head injury, especially so, when the finding of a right black eye was noted in the government hospital case notes. The question that arises is whether the omission (to diagnose the head injury) was a deliberate one or just a case of missed diagnosis. One can understand missing the diagnosis at the small, ill-equipped dispensary, but what about the full-fledged government hospital with a well-reputed medical college attached to it, and which serves as a referral centre to all the surrounding districts? If this omission was deliberately done at such an institute, due to pressures either from the police or any other source, or for monetary gains, then it certainly is a matter of concern and steps should be taken to punish such black sheep in the medical profession.

Case Report: 2

A fax message was received in our department one day (in 1997) in the evening from the deputy collector of Y taluka, stating that a person B had expired in police custody on seven days back. His post-mortem was done in the primary health centre of that taluka and the body was buried on the outskirts of the village. The wife of the deceased had raised doubts about the authenticity of the first post-mortem report as it failed to throw any light on the cause of the death of her husband. The cause of death as mentioned in the first post-mortem report was "Opinion reserved, viscera preserved". The situation in the village was very tense during these 7-8 days as the wife of the deceased and her supporters were constantly demanding for a re-post-mortem and there was a delay on the part of the authorities to take a decision. At last, due to political pressure, the authorities decided to carry out a re-post-mortem and accordingly sent a fax message to our department.

Next day the exhumation was carried out in my presence by the special executive magistrate of that area. The deputy collector of that taluka, the police inspector of the concerned police station and the deputy superintendent of the area were also present. It was rainy season. The grave was located on a slope so it was not waterlogged. However, water had accumulated at a short distance from the grave. The soil of the grave was moist due to the rains on the previous night. After exhumation the body was sealed and shifted to our mortuary for post-mortem. The post-mortem was carried out same day between 6 and 8.15 p.m.

Post-mortem findings: It was the body of a 35-year-old male. The body was partly decomposed and partly showed changes of adipocere formation. This is a natural means of preservation of a dead body, by which, in a damp, warm environment the body fats get converted into higher fatty acids, and so the features are well preserved and the injuries can be recognised. The skin over the body had loosened and was easily removable. The underlying body surface was white and waxy.

The following injuries were found (in addition to the post-mortem incisions of the first post-mortem examination over the head, chest and abdomen):

(1) 14 large contusions on the back and buttocks, and the posterior aspects of both thighs and calves were contused at places, (2) there was evidence of extravasated blood below the layers of the scalp in the left parieto-occipital and right parietal regions, (3) there was evidence of ante-mortem fractures at posterior aspects of both parietal bones.

The available viscera were preserved for chemical analysis and pieces of the skull bones were sent for histopathological examination. The cause of death arrived at was, "Evidence of multiple contusions present over the body. Skull bone pieces sent for histo-pathological examination. Final opinion kept pending till then". The chemical analysis report was received after a fortnight. It detected ethyl alcohol in the stomach and intestines (17 mg/100 ml.), liver, spleen and kidneys (25 mg/100 ml.). The histo-pathological report was inconclusive. The final opinion regarding the cause of death was given as "Death due to multiple blunt injuries with evidence of head injury". After receiving the advance death certificate, the police officers responsible for the custody of the deceased were suspended with immediate effect. And after obtaining the final cause of death they were all booked under Section 302 of the Indian Penal Code.

Discussion: When the second post-mortem (PM), done 8 days after the first PM could reveal these findings it is improbable that the doctor who conducted the first PM did not find anything to which death could be attributed. Therefore, it is very clear that in this case a fake PM report was prepared, either under pressure or for monetary gains. If the re-post-mortem had not been done then the first doctor would have given the final cause of death as alcohol intoxication, since ethyl alcohol was detected in the viscera of the deceased, though in minute quantities. The interesting part of this case was that the first post-mortem report as revealed to me by the state CID at a later date also contained findings of many injuries including the fracture of the vault of the skull. How did this happen? Why then the doctor kept the cause of death reserved?

8

Who Cares for Torture Victims? The West Bengal Experience

Nilanjan Dutta

Torture, as a phenomenon is not new. In Bengal (and similar examples can be found elsewhere, too), the colonial police system owed its origins to the state's need to systematise rent collection rather than in its law-keeping responsibilities in the modern ethical sense. Coercion was congenital to this system.

This coercive machinery, empowered by a series of repressive legislations, came in handy for the colonial rulers for suppressing the national liberation movement. Torture had become the order of the day by the beginning of the 20th century. Among its multiple uses, the extortion of confession, replaced the extortion of rent as the major one. Confession is an important theme in the theo-legal jurisprudence of the Western tradition (down to the point of, if we are allowed a little digression, l'affair Clinton) that was globalised by imperialism. It is also a convenient tool of summary justice, which the state uses to produce quick results, as a sort of magic remedy for both its own woes and those of the people. Thus, it also became established as a method of crime "investigation".

The post-colonial state has been conveniently using the coercive apparatus that imperialism had set up. The infliction of pain - both physical and mental - apart from making one confess, can break the victim down to submission, collaboration or obliteration. Torture not only scares, it kills. The victim may be anybody whom the state and its agents want to break down - a revolutionary, a criminal, or simply one who has to be brought over. Torture may be practised by anybody from a position of power on anybody who is powerless in a given situation. In fact, we have instances around us of torture by the more powerful members of the family (in a majority of cases, male), by criminals, by landlords and their henchmen, by mobs acting in the name of justice, and even by rebels professing egalitarianism. However, we have reasons to be particularly concerned about the torture sponsored and sanctioned by the state.

The state is the most powerful social entity in the power structure, which needs torture in order to be operative, and exploits this advantageous position to the maximum. An individual, who is the ultimate target of torture, is not as helpless before any other agency as he is before the state. The sanction of the state is the ultimate socio-legal sanction, and is given in the name of the whole body of citizens that it claims to represent. Agencies, such as the police and the armed forces, acting on its behalf, have this sanction automatically. When this sanction is for torture, a practice that dehumanises human beings, it gets the general stamp of approval. The "spectacle of suffering", to borrow Michel Foucault's description, has become an integral, though unacknowledged part of statecraft. No government, colonial or post-colonial has been able to do without it. In West Bengal (and earlier in undivided Bengal) we have seen this practice continuing under the widest variety of political rulers: colonialists, nationalists, as well as the leftists. Here we shall take a close look at our recent experience.

Intervention

Torture by the state agencies is thus a major issue for any initiative concerning human rights. In most cases, intervention in this type of violation of human rights involves two processes. First, the incident is highlighted by the activists and the media, or sometimes by the media before the activists, and sometimes the other way round. The chances and the extent of redress depend upon the strength of consequent public action.

In the 1990s, public litigation by torture victims and their family members, often assisted by human rights groups, have become more frequent than in the past. The West Bengal Human Rights Commission receives many petitions in this regard and recommends actions against the guilty policemen. In spite of its legal operational limitations, the commission has been able to make at least many policemen think twice before getting into the act. The latter, interestingly the 'elite' officers in particular, can be heard lamenting regularly in the media about the police being rendered 'toothless' against criminals by the human rights 'bogey' And to boost their 'morale' at 'crime conferences', home minister Buddhadeb Bhattacharjee had to deliver sermons, such as, "Be ruthless with criminals. You don't have to worry about the Human Rights Commission, we will take care of them."

Some redress is being offered by the state to the victims or their kin, usually in the form of monetary compensation, and initiation of legal proceedings against the perpetrators of the crime.

- Sheikh Nazrul, a boy from the district of Burdwan, was taken into custody by the Khandaghosh police station on April 10, 1997, on charges of theft. In the police diary, however, the date of arrest was noted as April 12. He was later admitted to the local primary health centre, and subsequently to the Burdhaman Medical College, with injuries that he complained had been caused by thrashing he received at the hands of the officer in charge (OC), and a few other policemen. He had been severely kicked on his chest, back, and stomach. The SHRC investigated the complaint, and following the corroboration of the doctor recommended that charges be recorded in the policemen's service books, and the OC not be given the charge of any police station for the next three years; a payment of Rs. 15,000 be made to the victim's family, which, if the government decides, could be realised from the policemen.
- Pramatha Kayal, of village Rameswar, South 24-Parganas district, was detained for about two weeks at the Kulpi police station. He was produced in the court on January 24 and granted bail. While in custody, he was denied food and physically tortured. His family members lodged a complaint against this treatment at the sub-divisional judicial magistrate's court in Diamond Harbour and the SHRC. A probe by the latter revealed that the OC of Kulpi had been demanding Rs 20,000 from the victim's family, which they could not pay. The commission recommended a CID enquiry, a criminal prosecution of the OC, the two other police officers were denied charge of any police station or circle for three years, and a compensation was awarded of Rs 20,000 to the victim.
- Raju Chakrabarty of Ranaghat, Nadia, a poor boy of 16, was detained on December 25, 1993, by the night watchman of the local market where he was roaming around with a loaf of bread in hand. The guard beat him up accusing him of having stolen the bread and handed him over to the police. Unable to bear the thrashing at the police station, he died the next day. The boy's father filed a case, with APDR support, at the Ranaghat

court. The sessions judge, Nadia accepted prima facie the complaint against the police on August 19, 1995 and ordered a CBI investigation. The state has, however, gone in for appeal and the case is still pending.

- Sheikh Azad, alleged to be a criminal of the Kolkata port area, was arrested on December 28, 1994, along with two others, and severely beaten at the Kolkata Police central lock-up. He was removed to hospital and died on April 10, 1995. His newly married wife, Ruksana Begum, challenged the police version that he died due to tuberculosis and is currently engaged in a legal battle.
- Dulal Ghoral died at the Panskura police station, Midnapore district, in September 1995, where he had been taken for interrogation in connection with a criminal case. The Lawyers Forum for Human Rights (LFHR) filed a writ at the Calcutta high court. In January 1997, a Division Bench held that the police had not only beaten the victim to death but also manipulated records to extricate themselves. The court ordered the officer in charge to be prosecuted and a compensation of Rs. 25,000 be paid to the kin.
- Debu Pramanik was illegally detained for 60 hours at the Chinsura police station, Hooghly district, before being produced in court on July12, 1996, on charges of bootlegging. Bearing severe injuries from the beating he received while in custody, he was released on bail, but succumbed on the way home. The Hooghly branch of the APDR filed a petition before the SHRC on July16, 1996. The commission, after investigating, found that severe torture had resulted in Pramanik's death. It awarded a compensation of Rs 20,000 to his family and recommended the prosecution of the officer in charge, which the government accepted.
- Subhas Das, another alleged bootlegger, was taken to Bhawanipore police station, Kolkata, in 1995, where he was reportedly beaten to death. The LFDR, assisted by the APDR, filed a case at the Calcutta High Court. The case created two important precedents. First, the High Court entrusted the inquiry to the district and sessions judge, Alipore, and not to any investigating agency. The judge, in his report submitted

before the High Court in February 1997, upheld the contentions of the human rights bodies. Second, the High Court, in awarding the compensation showed rare ingenuity. Das had a wife, but for quite some time he had been living with another woman. Criminal proceedings were initiated against the officer in charge, who, however, has gone in for appeal.

Care

There is seldom any follow-up done on the subject or the torture victim. But human rights activism cannot concentrate on the 'rights' component without taking into consideration the human being, the possessor of these rights. Therefore, the Centre for Care of Torture Victim (CCTV) was formed in Kolkata by a group of doctors and activists in November 1997 with the broad objectives of:

(1) Identification, treatment and rehabilitation of victims of torture (though the focus is on state-inflicted torture, the organisation has included in its purview torture by domestic, political and other agencies as well, because it believes that the practice cannot be justified under any circumstances in the interest of a humane society),

(2) Developing awareness among the people, professionals and administrators on the problem of torture and its prevention,

(3) Capacity building and research on medical aspects of torture victims, and

(4) Considering and expressing views on all questions and laws pertaining to torture and torture victims.

The problem is vast and complex and both human and material resources of the organisation are limited. With the active co-operation of several other human rights, medical and voluntary organisations, the CCTV has taken up more than 20 cases in the past one year. Working with these cases has brought up a number of issues, which need to be pondered. We present here three cases as examples.

Case: 1

Male, 46 years, a radical political activist was arrested in Kolkata in 1970 and detained under the Preventive Detention Act for about a year. He was subjected to violence during arrest, and during his initial month in police custody was tortured in order to extract information about his revolutionary activities. The methods used included abusive interrogation (which could continue for days together or could take place at any time of the day or night), deprivation of sleep, beating all over the body with sticks and fists, kicking and trampling with boots, burning with cigarettes and breaking of finger joints. The victim's house was ransacked, his family members threatened, and his elder brother was also detained.

No medical care had been given to him during his detention, except for the treatment of a broken thumb at the jail hospital. Under private medical care since his release, he recovered to some extent and took up the profession of a designer. But a couple of years back, he relapsed into the illness that had struck him after the torture. There was excessive tiredness, spinal pain and stiffness of the torso. He could no longer work on the drawing board, and doctors, including the orthopaedist at the CCTV, could not say when he would be able to go back to his professional life. With two children, he would have faced dire financial difficulties had not his wife been supplementing the family income.

Case: 2

Female, 21 years, with college education and nursing training from a Muslim family of Murshidabad district, was cycling home after work on a public road in August 1998. It was about 6 in the evening and the rains had just stopped. Trying to bypass a truck on the way she skidded into mud-water, which, allegedly splashed and spoiled the clothes of two Border Security Force personnel passing by. They immediately pounced on her while she lay on the ground with her bicycle, and started abusing and beating her with fists. The assault, on an open road, continued until a local woman saved her. The blows mostly fell between the back of her head and the lower portion of her body, as she had fallen on the ground face down.

After three months, of which the initial fortnight was spent in a hospital, the victim is still suffering from acute headache, sleeplessness, nightmare, the fear of being killed, and several other physical and mental problems. She reacts as violently to a pat as she would to an electric shock. The CCTV has placed her under neurological and psychiatric care.

Case: 3

Male, 38 years, was fired upon by the police on a busy street on the northern fringe of Kolkata in June 1983. The firing was apparently aimed at quelling an agitating crowd protesting against alleged police negligence over a traffic accident. The victim was not part of the crowd but a passerby. A bullet pierced him behind the right knee. The local police took him to a government hospital where he had to spend about a year. A limb-saving surgery was done. Nobody from the police or the administration ever turned up during or after the hospitalisation, which had to be paid for by him.

Following his release from the hospital, the victim's condition has been fluctuating for the last 15 years. At present, his wound still bleeds and there is pus formation. He complains of pain and difficulty in walking. He was self-employed before the incident, is now totally dependent on his mother's meagre family pension. The CCTV has recently taken up the case and is trying to provide specialist treatment. The injury, long hospital confinement, continuing illness, loss of income, dependency and frustration has caused deep anguish and trauma in the victim. This is a case of prolonged suffering of an innocent person caused by the state, and which is tantamount to torture. So typical of the state, it has not taken any responsibility of the victim at any point.

Needs

The above studies, varied as they are in nature and context, underline the need for specialised medical and social support systems for the victims of torture. There is also a gap between the available knowledge on the effects of torture on the body, mind, livelihood and social/familial condition of the victims and the ground reality, and which needs to be addressed.

For any support group, there are three important and immediate functions: (1) collection of information about torture cases and contacting the victims or their families, (2) assessing the support available and required, and (3) follow-up of each case with expert help. The scope for improving the support mechanism, particularly for those suffering from grievous injury, post-traumatic stress disorder, and economical handicap, should be explored in greater depth. While we should not shy away from fixing responsibility on the state and pressurise it for all possible forms of compensation, society should form the backbone of this support structure. If a society fails to take up this challenge it will only clear the way for its own derogation. After all, torture thrives on the culture of silence that is fatal for the society.

9

The Role of Legislation and Judicary in State Violence

Monica Sakhrani

'State violence' is any act or omission on the part of the state and its agencies, which hampers or impairs the physical and/or psychological development of the individual. It would include any act, which impinges on the social, cultural, economic, political and civil rights of individuals, whether the same is legal or extralegal. Thus, violence would not only include torture and other forms of custodial violence but also include laws, which target specific groups and individuals, and interpretations by the judiciary which favour state violence.

Role of legislation

Law is the system of rights, which devolves through one's caste, gender, religion, class and nationality. A right is a claim, which has a nature of title conferred by established legal authority, publicly and unambiguously announced by law, and excludes access by others to it. Infringement of the right has sanctions prescribed by law, which may be remedial in nature, as in the case of infringement of civil rights, or punitive in the case of infringement of criminal law. This division of illegalities into civil and criminal wrongs is to prevent transfer/loss of power and maintenance of political and economic status quo. Thus, most "blue-collar" illegalities committed by the poor are governed by criminal law, and "white-collar" illegalities committed by bourgeoisie enter the domain of civil law. The state places at the disposal of the bearer of criminal law rights, the entire coercive machinery of the state, which can be activated on a threat to the rights. The state, thus, exclusively appropriates the right to punish "offenders". The corollary to this is that the responsibility of punishing state excesses also lies with the state.

Preventive detention laws

The Constitution of India permits the implementation of preventive detention laws and denial of access to the courts in cases of preventive detention (Article 22(3) to (7)). Post-Independence India can boast of only a two-year period (from 1969 to 1971) without preventive detention legislation. Each successive preventive detention legislation; has been more repressive than its predecessor. The present National Security Act prohibits representation by a lawyer. The Supreme Court, while upholding the constitutionality of the Act in A. K. Roy's case (AIR 1982 SC 710), stated, "Howsoever much would have liked to hold otherwise, we experience serious difficulty in taking the view that the procedure of the advisory boards in which the detenu is denied the right of legal representation is unfair, unjust or unreasonable. If Article 22 were silent on the question of the right of legal representation it would have been possible, indeed right and proper, to hold that the detenu cannot be denied the right of legal representation in the proceedings before the Advisory Board. It is unfortunate that courts have been deprived of the choice by the express language of Article 22(3)(b) read with Article 22(1)".

The courts have consistently upheld the preventive detention laws. In A.K. Roy's case, the Supreme Court abrogated the power of judicial review on grounds that the courts are not equipped to deal with cases where the person has not yet committed an offence but is likely to do so.

Legitimate state violence

It is widely accepted that poverty is an important factor leading to crime. A dramatic example of this is that most contract killers are poor, unemployed, illiterate, male youth who are willing to kill for as little at Rs. 2,000. Another example is the high crime rate in slums. Another indicator is that 31.7 per cent of the cases registered in India in 1995 were theft cases (Crime in India, 1995). However, the flip side of this is that most crimes affect the poor. Studies reveal that most victims of abuse are the poor. However, cases by the poor are rarely registered, while cases against them are frequently done so. In fact, it would not be an exaggeration to state that in India poverty is a crime. This fact is apparent by even a causal analysis of the penal provisions.

- Ticket-less travelling is an offence under the Railways Act
- Begging is an offence under the Prevention of Begging Act
- Hawking without a licence is a cognisable office, though the Mumbai Municipal Corporation rarely issues licences, and there are no hawking zones. This is because the official fines collected from hawkers generate revenue of over Rs. 1 crore per month for the Corporation (The Times of India, November 9,1998)

- Prostitutes are punished for soliciting while the clients are not
- While embezzlement by a servant is punishable with imprisonment up to seven years, withholding of salary by employer is only a contractual breach
- Even in the few penal provisions in labour laws, where the penalties in the form of petty fines make it more profitable for the employers to flout the same, the prosecution; cannot be launched by the aggrieved parties except with the permission of the inspector, within a stipulated period.
- Public housing in India is non-existent, so is legal housing for the urban poor, who cannot afford the exorbitant rents. But "squatting" is an offence.

A typical demolition by the authorities is conducted in this manner: "On February 24, 1995, the demolition squad burnt 125 structures at Maharashtra Nagar, Bandra (East), Mumbai, during a demolition. Not only were the structures burnt but also were the personal belongings and documents of the residents. Four children and a man were injured and were treated for burns at the L.T.M.G. Hospital, Sion. Women, who protested the demolition, were beaten and arrested, and later released on payment of a fine of Rs 200 each." (Adenwalla M., "Evicting the Right to Shelter," Lawyers Collective, September 1998)

Arrests during demolitions are routine. In many cases the people are accused of setting their own houses on fire. The list is endless. There were 411 legislations containing penal provisions in Maharashtra in 1995 (Crime in India 1995). Furthermore, most of the offences committed by the poor are cognisable, giving the police the power to arrest any person suspected of having committed the same (Section 41, Code of Criminal Procedure). The National Police Commission in its Third Report has observed that the single most cause of corruption in the police force is the power to arrest. The Commission has also stated that nearly 60 per cent of the arrests were either unnecessary, or unjustified, and that such unjustified police action accounted for 43.2 per cent of the expenditure of the jails (As quoted by the Supreme Court in Joginder Kumar v/s State of UP, 1994 Cri.L.J.1981). Thus, the poor are the most likely victims of the abuse of authority.

The poor are also likely to stay in prison for the longest. The bail system in India is property-based and anti-poor. Hence, the prison population comprises around 75 per cent under-trials, many of whom are in jail because of their inability to furnish bail. The period of under-trial detention is not set off against the sentence in lieu of a fine (Section 428, Cr.P.C). Many mentally ill persons and juveniles are also in jail. Several persons are incarcerated for periods beyond the maximum punishment imposable by law due to their inability to afford lawyers. Though legal aid is provided for in law for indigent persons, in practice, most under-trials are denied legal aid. The courts also prefer to 'plea bargain' with the accused, many of whom plead guilty in order to be let off. This pulls them further into crime, creating records, which make them 'habitual offenders'. Detention of 'habitual' is permissible by institution of chapter cases (Chapter VIII, Cr.P.C), externment proceedings (Mumbai Police Act, Section 56), through incarceration in preventive detention laws or through the exercise of the preventive powers of arrest by the police (Section 1511, Cr.P.C.). Taking of photographs, fingerprints, and surveillance of the convicts is permissible under law. A criminal antecedent is also an important factor considered by the courts in the granting of or denial of bail.

The purpose of punishment is ostensibly deterrence and/or reformation, but incarceration has the opposite effect. It increases recidivism by exposing persons to criminals of different hues, by its negative labelling, by pushing families to destitution, and by failing to address core issues, which lead to crime. In criminal law 'actus reas' and 'mens rea', i.e., the physical act and the intention to do so, are the relevant considerations. Motive is irrelevant. Hence, the soico-political and economic factors, which perpetuate crime, are beyond the scope of law and the courts. This individualisation of crime justifies punishment, the purpose of which is to prevent organised rebellion.

Case for Custodial Violence

The number of custodial deaths in India doubled from 444 in 1995-96 to 888 in 1996-97 with Maharashtra leading the brigade with 201 deaths. The "Crime in India 1995" report of the National Crimes Record Bureau states that incidence of police firing increased by eight per cent in 1995 as compared to the previous year. In Mumbai 135 "encounter deaths" took place between 1995 and 1997, while in November 1998 itself there were such 15 deaths. The Maharashtra government has gone on record stating that "the encounter policy will continue", and these extra-judicial killings are being defended vociferously by the state in public interest petitions pending before the Bombay High Court. Various citizens groups representing bourgeoisie class interests have intervened in these petitions supporting the "encounter policy."

Prosecution and conviction of officers for abuse of authority or misuse of the same, is rare. Often no legal steps are taken, including the mandatory provisions required by law in investigating these deaths. The 1992 Amnesty International Report on Torture, Rape and Deaths in Custody found that of the 415 custodial deaths between 1985 and 1992, in only 42 of them were magisterial enquiries held, and in only three cases were police officers convicted. This was despite the mandatory requirement of inquests in all cases of custodial death under Section 176 Cr.P.C. The law also protects police officials in cases of use of violence. Section 46 of the Cr.P.C. permits a police officer effecting arrest to use force - up to causing of death - while arresting a person accused of having committed an offence punishable with death or life imprisonment. Section 197 of the Cr.P.C. stipulates that all prosecutions against police officers accused of any offence, alleged to have been committed by them while acting or purporting to act in the discharge of their official duty, shall be initiated after obtaining the sanction of the state government. Section 161 of the Bombay Police Act further states that suits or prosecutions in respect of acts done by police officers under colour of duty, or in excess of authority, shall be dismissed if instituted more than six months after the date of the act complained of. These provisions literally help the police get away with murder.

The Amnesty International in its report, "Amnesty International and India" deals with factors, which encourage custodial violence by the police. "... The sense of impunity generated by the infrequency with which the police have been held publicly accountable for their actions, the rare convictions of those responsible for rape or deaths in custody, and the length of legal proceedings, further encourage the perception that resorting to torture is acceptable. Police are given wide powers under a variety of legislations, which allows them to arrest, detain, and investigate. Detainees can be kept in police custody for long periods, particularly under legislation permitting preventive detention, during which they are at a risk of being tortured and ill-treated. In violation of the Indian law and police procedure, the practice of unrecorded police detention is common, and there is little doubt that it facilitates police abuse, such as beatings and other forms of ill-treatment, or torture, such as rape. Moreover, lawyers and relatives are routinely denied access by the police to people held in custody. Most of the torture and ill-treatment in India occurs during the first stage of detention in police custody, when access to outsiders is routinely denied. Indian laws are virtually silent on the procedure for questioning suspects in police custody, and no provisions exist detailing safeguards in the Criminal Procedure Code."

Many special legislation, such as The Narcotics Drugs And Psychotropic Substances Act, shift the burden of proof on the accused. This is contrary to the basic principle of criminal jurisprudence that states that the prosecution must prove its case. Section 27 of the Indian Evidence Act permits confessions made to police officers to be used as evidence if they result in any recovery of article, or discovery of fact relating to the offence. This encourages the use of third degree in the investigation of cases. Section 15 of the now repealed Terrorist and Disruptive Activities (Prevention) Act (TADA) permitted confessional statements recorded by the police to be used as evidence against the accused, provided the same are voluntary. How these "voluntary confessions" are obtained is described graphically in an eye witness account titled, "Voices from the Draconian Dungeons", detailing instances of torture during investigation of the Bomb Blasts case by the Mumbai Police.

An example: "One day the police took her (Noorjahan, wife of accused Shahnawaz Abdul Qader Qureshi, 19 members of whose family were illegally detained by the police during investigation), along with her 45-day-old infant, to the Dadar Police Station. Her husband was already there. Due to electric shocks administered to him, his face had turned black. Noorjahan was molested and humiliated in the most degrading manner. Suddenly an officer orders his men to undress her. Her husband, who could hardly speak due to his condition, pleaded not to touch her. Shahnawaz was thus left with no choice but to agree to sign the papers. His sister's mother-in-law, Zubaidabi, 60, became mad during detention. The family was kept under unlawful detention for a period of one month" (Pages 13 and 14).

Role of Medical Profession

The Supreme Court in D.K. Basu v/s State of West Bengal (1997 Cri.L.J. 743) has laid down guidelines, as preventive measures, to be followed in all cases of arrest and detention. They include:

- Police personnel to have accurate and clear identification to be entered into a register
- Memo of arrest to be prepared attested by at least one witness

- Information of arrest to family friend of arrestee within 8 to 12 hours after arrest
- Medical examination of arrestee at his request at the time of arrest and major and minor injuries, if any, present on his/her body to be recorded
- Medical examination every 48 hours during detention in custody by a doctor on the panel of approved doctors appointed by the Director of Health Services of the concerned state or Union territory. Director, Health Services should prepare such a panel for all tehsils and districts as well
- Copies of all the documents to be sent to the illaqa magistrate.

Medical professionals play a crucial role in the detection of torture, apart from their recognised role as providing treatment for torture and trauma. The profession could also help in accurately identifying the incidents of torture and cases of custodial violence as they have access to the victims. However, in most cases the doctors attached to prison hospitals, and even public hospitals are unwilling to even accurately record the injuries observed on the victim, thus playing the role of protectors of the perpetrators of violence and do not consider themselves accountable to their patients (victims of torture), nor the judiciary under whose custody the patient is. Medical professionals also fail to document the psychological trauma, especially among women. The most shocking failure, however, is not in their complicity in covering-up torture, but in failing to provide adequate treatment to detainees. The single most cause of death in prisons is not custodial violence but lack of medical care, with people dying due to malaria, diabetes and heart attacks, after being denied proper treatment, despite funds being earmarked for the same.

Role of the Judiciary

"There are several types of separatist and terrorist activities in several parts of the country. They have to be subdued. Whether they should be fought politically, or be dealt with by force, is a matter of policy for the government to determine. The court may not be the appropriate forum to determine these questions" (Justices B.P. Jeevan Reddy and Suhas C. Sen, People's Union for Civil Liberties -v-Union of India, 1997 (3) SCC, 433).

This remark sums up the attitudes of the judiciary in case of state violence. In the aforesaid case, the enquiry by the district judge into an encounter killing instituted by the Supreme Court had concluded that there was no encounter. The Supreme Court ordered compensation to be paid to the victims. No direction for prosecution was given. This has been the response of the judiciary in almost all cases of gross violations of fundamental rights. The message that the courts seem to be sending is that no rights are sacrosanct and can be violated at a price.

The Supreme Court has also consistently upheld the constitutionality of all legislations, which give special powers of arrest and detention to the state agencies and provide for harsher penalties. It has consistently upheld capital punishment. Every post independence preventive detention legislation, from the Preventive Detention Act (A.K.Gopalan v/s Sate of Madras, AIR 1950, SC 27) to the National Security Act (A.K. Roy v/s Union of India, AIR 1982 SC 710); has been upheld. The Supreme Court during the emergency abdicated its right to issue writs to enforce rights of personal liberty (ADM Jabalpu v/s S.S. Shukla, 1976 Sup. S.C,R.172). The Bombay High Court has upheld externment proceedings and the power of the police to detain persons for up to one month under its preventive powers of arrest. The Supreme Court in Madhu Limaye's case (AIR 1971 SC 2486) has held that the power of an executive magistrate (power exercised by the assistant commissioner of police) to require bond of good behaviour from persons, and detain them for their failure to furnish the required surety, or breach of conditions of bond under Chapter VIII of the Cr.P.C.; is not in violation of Article 19. The Supreme Court also upheld the Terrorist and Disruptive Activities (Prevention) Act (Kartar Singh v/s State of Punjab, 1994 (3) SCC 569). This was done despite the misuse of TADA, which was routinely applied to even robbery cases. In Sanjay Dutt's case (JT 1994 (5) SC 540) the Supreme Court held that the onus was on the accused to prove that the possession of arm in a designated area was not for purposes of terrorist activity. Recently the Supreme Court upheld the Armed Forces (Special Powers) Act that empowers non-commissioned officers affecting the arrest of any person, who is acting in contravention of any law or order in force in "disturbed" areas, to use force to the extent of causing death of the said person. The Supreme Court held that the likelihood of misuse or abuse of powers by such junior officers does not render the provision invalid. The court also stated that if the legislature is competent to enact a law, then its motive, whether bona-fide or mala-fide, is not relevant. (Naga People's Movement of Human Rights v/s Union of India, 1998 (2) SCC 109)

The courts have failed to check the abuse of authority by state agencies and rarely punished the contempt of the directions issued by the

Supreme Court for protection of human rights. The Supreme Court in M.P. Dwivedi case (1996 (4) SCC 142) accepted the explanation of the police officers who handcuffed activists that they were not aware of the specific directions of the Supreme Court, which state that police are not to handcuff the accused without the permission of the magistrates. The Supreme Court has not laid down a clear policy on the granting of bail on personal recognisant bond in petty cases, or when the accused are poor, despite expressing concern on a series of judgements that the bail provision was anti-poor. The apex court has also not specifically laid down the responsibility of the magistrates to check custodial violence, and it is not mandatory for the magistrate to ask the accused produced before him/her whether he was subjected to torture. This prejudices the accused; who may be too scared to voluntarily complain of torture. Magistrates, while granting remand, routinely note that the accused made no complaint of torture - without even questioning the accused about it. It is only when the accused voluntarily discloses of torture that a noting is made in the remand application. That apart, little else is done. Magistrates rarely follow the directions of the Supreme Court. There is no instance of a magistrate visiting a lock-up. The Supreme Court has stated that the presence of the accused is not a mandatory requirement for the grant of remand, and remands are routinely granted in the absence of the accused. In cases where extreme injuries are caused due to torture, the accused are rarely produced before the remand court, and the ill treatment goes unchecked. This encourages the use of third degree. Rarely is a case quashed when the accused is tortured. The appalling apathy of the courts can also be seen in the delay in conducting trials, in long periods of incarceration of persons as under-trials, and in stringent conditions of bail.

Conclusion

In conclusion, it can be said that the legal and judicial system aid and abet state violence, whether it be through the mass of penal legislations, their selective implementations, the refusal of the judiciary to monitor the administration of criminal justice, and the system of penalties imposable by law. The reason for this is that criminal law "was made for the few and it was brought to bear upon others, that in principle it applies to all citizens, but that it is addressed principally to the most numerous and least enlightened classes; that unlike political and civil laws, their application does not concern everybody equally; that in the courts society as a whole does not judge one of its members, but that a social category with an interest in order judges another that is dedicated to disorder: 'visit the places where people are judged, imprisoned or executed ….. one thing will strike you everywhere, everywhere you will see two quite distinct classes of men, one of which always meets on the seats of the accusers and judges, the other on the benches of the accused', which is explained by the fact that the latter, for lack of resources and education, do not know 'how to remain within the limits of legal probity'" (Michel Foucault, 1977, Page 276).

10

Violence to the Psyche: Costs of Surviving Violence in Kashmir

Kishwar Ahmed-Shirali

They say things are getting better. February 1998, women go about their tasks in silence. Nothing feels good, no gatherings, no TV, no 'wasvan', nothing. There are worries and fears, about children's health, schooling, and most of all, safety. Mothers at sundown wait with dread in their hearts for their sons and men to return. Daughters are not allowed out at all.

- A 14-year-old son has recurrent fever, and fainting spells as well. A neurologist in Jammu is consulted. The EEG is found to be normal. Some pills are prescribed. He tells me he has nightmares and just before fainting, he is afraid. His house is next to the beleaguered mosque, Hazratbal. The elder brother cannot sleep without the sound of rapid firing.
- A 14-year-old girl in the OPD of the Psychiatric Diseases Hospital has pain and burning sensations in the eyes and thighs. The doctors can't find anything wrong. The father, very strict and 'tez' (harsh) would not allow her out, apart from going to school. The mother who was accompanying her, said, she also had pain in her legs. She drew a small girl in a frock, for "Draw a Person Test", and wrote a paragraph about her, then scratched out the face and the paragraph; indicating a low, negative self image, denial and fears about being seen and seeing.

Women attending the OPD of a district hospital with various psychosomatic and gynecological complaints (N=24, age 17-50 years); were also given "Draw a Woman Test". The results showed: 50 per cent low self esteem; 40 per cent average; 10 per cent good self worth; 28 per cent lack of autonomy; 25 per cent denial of body, 38 per cent decorative-selves; 12 per cent veiled faces, reluctance, avoidance of public (male) gaze; 62 per cent non-communicative (eyes), could be cultural or withdrawal/anxieties/fears as in depression/mourning; and 50 per cent had feelings of insecurity, 1/3rd projected loss of support (no legs).

Most doctors and medical/social welfare officials believed that the 'general turbulence' since 1989 had caused a general paralysis of health services and a simultaneous increase (60-70 per cent) in mental, psychosomatic problems, 'panic abortions' and Ceasarian births, to avoid night deliveries. Curiously, 'medicate' shops had also increased. Psychiatrists reported that there was a rise in help-seeking behaviour from 1990. Suicide is a sin in Islam. However, suicide attempts have increased alarmingly, especially among adolescent girls and young rural women.

As a member of an NGO-sponsored Mental Health Needs Assessment team, which visited the Valley in February-March 1998, I was critical of the absence of women mental health personnel. In May, I was invited to join a private clinic for stress-related diseases (psychiatry, cardiology, and endocrinology). I worked there for three months and met 319 persons (women 217, men 102) and their families, from inner city/ suburban, rural, mountain border regions. They were from the upper/middle class and the working class, and were businessmen, government servants, doctors, teachers, scientists, politicians, agriculturalists and the landed, labourers (daily wages, unemployed), dairymen (gujjars), fishermen, craftsmen, and houseboat men. They had all been to general practitioners, neurologists, and psychiatrists, and to their local healers (pir babas). I was involved in psychosocial and clinical assessment, case histories, projective and IQ testing, individual/group/family therapy and reiki, as needed.

Stress has acquired many faces. The old, the young, and even the very young have been devastated by the ongoing climate of violence, which like AIDS engulfs all aspects of life in the Valley. Nobody was immune to it. Family dynamics, the parent-child or man-woman relation, offices, services and businesses had all been corrupted.

A six-year-old was silent and withdrawn, a ten-year-old smashed the TV and mirrors, a 16–year-old ran away, and an 18-year-old had a headache and body-ache, a 21–year-old victim of interrogation was unconscious for a month, a 30-year-old complained of sexual dysfunction due to electric torture to the body/penis, some were sexually abused when they were nine-ten years old. A 42–year-old businessman weeps, a 47-year-old was torn with guilt about incestuous feelings, as he was a victim of child abuse and current violence. These were some of the male distresses.

For women the distress goes deeper. An eight-year-old talks, dresses and behaves like an old woman, a ten-year-old is not studying, a 12–year-old sees fairies calling her, a 13–year-old has fainting spells and scratches her whole body, a 14-year-old tears her hair, cuts her wrists, cries 'dam dam' (suffocation) and faints. A young pir sexually abuses a 14-year-old when he was called in to cure her fainting spells. A 15–year-old insists on disco dancing on the streets. A 17–year-old sent for religious studies to Ahmedabad is anorexic, hears horses neighing and cats yowling, while locked in a boarding room at night. An 18-year-old hates being a woman and wants to hang out with the boys. A 20–year-old runs away from home and wants to die. A 24–year-old lecturer has an existential crisis. A 28–year-old employed in a hospital to be married abroad, is terrified of roads. A young mother has severe migraine, she feels as if the back of her head is locked, and if opened, she will die. An old Pir sexually abused her when she was a teenager. Another attractive divorcee, who remarried a younger man, has burning sensations all over her body - she was sexually abused as a child. Hysterical fainting is almost universal.

In older women, distresses result from family violence, second marriages, sons in lockup, widowhood, daughters returning home after marital problems, somatic problems with sexual distress, inability to control grown-up children and husbands, loss of support, surgery (six women had abdominal surgery) from being over-tested and over-medicated. Helplessness and hopelessness, depression and insecurity, combined with low self-worth (projective test findings), further fragment their fragile selves.

During curfew/hartal/unemployment and the long, cold, winter months, the family dynamics get more exacerbated - feeding on the sounds of women wailing and grenades exploding. Violence turns on itself.

In Kashmiri families, children are over-indulged and over-protected in all classes, both sons and daughters. This has increased now, perhaps due to the general climate of fear and anxiety. Women are socialised with a "princess-complex" of high expectations, but with the harsh realities of violence and death, they are unable to cope. Almost everyone had a close family member tortured, kidnapped or killed. Little children were a witness to all, leaving deep scars on their psyche.

The broadly overlapping patterns observed were tentatively recorded. The incidence percentage is given below:

Symptoms	Female N=217			Male N=102		
	Case	%	Age Rank	Case	%	Rank
	96	44.2	7-35	15	15	10-12
Depression	78	35.9	16-65	38	38	6-50
Functional Somatic	20	9.2	12-15	-	-	-
Sexual Dysfunction	-	-	-	17	17	25-34
Acting out	-	-	-	3	3	10-16
Addiction	-	-	-	1	1	22
Pain	1	0.5	25	-	-	-
Phobia	1	0.5	28	-	-	-
Obsessive	1	0.5	64	-	-	-
Paranoia	1	0.5	36	-	-	-
Dissociation	1	0.5	38	-	-	-
Incest	-	-	-	1	1	47
IQ Testing	18	8.2	3-14	25	25	4-16

* Information available for only 100.

Conclusions

The urgent needs are psychosocial humanistic/holistic care-givers to help cope with post traumatic stress disorders, at various age levels, to allay fears, anxieties, guilt, and most of all, restore hope and faith in themselves. NGOs need to step in to help revitalise the community-based, preventive health services. Women's awareness support groups, stress management, sex education, coping strategies are sorely needed. Otherwise, I am afraid, reactionary/fundamentalist and even market forces are already reaping the horrendous harvest.

11

Effect of Slum Demolition on Children

Mani Mistry, Lalitha D'Souza

The investigating team was invited to study the health status of the people of Ambedkar Nagar by Ms Mahrook Adenwala, lawyer and housing rights activist, who has been actively involved with the legal aspect of the demolitions that have plagued the people of Ambedkar Nagar through the past decade.

Introduction

This paper reports on a study of the health condition of children in the slum of Ambedkar Nagar, in Colaba, Mumbai. It notes that the health of the children living in this slum is appalling. Over three quarters are malnourished. Infection in this impoverished environment is rife. It is reported that this slum has been demolished no less than 45 times to date. Repeated evictions mean that these slum-dwellers slowly lose their capability to absorb the impact of further demolitions. The consequences of this are reflected in the health of the children.

The Context

On the May 18, 1998, approximately 5,000 people living in 1,500 huts were forcibly evicted from their homes in Ambedkar Nagar slum. This slum was situated in Cuffe Parade near the southern tip of Mumbai. Within a few days a slum in which many people had lived for over ten years had been flattened and finally cleared with bulldozers and earth-moving machinery. A ten-foot high wall had been built and topped with razor wire around the 8,000 square metre site. All that remained after the eviction was a single temple to the Hindu deity, Ganesh.

The successful eviction of May 18 was not the first time that an attempt had been made to evict the residents from Ambedkar Nagar. The residents of the slum have claimed that there were 45 previous attempts to evict them from their homes; the Collector of Mumbai, Mr Sanjay Chahande, confirmed these facts. Each time the slum-dwellers' homes were destroyed, they had to rebuild them. An eviction attempt in April 1997 demonstrates how devastating these evictions are. On this occasion the collector had issued notices of the eviction in advance. A list was prepared of 106 families who would be given alternative pitches in the resettlement area because they could show acceptable proof of residence prior to January 1,1995. Among the slum-dwellers there was considerable confusion, as no one was sure whose names were on the list and whose names were not. The demolition squad moved in at 11 in the morning to start the eviction process, accompanied by armed police. Shortly after the start of the demolition, a fire broke out. The fire brigade arrived one hour later, and hosed the area for about ten minutes before they ran out of water. This fire destroyed 600 hutments and it stopped the eviction.

For many of the slum-dwellers, their huts had been destroyed either by fire or by demolition over and over again. In addition, the residents also report that on several other occasions the demolition squad came to the slum and demolished huts, which were considered illegal. These summary demolitions did not constitute full-scale eviction; nonetheless, they left many families temporarily homeless. The materials from which their homes were built were loaded into trucks and driven away. The residents could pay the BMC a fine and retrieve the plastic, tin sheeting, and bamboo, from which their huts were made, or, as was reported by the residents, they went out and bought new materials to re-build their homes.

The history given by the residents, corroborated on at least two occasions by newspaper reports, is of regular and systematic eviction attempts by the BMC over about ten years. On each occasion the slum-dwellers were rendered homeless, they were obliged to spend approximately Rs. 500—a large amount of money given their meagre income—to rebuild a shelter for themselves and their families.

On May 18 the eviction was total. The collector managed to evict and exclude the slum-dwellers from the site. Their homes, water tanks and shops were all destroyed. In addition, the bulldozing of the slum-dwellers' huts was carried out with such haste that no transit shelter was made for them at all. An imposing ten-foot-high wall, topped with razor wire, was hastily erected around the site.

No alternative shelters were provided. The slum-dwellers were forced to live out in the open in the searing heat of a Mumbai summer. It was not long before the children started to fall ill. By the evening of the eviction day, many children were suffering from sunburns and sunstroke. The Asian Age newspaper reported that by the next day ten children had been admitted to the nearby Albless and Cama Hospital with acute sunstroke and dehydration (Asian Age, 1998). The residents in the slum confirmed this report.

By the time this investigation was carried out, three months after the eviction, the slum-dwellers had resettled onto a much smaller boggy area to the west of the original site. The slum-dwellers feared that another demolition was imminent. The collector had allocated new plots to those residents of the original slum who could prove according to the 'legal' requirements that they were residents of Ambedkar Nagar on or before January 1,1995, (entitlement to reallocation is through proof of residence through ration card, photopass or election card prior to January 1,1995). However, the majority of the inhabitants of the original slum had not been able to demonstrate their right of tenure, either because they did not hold the appropriate papers, or, as was evident from our investigation and a survey carried out by Navara Hakk prior to the eviction, many of the households were inadequately surveyed.. These slum-dwellers had been obliged to make do with whatever space they could find in the resettlement site.

Many residents showed this team of researchers ration cards dated prior to January 1,1995, asking why they were not allotted alternative pitches. Community leaders among these groups took on the task of 'allocating' space to households. Thus, in addition to the expenditure these people have had to make in rebuilding their homes they were also forced to pay bribes to slum-landlords. Their problems got compounded as rumours of another survey of the slum spread. Associated with this rumour was the widespread belief that a further eviction would follow. Even the letters issued by the collector's office to the households with legal proof of residence included a statement to the effect that the arrangement was a temporary one.

The residents of Ambedkar Nagar have lost their homes many times over the years. They are now unsure as to whether they will have their huts demolished again. They are reluctant or afraid to invest in adequate shelter for themselves and their children. In addition, they do not have the resources to invest in service infrastructure like water supply, nor do they have the organisations to demand services like toilets, or paving, guttering and garbage disposal facilities. It is in the context of a slum population who have had to constantly reinvest in providing themselves with adequate shelter and services, and are now unsure as to their future, that this investigation was conducted.

The Health Condition of the Residents of Ambedkar Nagar

This investigation of the health condition of the residents of Ambedkar Nagar was carried out over three months between August and November 1998. The investigating team selected a sample of 100 children, aged 0-10 years, in order to understand the health condition of the population. The sample children were selected using a stratified random sampling technique, which relied on a survey of the slum conducted by the research team along with the residents. This survey enumerated the number of children living in each hut. The sample was stratified into four areas, which were mapped by the residents in the slum in general meetings, and reflected their perceived right of tenure. These four areas are shown in Table 1.1.

Table 1.1: The four areas of the slum defined by the residents of the slum with reference to right of tenure

Area	No. of Huts	Children 0-10 yrs	Resettlement Sites allotted by	Perception of tenure
I	227	794	Collector	Name on the electoral roll and existing ration card.
II	50	147	Local Leaders and slum lords	Householders not having names on the electoral rolls, but having other proof of residence prior to January 1,1995 (example: ration cards)
III	150	480	Local Leaders	No proof of residence prior to January 1,1995, but resident in demoloshed slum
IV	60	216	Self	Unclear

The sample was selected to reflect the proportion of children in each area. Therefore, 48 children were selected from Area I, 10 from Area II, 29 from Area III and 13 from Area IV. Each child was given a non-invasive clinical examination by an experienced paediatrician, the intention of which was to identify signs of infection and malnutrition. In addition, the height (or length in children <1yr) and weight of each child was recorded. Accurate birth dates were only available for 23 of the children so body mass index (BMI) was used to calculate nutritional status, as this is an age-independent index.

A second examination of the children was conducted three months after the first. It was hoped that the same children would again be examined and measured. Unfortunately, only 19 per cent of the children from the first sample of the first survey were available in the slum. Most of them had returned to their village of origin, as there were rumours that another eviction attempt was likely. One child was reported to have died. The children who were still in the slum from the first survey were examined, and in addition, a further 81 were selected. The same method of selection was used as in the first survey.

In addition to the evaluation of the health status among children, qualitative research was conducted in the slum. This approach can be conveniently divided into three stages. (1) The first was general meetings with residents in the slum in which the researchers sought to understand the events following the eviction—the settlement patterns and re-building activities in the aftermath of the eviction. These also allowed the researchers to understand the employment activities and histories of the slum-dwellers. These general meetings, which were an open forum, also facilitated the mapping of the slum into the four areas discussed in Table 1.1. (2) The general meetings were followed by focus group meetings in each of the four areas involving women from the areas. Each meeting examined the effects of the eviction, the process of re-building the huts, impediments on building, service provision, and concerns about their health and that of their families. (3) The focus groups were followed by open-ended interviews, which allowed for much more detailed case studies to be developed. Two women were selected from each of the focus group meetings. The criteria for selection was that they had expressed views and experiences that were similar to those discussed in less detail in the focus group meetings (Kruegar, 1994, Patton, 1990).

The Results from the Health Survey

The observations made in the clinical examinations are detailed in Table 1.2. Figure 1.1 shows a histogram for the BMI in both August and November.

Table 1.2: Proportion of children with symptoms

Symptom	Grading	Survey One	Survey Two
		n=100	n=100
Vitamin A deficiency	Mild	24	25
	Moderate	8	9
Vitamin D deficiency		4	2
Clinical anaemia		72	87
Clinical signs of Kwashiorkor		3	2
Clinical signs of Marasmus		3	3
Fever	Infection	7	6
	Suspected Malaria (blood smear not taken)	-	1
Diarrhoea	History from child	17	9
	History from mother	5	4
Skin infection	Fungal	12	15
	Scabies	6	6
Worm infestation	History from mother	13	19
Lice infestation		11	16
Injuries	New and old	9	8
	Burns	1	0
Middle ear infection		5	8
Upper respiratory tract infection		54	33

Figure 1.1 A histogram for Body Mass Index(BMI) in Ambedkar Nagar for children aged 0-10 year in August (n=100) and November (n=100).

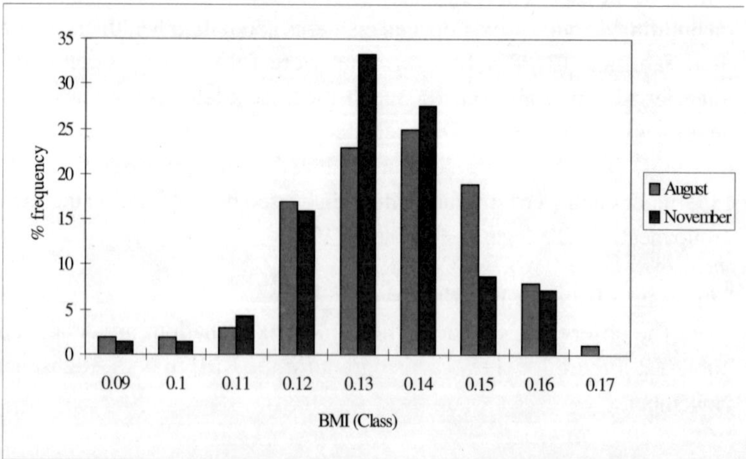

Discussion

The children in this slum were suffering. The clinical manifestations of malnutrition and infection were alarming. The children's nutritional status was a cause for considerable concern. An accepted normal range for the BMI is 0.15–0.16 (Ghai, 1982). In August, only 28 per cent of the children had a normal, or slightly higher than normal BMI. In November, the number of children in this range was 16 per cent. The remainder, 72 per cent in August and a staggering 84 per cent in November, fell below the accepted normal range for BMI. Part of the difference in the number of children in the normal range or above can be accounted for by the lack of breast-fed babies in the second survey. In the first survey, one child with a BMI of 0.174, and two of the babies with a BMI, which fell in the range of 0.16-0.17, were breast-fed. At the other end of the scale, 8 per cent of the children had a BMI below 0.12 in August. In November, 6 per cent had a BMI of less than 0.12. The only child that the researchers know had died in the intervening three months had a BMI of 0.092 in August. He also displayed florid signs of kwashiorkor and xerophthlmia at the time of this survey. His mother reported that he fell sick one evening with fever and was taken to a private practitioner who dispensed a packet of medicines. The next morning the child died. He was eight years old.

The other signs of malnourishment in this population were disturbing as well. Vitamin A and D deficiency were high in this population. It is now widely recognised that children displaying signs of mild vitamin A deficiency have a greater chance of dying in the next three months (Sommer, Tarwotjo, Hussaini and Susanto, 1983); 32 per cent of the children displayed florid signs of vitamin A deficiency in August, 34 per cent in November. Clinical anaemia affected over three quarters of the children in both cohorts. It was evident that even if the child's BMI was nearing the normal range (the modal BMI in August was 0.146, in November 0.139) many of these children were receiving a diet, which did not contain adequate quantities of essential nutrients.

There is only one other survey of nutritional status amongst children in the slums of Mumbai that the researchers are aware of. This survey, using different indices from those used in the survey conducted here, reported that approximately half the children in their survey were moderately to severely malnourished (Geetha and Swaminathan, 1986). The indications from the surveys conducted in both August and November in Ambedkar Nagar indicate that the children were more malnourished in this slum. The qualitative research undertaken as part of this research provided evidence as to why this may be the case. The survey mentioned above was conducted by Geetha and Swaminathan (1986), in a slum in Dindoshi, a suburb of Mumbai. It was a resettlement camp provided by the BMC for slum-dwellers who were moved from a site in Cloaba, which was near Ambedkar Nagar, the subject of this study. These slum-dwellers, although poor, had not faced eviction from the new site in the last ten years. But, in Ambedkar Nagar the slum population had repeatedly faced eviction. As was reported above, many of the slum-dwellers had lost their homes as many as 45 times. Each time they had to rebuild the structures at considerable expense.

The slum-dwellers in the focus groups described a series of 'coping mechanisms' (Corbett, 1988) they had developed, like many poor households in Mumbai, to absorb the impact of disaster. These included small savings, often held in the community, which they were able to draw upon to finance the rebuilding of their homes and to maintain their food intake. Once depleted after multiple eviction attempts, the slum-dwellers were obliged to turn to another form of household saving, that of household possessions, including jewellery and brass vessels. These too had long been sold to rebuild homes and feed the household. In subsequent demolitions, they had been obliged to take out loans from loan sharks each time their homes were destroyed. The interest rates on these loans were reported to be very high, at times in excess of 100 per cent. They did not get a chance to gain economic stability and food security. On each occasion, the household economy had become more imperilled. "Less food," one respondent noted, "is available in our house each time our hut is destroyed." This experience was often repeated by respondents in the research.

Repeated demolitions also meant that people just did not get enough time and opportunity to establish their homes and environments. They always had to cope with the filth and confusion of a new area. Nor did they not get an opportunity to establish their proof of residence for the minimum duration required. Thus they were always a step behind.

With the threat of eviction the slum-dwellers had been forced to flee the city for the village. It was impossible to comment on the conditions these people faced in their home village, but what was certain was that they have had to relinquish the possibility of their paid employment in Mumbai. Many of the slum-dwellers worked as either labourers carrying mud at construction sites, or were cleaning fish at the Sasson Dock, which was two kilometres from Ambedkar Nagar.

The slum-dwellers who remained in Ambedkar Nagar were unwilling to make large investments in re-building their homes because of the threat of eviction. Many of the huts above the high-tide line had mud floors, only a small number had been able to commit themselves to the expense of concreting them.

In the areas of the slum where there was a regular inundation of seawater, the condition of the huts remained appalling. Much of these people's lives were spent living on flimsy platforms as the water washed through their homes.

There were no water taps in the slum. During the first round of this investigation, water was only available from a tanker, which was parked about 500 meters from the slum entrance or it could be bought for Rs 2 for a 20 litre handa (water vessel) from the nearby MHADA transit camp. The malnutrition of the children undoubtedly meant that they were more likely to pick up any opportunistic infection. The limited quantity of water for hygiene needs made the situation much worse. Skin infections were widespread among the children. The probability of feaco-oral transmission and diarrhoeal disease were noted to be high due to the lack of water and poor sanitary conditions. Most of the residents had no access to a latrine. They used an area adjacent to the new settlement for open defaecation. When the tide came in the contaminated water was washed into the huts and lanes. Children were seen to be playing in deep pools of filthy water in which faecal matter was seen to be floating. Inside the huts, dampness prevailed. The poor environmental conditions lend themselves to upper respiratory tract infection and possible pneumonia. This was a population at severe risk of disability and premature death.

Conclusion

The evicted slum-dwellers of Ambedkar Nagar have faced multiple evictions and summary demolitions over the last ten years. This has had a profound effect on their ability to withstand these repeated disasters. The successful demolition of May 18 left these slum-dwellers homeless for a considerable period, before they built alternative accommodation. Even now, the threat of further eviction hangs over their heads. The children's health is appalling. Over three-quarters of the children are malnourished. The expenses incurred through repeated eviction means that the households no longer have the resources to adequately feed their children. Their health condition is also a reflection of an environment, which is not fit for living and in which even the most basic service provision is unavailable. The BMC and the state government had provided this site. It is clear that repeated eviction by the BMC and the action of its officials have compounded the health problems of these people.

We express concern for short- and long-term ill effects on the growth and development, and safety of the children, who are repeatedly evicted from their homes. Under-nutrition, disease and emotional stress are the result of both being evicted from their homes and watching their parents find ways of coping with repeated and violent demolitions.

This study raises a few questions. Can the Municipal Corporation of Greater Mumbai, which is responsible for the health of the city, remain oblivious of the devastating effect of the demolitions carried out by them on the health and safety of children? No attempt is being made by the state to study the problem. And predictably, there are no preventive measures instituted to avoid the ill effects on the health of the children.

Recommendations

- Medical facilities are not provided at the site, shelters are not provided to keep children, women and the old from exposure to harsh weather conditions.
- Identification of resettlement plots which are fit for human dwelling.
- Allotment of pitches by name prior to the demolitions.
- Prior provision of basic amenities, such as water and sanitation, at the resettlement site.
- After allotment of pitches, a minimum of eight days should be allowed for the change in residence.
- Therefore demolition should be carried out only when homes are vacated.
- Shelters to be provided for transit period.
- Exposure to harsh weather conditions must be taken into consideration while deciding the time for demolition.
- Medical cover to be provided at the site.
- Maximum efforts should be made to provide permanent, rather than temporary sites.

Acknowledgements

The children and other residents of Ambedkar Nagar, Colaba, Mumbai.

Nick Emmel PhD, Nuffield Institute for Health, University of Leeds, UK.

12

The Law and Homosexual in India

Sherry Joseph

While talking about law and homosexuality, I am reminded of a story of a washer-man and his donkey. The donkey refused to move with the heavy bundle of clothes on his back from his house to the pond. The washer-man nailed a carrot to a stick, which was tied in front of the animal's mouth. The donkey kept on moving with a view to eat the priced vegetable – the donkey went on but the carrot was un-reachable. In the field of jurisprudence this shows how some laws – the proverbial ass, pursue, perpetually, the carrot of the moral ideal.

Homosexuality has an ancient history in India. Ancient texts like the Rig Veda, which dates back to around 1,500 BC, and sculptures and vestiges depict sexual acts between women as revelations of a feminine world where sexuality was based on pleasure and fertility (Giti Thadani, 1991). The description of homosexual acts in the Kamasutra, the harems of young boys kept by Muslim nawabs and Hindu aristocrats, male homosexuality in Medieval Muslim history, corroborations of sodomy in Tantric rituals are some historical evidences of same-sex relationships (Sherry Joseph, under publication).

However, these experiences started losing their significance with the advent of Vedic Brahmanism and, later on, of British colonialism. Thadani claims that Aryan invasion, dating to 1500 BC began to suppress homosexuality through the emerging dominance of patriarchy (Sherry, under publication). In the Manusmriti, there are references to punishments like loss of caste, heavy monetary fines and strokes of the whip for gay and lesbian behaviour. In the case of married women, it is mentioned that 'luring of maids' is to be punished by shaving the women bald, cutting off two fingers, and then parading her on a donkey. Manu's specifications of more severe punishments for married women can suggest either a wide prevalence of such relationships among married women, or a greater acceptance of these practices among unmarried women. In either cases, these references point to the tensions in the norms of compulsory heterosexuality prescribed by Brahmanical partite.

Both sexual systems coexisted, despite fluctuations in relative repression and freedom, until British Colonialism, when the destruction of images of homosexual expression and sexual expression in general became more systematic and blatant. The homophobic and Victorian puritanical values regarded the display of explicit sexual images as 'pornographic and evil'. The Western view, since the time of colonial expansion, has been strongly influenced by reproductive assumptions about sexuality. These puritanical values and attitudes were in turn mapped into the interpretation of sexual activity among colonial people, and which is evident from the responses to all forms of 'unnatural' sexual practices. The Indian psyche accepted the Western 'moral and psychological' idea of sexuality being 'pathological', rather than the natural expression of desire, which once used to be a part of Indian culture.

The last century witnessed major changes in the conception of homosexuality. Since 1974, homosexuality ceased to be considered an abnormal behaviour and was removed from the classification of mental disorder. It was also de-criminalised in different countries. Since then various states across the globe enacted anti-discriminatory or equal opportunity laws and policies to protect the rights of gays and lesbians. In 1994, South Africa became the first nation to constitutionally safeguard the rights of lesbians and gays. Canada, France, Luxembourg, Holland, Slovenia, Spain, Norway, Denmark, Sweden and New Zealand also have similar laws. In 1996, the US Supreme Court ordered that no state could pass legislation that discriminated against homosexuals. In India, so far, no such progressive changes have taken place, and homosexuals remain victims of violence in different forms supported by the state and society. This paper attempts to see how the state, through the legal machinery, violates the rights of the homosexuals.

Is homosexuality a crime?

A frequently asked question is whether homosexuality is a crime or not in India. An affirmation would be the most frequent answer. How do the Indian laws view homosexuality?

There is no explicit mention of homosexuality or homophilia in any of the statute books of India. (Homophilia emphasises love-philia instead of only sexual behaviour. It focuses on affectionate and erotic desire instead of viewing homosexuals as 'certain kind of people'). A person cannot be prosecuted for being a homosexual or homophilic. However, the sexual act of sodomy is a criminal offence. The major provisions of criminalisation of same-sex acts are found in the Section 377 of the Indian Penal Code (IPC) of 1860. Section 377 of IPC reads, "Of unnatural offences: Whoever voluntarily has carnal intercourse against the order of nature with any man, woman or animal shall be punished with imprisonment for life or imprisonment of either description for a term which may extend to 10 years and shall also be liable to fine". Explanation: Penetration is sufficient to constitute carnal intercourse necessary for the offence described in this section

What does this non-bailable and cognisable offence imply? It is based on centuries old misconception that sodomy and homosexuality is the same thing. A homosexual man is viewed as a 'type of person' who has only anal intercourse with his partner. However, the emotional attachments, fantasies, and affectionate and erotic desires have not been given due consideration. Thus, de jure, it is an attempt to criminalise sodomy while de facto it is an attempt to criminalise and stigmatise homosexuality. Hence, conventionally, homosexuality is considered an offence under the IPC.

In the history of the statute from 1860 to 1992, there were only 30 cases in the high courts and Supreme Court (Shamona, 1992). The small number of cases filed under this section shows that the section is redundant and outdated and needs to be repealed.

This section raises interesting questions like what is 'natural'? What is the 'order of nature'? "Nature' conceived by whom? And 'order' perceived by whom? Even if one assumes that the 'order of nature' is penile-vaginal intercourse between a man and woman, Section 377 remains ambiguous about which sexual acts it seeks to prescribe. For some reason, sodomy between males, and male and female, as well as bestiality has been considered 'carnal intercourse' against the order of nature. However, there are no reported judgements of the high courts or the Supreme Court declaring that cunnilingus or fellatio will be considered an offence punishable under Section 377 of the IPC.

Even though this section does not distinguish sodomy between males and between male and female, it is targeted against males, more so than females. In 1992, 18 men were arrested from a park in New Delhi on the suspicion that they were homosexuals. After protest and demonstration by gays, lesbians and human rights groups, they were released from police custody after a petty case was filed against them. In fact, they were not indicted under Section 377 but under the provision of public nuisance under the Delhi Police Act. There are similar sections in the Police Acts of different states of India. The police and heterosexuals use this section to blackmail gay men, and other men who also have sex with men to extort money and valuables from them. This more so happens in parks, certain streets and public toilets, which function as an informal sexual networking area for homosexual men.

This section has been used to intimidate women, particularly in the case of women who have run away together, or if they make their relationship known. In 1987, Tarulata/Tarun Kumar underwent a female to male sex change operation and married Lila in 1989. Lila's father filed a petition in the Gujarat High Court saying that it was a lesbian relationship and that the marriage be annulled. The petition contends that, "Tarun Kumar possesses neither the male organ nor any natural mechanism of cohabitation, sexual intercourse and procreation of children". Adoption of any unnatural mechanisms does not create manhood and as such, Tarun Kumar was not a male. The petition called for criminal action under Section 377, and the case is now pending in the Gujarat High Court.

No distinction is being made between consensual and coercive sex. From 1860 to 1992, out of the 30 cases, 18 were non-consensual, four were consensual of which three were before 1940 and 8 were unspecified. In a judgement (Fazal Rab v/s State of Bihar) the Supreme Court was dealing with a case where a man had homosexual relations with a boy, and with the latter's consent. The Supreme Court in 1983 observed that: "The offence is one under Section 377, of the IPC, which implies sexual perversity. No force appears to have been used... neither omissions of permissive society nor the fact that in some countries homosexuality has ceased to be an offence, has influenced our thinking." Considering the consent of the boy, the Supreme Court reduced the sentence from three years rigorous imprisonment to six months rigorous imprisonment. Under this clause, a third party can sue the partners who voluntarily enter into sodomy, thereby infringing on the right to personal liberty and privacy as enshrined in the Fundamental Rights of the Constitution.

Heterosexual couples engaged in sodomy can also be indicted under this section. Marriage is taken as an implied consent by the wife; for 'normal' intercourse and not for anal intercourse. If the wife consented, both are guilty, if she did not, the husband alone is guilty. Under Section 13 of the Hindu Marriage Act, 1855 and Section 11 of the Indian Divorce

Act, 1869, a wife can apply for divorce if the husband has been guilty of sodomy/bestiality.

This section (377) is mostly used to register cases of child sexual abuse, since the rape laws do not have scope to include male rape. On the other hand the term 'Against the order of nature', is broad enough to include sexual abuse of male children. From 1860 to 1992, 15 out of the 30 cases registered were assault on minors.

Constitution and Other Provisions

The Indian Constitution states that "there shall be no discrimination on the basis of the sex of a person" which is a Fundamental Right of the citizen. The term 'sex', although refers to the biological sex of a person as male or female, is broad enough to include sexual orientation in the present context.

Section 292 of the IPC refers to obscenity, and there is ample scope to include homosexuality under this section. Last year, a parcel from the US containing a few copies of gay and lesbian magazine for South Asians was sent to a gay group in Kolkata for distribution and subscription. The Customs authorities confiscated it. They contended that as per law the publication amounted to obscenity and was offensive to the morality of the country. The case was closed when the addressee discarded the parcel, seeing no way out.

The concept of family refers to a universal, permanent, and pervasive institution, characterised by socially approved sexual access and reproduction, common residence, domestic services, and economic co-operation. Let me quote two instances of alternative marriage system existing in India. Amongst the Nair community in South India, who followed the matrilineal system of descent, several men could have access to a woman through the Tali rites, and subsequent sambandham unions. The Tali chain and locket worn around the neck was tied by a man of appropriate ritual status on behalf of his sub-caste, which acquired sexual rights over the woman concerned. These rights were extended to any member of the higher caste, usually Namboodiri, who was attracted to and was found acceptable for the woman. Men who had sambandham relations did not have any exclusive rights as husband or as father; the woman could withdraw the sexual access allowed to them any time, if she so wished. The right over her progeny was vested in her tarawad (household of matrilineal kin). In the Nair-Namboodiri sambandham, the latter could not ever dine with his wife or children, not to speak of sharing any domestic chores or economic activity.

In a small village called Angaar, in Gujarat, among the Kutchi community a ritualistic transgender marriage is performed during the time of the Holi festival. This wedding, which is being celebrated every year for the past 150 years, is unusual because Ishaak, the bridegroom, and Ishakali, the bride, are both men.

In spite of the existence of alternative marriage systems and customs, the conventional definition of a family includes a man and a woman along with their resultant children. This definition is based on the notion of compulsory heterosexuality and homophobia. At present, there is no legislation in India where same-sex couples can register as domestic partners, or undertake civic contract unions.

Under the labour laws, the provision under 'moral turpitude' is anti-homosexual. Mere claim of an employee is enough for dismissal from the job. A relationship not based on blood or marriage is not entitled for social security benefits under the Employee Provident Fund Act, the Pension Act, the Workmen Compensation Act, the Insurance Act, the Housing Act, etc.

The legal status of homosexuality in the Indian Armed Forces follows the model set by Section 377 of the IPC. Section 46 of chapter VI—offences of the Army Act, 1950, states: "Any person subject to this Act who is guilty of any disgraceful conduct of a crude, indecent or unnatural kind shall, on conviction by court-martial, be liable to suffer imprisonment for a term which may extend to seven years or much less punishments as is in this Act mentioned". Similar provisions exist in the Air Force Act and the Navy Act.

Legal Remedy

In 1994, a controversy emerged when a medical team visited the Tihar Jail in Delhi and reported a high incidence of sodomy in the male wards. They recommended making provisions for condoms, as there was a risk of HIV infection being transmitted to the jail inmates. The jail authorities abstained from making provisions for condoms since it would mean that they were approving a crime and aiding and abetting an offence under the IPC.

A human rights activist group has filed Public Interest Litigation in the Delhi High Court. The petition challenges the constitutional validity of Section 377 of the IPC and advocates supply of condoms to jail inmates, with a plea to restrain the authorities from segregating or isolating prisoners with homosexual orientations or those suffering from HIV/AIDS. The petition urges that Section 377 is obsolete, and must be struck down as being unconstitutional on the grounds that Right for Privacy is part and parcel of the Fundamental Rights of Life and Liberty under Article 21 of the Constitution and recognised by the 1948 International Convention on Human Rights. Section 377 is a violation of Article 14 of the Constitution since it discriminates persons on the basis of their sexual orientation. Having been enacted in 1860, Section 377 is archaic, absurd, and implemented by the British in all its colonies, including India, but now has been repealed in England, the country of origin. The initial response of the judges during the hearing of the petition was quite homophobic. They questioned whether the petitioner wanted to promote 'free sex and pervasive sex'. When a senior advocate appeared for the petitioner, the judges quickly changed their attitude and heard the petition with sympathy. The case is pending for argument in the court.

This is the only case, which has been filed against the anti-discriminatory homosexual laws in India. The point of argument in this case is more from a sexual health perspective and less from the gay rights perspective. Given the Indian socio-cultural and political situation, it will take some time for the gays and lesbians to come forward to fight for their rights. However, in the last few years, an increasing number of gay groups throughout the country are giving serious thought to the problems faced by them.

We know that the law enacted in any country is often the product of a majoritarian, popular consensus. Some of the laws reflect the prejudices and myths of the dominant ideologies circulating in these societies, and thus try marginalising minority groups, like homosexuals. Shouldn't the law help counter the prejudices and protect the rights of the marginalised section?

Part-IV
Caste and Communal Violence

13

Lesser Humans : Scavengers of Indian Republic

Martin Macwan

Three years of working with the scavengers

So much has been written on and around the issue, including reports by the various commissions set up by various governments. Hundreds of recommendations have been made and schemes drawn up, without anyone ever being serious about it. If 50 years of independence have to be summarised by the scavengers (Bhangis), it will be thus: "We trust no one."

Therefore, I do not wish to add any more material to the subject, which is theoretical and impotent. The nation has patted its back several times for evolving various plans and felt content, in spite of knowing that their inaction has only strengthened the privileged. So, if we cannot wipe someone's tears, why deceive them with promises that we fail to keep again and again.

Personally, it has been a shock to me. In spite of working with Dalits for many years, this issue never hit me hard, until about two years ago. I only wish to narrate here the facts that my colleagues and I have come across. These facts throw light on the life of scavengers. I feel, these facts tell a story of scavengers, but more than that, it tells the story of the state, which has maintained a status quo.

These are facts that describe the scavengers as they are today. Any attempt to theorise these facts only helps to wash away the guilt of those who are in public life. If they are only an embarrassment to the nation and its leaders, I wish to increase it. These are hard realities that exist today in 1998. They affect around 8,00,000 families in India.

1. Forced labour of the filthy kind

1.1 Dry latrines have to be cleaned: Vado varvano chhe: There are various kinds of dry latrines in urban and rural areas. These units are either in private homes or managed by local self-governments.

1.2 I still have to clean up the waste: *Vassida varvana baki chhe:* Vassida means dung of animals, along with other filth that is scattered all over. They need to be collected and dumped at a designated place. The village has a sizeable number of cattle. The dung, mixed with hay, is dumped at a site to make manure. The excreta of very young babies are also mixed in the collection. Vassida is collected manually by Bhangis in shallow plates made of tin and dumped. The dumping grounds are often near their homes. After the dumping is over, the tin plates are cleaned to save them from corrosion. The contents that stick to it are mixed with dry soil and wiped clean with hands. Some food is given to the Bhangis daily for these labours. At the end of the threshing season, they are given 10-15 kilos of grain.

1.3 Vadoliyu: There are communities like feudal lords and Muslims, who are considered high caste but are poor. Their women live in enclosures. Curtailing women's freedom has forced them to a small dry latrine known as vadoliyu. There is a hand dug small pit in the ground, not deeper than one foot, in which human excreta is discarded. It has two bricks, one on either side to serve as foot-rest. For privacy, jute bags are hung across four wooden pillars dug in the four corners of the pit.

1.4 Dabba jajroo: The rich in the village build a proper toilet, which is at a corner of their castle-like house. The excreta and waste from the toilet gathers in a tin box, which is then removed from an outlet in the wall. This outlet is at the rear and the removal of this box cannot be seen from the inner parts of the house.

1.5 Gutter latrine: The open gutters for disposal of filth are connected to every house with bathrooms. The children, and even adults under cover of darkness defecate directly in these gutters where excreta mix with plenty of dirty water and other filth.

1.6 Vada jajroo: In every big village the local government demarcates separate plots of land for men and women to be used as open toilet. The plots are covered from all sides with a three- to four-foot-high wall, with an open entrance at some point. In a larger village there may be several such wada latrines.

1.7 Khada jajroo: A properly built latrine is connected to a soak pit at the rear. The bathroom is also connected to the pit. The mixture of water and excreta never leaves the pit dry. When the pit is full, which is neck-deep, someone gets into it to clean it. He remains in that filth for three to four hours.

1.8 Village community latrines: These are of various kinds. There is one type of properly built latrine, without tub, where the disposal is led through a hole to the common open-drain at the rear.

The other kind comprises a place like a big hall, with two rows of toilets, on either side. The distance between the rows, which are one-and-a-half feet above the ground, is approximately three feet. Only two footrests separate a person from the one sitting next. People who utilise this come with only one small tin of water to wash themselves. The disposal remains right there. It is collected with two tin plates and emptied in a bamboo basket for disposal. The basket is either carried on the head or the shoulder. At times, the basket can be full of worms, which breed very fast in the waste having been left indisposed for a day or two.

The only people, who dispose human waste, are the Bhangis or scavengers. Most of them are women. Their day starts early in the morning with the foul smell of shit, and it ends with the same foul smell as their houses are close to all types of latrines.

The owners of private dry latrines pay them Rs 5 per month (12 US cents), and a piece of bread everyday. The piece of bread is tied in the sari and can be seen hanging in front of their belly, while they are busy working-hands soiled with filth.

The local self-governments, which employ these people through government grants, do not follow uniform standards of payment. Some bodies pay Rs 50 per month ($1.25) while others pay Rs. 600 a month. In some cases, the salaries have not been revised for the last 20 years or more. In semi-urban areas, the payments are higher, although there is unequal payment for men and women. The grants used for these payments through self-governments are part of the World Bank loan given to the nation under various development programmes.

The workload never decreases because it is linked with population increase. So, when mothers are sick and unable to work, but cannot afford to take leave, the children join them as a helping hand. The children then face seclusion in schools, where other children, and sometimes teachers, smell stink from them.

1.9 You drag away that (dead) dog: Aalya, kutru dhahaidi kadh: There are some animals, which are useless after death. They are also considered inauspicious. Dogs and cats are from this category. Many Hindus shall return home halfway if a cat crosses their way. When cats and dogs die, they have to be discarded. Members of the Dalit community are summoned to discard such animals, only where there are no Bhangis. There have been incidents of physical attacks on Dalits for their refusal to do so.

The dead animal is tied with strings and then pulled out of the village, while all others who are passing by go off the road, covering their nose and mouth with their hands. This is to save them from the foul smell that may bring impurity, and thus force them to have a bath.

1.10 Railway tracks and excreta: Even when trains stop at stations, there are some passengers who continue to defecate. Excreta, in this case, are trapped between rubble stones. The only way to remove them is by scrapping with wire brooms.

1.11 Manholes: The metropolitan areas and big cities have flush latrines connected to sewage lines, which are very big in size. When they are blocked, the scavengers get in them through the manholes, and dive in the filthy water with a bucket to remove all kinds of substance, such as plastics, cloth, glass pieces, etc. In industrial pockets, chemical waste is channelled into these gutters or it seeps in like ground water.

In Ahmedabad, there were 32 manhole deaths in the past two years, where the victims had inhaled carbon monoxide while at work in the manhole.

1.12 Pathology laboratories: Only a Bhangi collects the stool and urine for pathology tests from the patients.

1.13 Post-mortem rooms: The dead bodies are handled by Bhangis. A Bhangi does the opening up of the dead body likewise it is his job to sew the dead body after the autopsy. In a murder case of a Dalit, where the body was exhumed after 17 days, I witnessed that the doctors were at a distance taking notes. The cutting of the body, the breaking of the skull, the removal of bones for examination, was done by a Bhangi.

1.14 Hospitals and maternity homes: Removing blood, urine, shit-stained bedclothes, is done by Bhangis. Cleaning soiled bodies of the ailing patients, or removal of waste and urine pans and cleaning them is done by Bhangis. The labour room tables in maternity homes are cleaned by Bhangis. Women carry out the hospital jobs. They are referred to as mahetrani.

2. Traditional Duties in Villages:

Not by choice but enforced by custom, tradition and imperatives of survival

2.1 Go, make the announcements: *Haad padi aav (Town crier):* In villages this medieval mode of communication is still popular. The Bhangi is asked to go from street to street to announce a meeting or give warning to cattle breeders for trampling crops, etc. In return he is paid a rupee or two.

2.2 Toran, dhol and dakla: A Bhangi does all jobs: tying buntings or festoons (toran) of tree leaves over the doorway, and cloth shade (mandap) in front of the house celebrating a wedding, or a festive day like the New Year Day; playing the drum (dhol) during wedding celebrations - which last for a couple of days - among all castes of the village; playing the small drum (dhakla) accompanied by wailing-like singing during the worship of the exclusive deity of the other sub-castes of Dalits.

The payments for such jobs are in cash and kind. Such jobs undertaken at wedding ceremonies can earn the Bhangis better money. Denial to perform any of the jobs can lead to serious consequences.

2.3 Go, give the bad news about the death: Ja melo aali aaay: News is of two kinds, good and bad. News about marriage, engagement, childbirth, especially of a male child, or a newly wed girl getting pregnant for the first time, is considered good news. News about death, especially of the young, is considered bad news. The person who gives good news is auspicious. The person who gives bad news is the contrary. People in the rural areas communicate largely through personal messages.

Good news, therefore, is sent through the Brahmins only. (Brahmins are priests. Even Dalits amongst themselves have a sub-caste of Brahmins). A Bhangi only gives the bad news. In return for his service, he is given some butter, jaggery and bread. He normally carries a bathing towel, which he spreads on the ground and sits after the news is delivered. The relative of the dead empties a cup of coarse grain in the towel. For the eatables, he has to borrow a utensil from a local person of his community.

He might sit in a corner, off the road, and eat the given food, or carry it back home for his family.

3. Some Traditional Practices

Internalisation of degradation

3.1 Eating evil or cursed food: Varelu, mantrelu khavanoo: Belief in black magic rituals persists among the rural and urban (non-Bhangi) poor of the so-called lower and middle castes, and sometimes in the upper castes as well. For example, black-magic treated food is left at the nearest crossroads to free a person from evil spirits. No one touches that food or offering, except, of course, the Bhangi who eats it as part of his life-long struggle against hunger.

3.2 Masters, please give us dinner: *Vadu aljo maa baap:* Vadu means dinner. Aljo means 'please be kind to give'. Maa baap, means mother and father literally, but in this context it means 'kind masters'. Whether it is a city or a village, in the evening, approximately when one is about to finish dinner, a person, mostly a woman, sometimes accompanied by a child, enters the street. Both are carrying aluminium utensils. She then shouts with maximum humility. "Vadu aljo maa baap" At some distance the same appeal is repeated and then meekly they go to a central place and wait. Both are barefoot. The woman has a bigger utensil, and the child a smaller one, for solid and liquid food, respectively.

One after another, any member of a family, mostly women and kids, come out with food, and from a little distance empty it into the utensils held by the woman and the child. Every time someone comes with food, the woman plays two functions. Firstly, to accept the food with expressions of gratitude in the eyes saying, "Lao maa baap" (Give us kind masters), and secondly, be vigilant that her child does not - even by accident -touch the one who gives the food. The most important thing is also to see that the child does not spill the food.

There is someone else also waiting in the street - the dogs. The family members come out of the house with two separate plates, one to be emptied in the utensils of these Bhangis, and the other on a big stone plate fixed at a place for the dogs. Sometimes the dogs sniff the food, and without touching it walk away.

After waiting for some time the woman and the child, on realising that no more food shall be coming their way, walk away to their house for dinner. Three kinds of food is given to them: (a) fresh but not consumed, (b) fresh, but which is in the form of leftovers in the plate, especially from the children's who cannot finish everything, and (c) the leftovers from the afternoon.

Children on either side simultaneously learn the ways on how to give and what to give, and how to receive things. Those who mainly come to ask for food are the Bhangis. Sometime even beggars come and beg for food, but they name the food that they would like to have, i.e., they would say, "Please give me some vegetables," etc.

3.3 Baa, would you please pour water for me?: Baa paani redi aljo: A woman of high caste is addressed as 'Baa' (mother). Dalits are not allowed in many villages to draw water from the well. The worst is that scavengers are not allowed access to the well meant for Dalits. They have to wait at the side, until a high caste woman has mercy on them and pours some water in their pots.

It is worse in the agriculture season when the sowing operations are on, and one has to wait for hours to get a pot of water.

3.4 A kind of wild grass: Dabhdo: Dabhdo, a kind of grass has multiple uses in villages, especially to save the family from the wrath of supernatural elements. A little Dabhdo is always put along with the dead body in the grave. It is also required when there is a sun eclipse, which is believed to bring disaster to the family. People believe that during an eclipse, Rahu, a demon, possesses the sun. . Therefore, during an eclipse, some Dabhdo is thrown on the roof of the house to save the family from likely disaster.

A Bhangi always handles Dabhdo on such occasions. If at all the wrath comes, it shall come on him.

3.5 Zampdo and Zampdi: Gods and goddesses can be divided into two groups: those of the upper castes, and those of the rural, lower caste poor who mostly have their own local village goddess (called Gramdevta). These local gods and goddesses are not a part of the classical Brahminical Hindu religion, and can be appeased only by "black" magic rituals.

There are some who bring love, compassion and wealth. There are others who bring wrath and disaster and have to be feared. It is interesting to note that all good gods (who promote welfare), i.e., Saraswati (goddess of education), Lakshmi (goddess of wealth), and Brahma (the creator), are worshipped by the high castes. They are painted as artistic and beautiful personalities, fair and attractive, with compassion in their eyes.

The bad gods (who bring destruction) - Meldi (who asks for child sacrifice), Kalka (black with a long tongue) – are; worshipped by the poor.

Hadaksha (the goddess of rabies) is worshipped by Bhangis. The gods for the poor promote only destruction and fear.

Similarly, it is believed that close contact with a Bhangi, whether dead or alive, is equally harmful. The ghost of a Bhangi male is known as Zampdo and that of the female Zampdi. All other ghosts can be appeased but not the Zampdo and the Zampdi.

Therefore, one does not find a Bhangi roaming around after dark during the pre-Diwali festivals. They are scared that they shall be the victims of supernatural elements. This is a good trick to keep Bhangis away during the fun and frolic, which is a major attraction of these festivals.

3.6 Burial cloth covering the dead body: *Kafan and loogdu:* The end of the life journey is death. The dead body of a male is covered with white cloth and that of the female with red cloth, known as kafan and loogdu respectively. Just before the body is laid to rest in the grave, the cloth is removed and hanged on a bushy shrub. After the burial, the Bhangi takes home the kafan for a new dress.

4. Prohibitions

4.1 Marriage procession cannot enter the village: *Jaan gaam mathi na kadhay:* The marriage procession of a Bhangi cannot enter the village from the main gate. Similarly, they cannot decorate themselves with jewellery or good shining clothes. There have been serious incidents of attacks on the scavengers for not having obeyed the above rules. They cannot hire music bands for the occasion, as is done by others. A young boy was beaten up because he had tucked his shirt in.

4.2 Can we celebrate a pre-marriage ceremony?: Phuleku pheravvu ke nahin?: Phuleku is a pre-wedding ceremony where the boy, with a garland around his neck, painted with turmeric powder (believed to be a skin purifier as well making the skin glisten) a knife and coconut in hand (knife to protect against evils) is invited around to all the families of his community. He is fed with sweets and given some money as gift. Normally, he is accompanied by his friends and young girls who, chant marriage songs.

In higher caste communities the same ceremony has added elements. The boy is on a horseback, and goes around on public roads accompanied by music bands and firecrackers.

Dalits are not allowed to do anything by which their ceremony matches with the one of the higher castes. There have been incidents of mass attack, where Dalits had tried to sit on horseback for the ceremony.

4.3 Which way shall we carry the dead?: *Maaiyaat kyan thi kadhshu?:* There is always a cause for worry when someone dies in the community. The dead body of Dalits cannot be carried out to the cemetery by the main village gate, for it would defile the village. Therefore, often, it is a long detour by the time the body reaches the final destination.

4.4 And, we dropped ourselves from the school: *Ane ame bhanta bhanta utri gaya:* Sangeeta, a 14-year-old, describes how her teachers pushed her to the last bench in the class. Earlier, she scored very good marks. But she, and other children as well, felt psychologically so harassed by the teacher that they dropped out of the school.

"I had dreams that one day I shall be a nurse or a doctor... but I have become a scavenger. All my dreams have been shattered." Unable to continue she breaks down in tears.

4.5 Can't you see? Have your eyes blasted off?: *Bhadto nathi? Ankho phuti gayee chhe?:* One hears this phrase quite often whenever a scavenger approaches a higher caste person and thereby comes within a close distance. The connotation is for untouchability. The former has to keep such a distance that his shadow does not fall on the latter.

4.6 Who will make flour for us? *Darav vanu dukh:* In many villages, the flourmills owned by high castes do not grind flour for scavengers. They have to cycle to other villages for the purpose. This is a major problem we have seen in the villages of Patdi taluka, Surendranagar district.

4.7 You, get up from here: *Ey utho ahinthi:* In a village called Zanand, 70 km from the state capital, scavengers find themselves in a difficult situation. All wastelands in the village have been encroached upon as the village is close to the river and the land is fertile. The problem for Bhangis is where do they go for toilet? Wherever they go—even when they are in the middle of the defecation process— someone or the other from the higher caste forces them to get up and go away. This applies even to women.

4.8 Sit on the floor: *Niche bes:* The Bhangi or other Dalits, though elected as members to the local self-government, are not allowed to sit on the chair. They have to sit on the floor. There are times when they are not summoned for meetings. Later, their signature or thumb impressions are acquired as proof of their having attended the meeting.

4.9 Is Mohan home?: *Mohan gher chhe?:* Mohanbhai is my colleague in his early forties. He belongs to the community. It was dark all over and we were waiting for the dinner to get ready. Someone shouted from the end of the street. On his return I inquired as to who was the caller and I learned that it was the village postman. The post is not delivered at home. Mohanbhai, however, being a development worker has the privilege of having his mail delivered at the end of the street.

4.10 Get Ram's cup: Ram patar utaril laav: 'Ram patar' is a name for the cup made from clay, kept separately for Dalits in almost all upper caste houses. It is placed over the outer pillar, under the roof. Therefore, when a Dalit goes to a upper caste house he is offered tea in that cup. After he drinks his tea, which is poured in the cup from above, he has to wash the cup (again the water for this purpose is poured from above) and keep it at its original place.

For Dalits, including scavengers, the very fact that a high caste person offered them tea is an occasion of pride. In a village, there are times when the exploitation is not direct. The community leaders are called in to mediate over a cup of tea. They hold quite a clout over the community. In cases of money borrowing from landlords, one has to go via these leaders.

5. Desperate search for subsidiary sources of income

5.1 Collecting bones from garbage: *Hadka vinvana:* Adults and children collect bones, which are picked up along with paper and glass pieces to be segregated and sold for a petty sum in the market.

5.2 Supda and Indhoni: Supda is like a flat plate made from straw. It is used for cleaning the grain before it is cooked, It separates the grain from the chaff. Indhoni is a small ring made of grass , which women place on their heads to support water pots.

For Bhangis the only 'clean' means of earning some money is to make these household articles, which are used by all castes. In the primitive barter economy of the village, the Bhangis are paid in kind (grain) and not cash. Buyers are few and far between. The only significance is that these articles are not considered as polluted by their touch, and that, in a small way, they are allowed to become artisans for a while.

6. Self-perception, and as Perceived by Others

6.1 Destiny inscribed by goddess fate on the sixth day after birth: ***Chhathhi na lekh:*** After a child is born a ceremony is conducted on the sixth day. A piece of paper and pencil is kept under the pillow of the sleeping, newborn baby. It is believed that Goddess Fate, or 'Vidhata', now insribes the fate of the newborn, which can never be undone. No wonder, most Bhangis believe their present fate to be divinely ordained.

6.2 Sir, we are like animals: *Saheb, ame rahya dhor:* Whenever you enter a scavenger colony and start a dialogue about their getting organised or fighting for their rights, someone or the other will say, "How can we understand all these? We are like animals."

6.3 Boys have names like Waste, Unclean, Dusty, Idiot, etc.: *Kachro, Melo, Dhudiyo and Bogho*: These are common names in the community. One can add more to the list. In Gujarat, all male names carry the -bhai (brother) and females the -ben (sister) suffix to their names. However, this is not allowed for a Bhangi or a Dalit. Even government records describe their names in the most insulting manner. The other castes, in fact, all communities in general address Dalits in the same insulting tone. On the other hand, an elderly Dalit dare not address a feudal kid without respect. In cities, now, they have better names.

6.4 He is completely rotten, very sick: *Akho ne akho haadi gayo chhe*: This is how a very sick person is described in the community. The phrase 'sadi javu' (rotten up) is used in the context of vegetables or fruits. A Planning Commission study on the health problems of the scavengers says that they are more vulnerable to anaemia, diarrhoea with vomiting, respiratory infections, skin diseases, jaundice, and other ailments as compared to others.

6.5 From where shall I start counting my sorrow?: *Dukh chyanthi ganvoo?:* Especially the old within Bhangis are in a pathetic condition. Crippled by age and negligence, they are a helpless lot. One repeatedly hears from them the wish of an early death.

6.6 Will you have tea?: *Cha piso?:* Even when the scavenger knows that you do not consider them to be low as others do, still, each time they will ensure by asking whether you'll have tea or water at their house. Those who believe in untouchability - as far as food is concerned - shall deny politely, "No, thanks, we just had." Scavengers get the message and ask such people, "If you want we can get tea made in the market for you."

In cases of major atrocities on Dalits, police protection is provided. Policemen from high castes will not take water from the Dalits. In such cases, the Dalits go to the high castes—even to those with whom they had a dispute—and request them to provide food and water to these policemen.

6.7 How about a Bhangi having sex with you?: *Taane bhangiya raakhe?*: This is the worst abuse one can direct to a non-Bhangi woman. It is provocative enough to murder the abuser.

6.8 Oh, I see! You are going around with a newspaper!: *Chhapu laine fare chhe?:* "A Few days before the high court struck down the system of manual scavenging in village Ranpur, Kishorbhai, a leader of the community, moved around with a broom in his hand. Now, he has bought a newspaper." This was the comment passed by a high caste merchant as he passed through the market area.

6.9 Brother of the Bhangi....Bhangi behaviour: *Bhangiya ni bhaee...Bhangiyaa weda:* Whenever someone from another community, except a Bhangi, behaves in an unpleasant manner, he and his behaviour is described as above. This is one of the most humiliating labels you can give to a non-Bhangi.

6.10 Bhangis have crossed their limit: *Mara haara bhangda phati gaya chhe*: This is a remark - full of contempt and full of intolerance - made by high castes, which also carries a bad connotation. Whenever a scavenger is finely dressed, or is going to college, or has purchased a vehicle, or has done something, which suggests that his financial or social position has improved, this remark follows. Mara haara means my brother-in-law, and phati gaya means they have crossed the boundary. In a crude sense, it means 'they have gone above their status.'

6.11 Scholarship for the 'children of persons engaged in filthy and unhygienic occupations': This is how the government has framed a scheme to financially assist school-going children, especially of Bhangis. The teacher is in charge of applying, securing and disbursing the scholarships from the government. The duties and powers of the teacher are discretionary.

There have been several cases where we had to intervene and force the teacher to pay up the scholarship money to the parents, and which had not been done for four years.

6.12 Loans for dhols and nagaras (drums): The Gujarat government has a special scheme for Bhangis. Financial aid is given if they want to purchase dhols and nagaras. The dhol is a drum tied around the neck and played. The nagara is a drum placed on the ground and beaten. This is in pursuance of the 'self-government programme', with a taste of 'entrepreneurial development'.

6.13 You do not have any business experience: *Tamne dhandha no anubhav nathi*: The Central government in the early 1990s started the National Scavengers Scheme. The aim was rehabilitation. The rehabilitation package consisted of part grant and part bank loan to the scavengers for anything else but scavenging. One Bhangi youth applied for the scheme. The government authorities approved the grant part of it and forwarded the application to the local bank for the loan part. The bankers told the youth, "Since you have no experience in business, we cannot give you a loan." The loan was needed as capital to buy and sell dress material. The loan amount was Rs 5,000 ($120) "How can I have experience, unless I do it?" was the argument of the pleading applicant.

7. Some Stories of Experience

7.1 The story of chhaniya ghaun: Chhaniya means something immersed in the dung of an animal, specifically in this case of a bullock, and ghaun in Gujarati means wheat. In a village called Vataman, in Ahmedabad district, my friend and colleague showed me that in the threshing season, the bullocks with their hooves thresh the wheat crop as they walk over it in circles. The process continues until the corn is separated from the hay.

During this exercise the bullocks eat a lot of the grain and suffer from diarrhoea. The indigestible corns come out with the dung in the form of a dribbling slurry.. There are people waiting to collect this slurry. They fill it in bamboo baskets and take home the stuff. Here they mix it with a lot of water, and then drain it off to collect the wheat that has settled at the bottom of the vessel. The wheat is then dried in the sun, and taken to the flourmill to be ground, and consumed. The wheat collected like this can take care of a family for two or three months.

The persons who do this, as I have seen so far, belong only to one community, i.e., the Bhangis. Lately, with an increased use of tractors and threshers, chhaniya ghaun is not easily available.

7.2 The story of Laxman: Laxman, an eight-year-old, is from the Vejalka village in Ahmedabad district. He is staying with his grandparents. His parents are away in search of work.. There is a small pan–cigarette shop in the village. The owner is a Patel—a high caste.

The place is a popular joint for poor children, because from here they entertain themselves by watching television, kept in a house next to the shop. It was a bad day in Laxman's life. He was so engrossed in watching a film on TV that he put his hand on the shop. The owner asked him to remove his hand. Laxman was too engrossed to hear that. The owner then threw a handful of wet lime paste (used in the pan) at Laxman, which fell on the latter's clothes. It is the second throw that went straight into the lad's eyes.

The eye specialist is not hopeful of saving Laxman's eye. I remember the day, two months back, when Laxman came to my office with his grandfather. He forgot his pain, as he concentrated on the refrigerator, closing and opening it and wondering at its coolness. He asked many questions about the refrigerator.

When I took him to an English newspaper office, on climbing the vehicle, he told his grandfather, "Papa, how nice this car is. Aren't we sitting in one for the first time?" All along the road in the city, the evening life flooded with lights amazed him, and his mouth fell open in amazement. I asked him whether he would go to school now. He said, "If I go now, the students and teachers will tease me by calling me blind, so I will go only after I am well."

7.3 I did not get the better part: ***Haaro maal mara bhag na ayo:*** The place is a village in the Vadhwan taluka of Surendranagar district. This has reference to the injustice being meted out to the complainant from the Bhangi community over the distribution of meat from a dead animal. When an animal dies in the village at least four people are required to drag the corpse to an assigned place, or where that place is far off , it is dragged to a secluded corner off the road.

The first stage is skinning, which requires skill. A well-discarded skin will fetch a better price in the market than the one with punctures. The second stage is to separate the meat according to its quality, as certain parts are considered better than the others. The third stage is distribution of the meat, where the survival of the fittest theory applies.

The quarrel was that the scavenger did not get a better part of the booty as another member who belonged to a higher caste cornered it - a Dalit. . And as the matter could not be resolved amicably, it resulted into a police complaint. The police was more than puzzled, not sure as to how to handle the matter, and sought the help of our organisation, i.e., Navsarjan.

Two of our colleagues reached the village to find that the aggrieved party had gathered outside the house of a retired police officer who, belonged to a non-Dalit high caste. It is a usual practice to seek counsel from the higher castes in resolving intra-community disputes. Surely, they were all standing outside the house making representations.

When the retired police officer came to know that two workers of our organisation had arrived, he invited them into the house. One dare not observe untouchability with the workers. One of the two workers was from the same community, a Bhangi. Suddenly there was hue and cry as the host offered drinking water to the workers. Those standing outside were saying, "Sir, he is our Bhangi, a low caste, therefore he cannot drink water from your house." The atmosphere was so charged that the aggrieved party had completely forgotten about their complaint.

Therefore, in all this the issue that had taken precedence was to save the master from any defilement that might befall him because of this act of their community member—drinking water in the house of a high caste.

The story itself is nauseating. However, in an area where 60 per cent of the population have to migrate in search of labour for more than six months in a year, the poorest who cannot do so have no option but to eat what is available.

The incident of the 1920s flashes through the mind, when Gandhiji gave a call to the Dalits to give up eating dead animals—a factor he thought distanced them from others. He received two letters in response. The first was from a teacher in rural Kolkta. He wrote that when he gave up eating dead animal meat, it was stuffed into his mouth by caste Hindus, saying that it was his religion to eat it. The second letter was from a businessman from Mumbai. He was apprehensive that if Dalits gave up eating dead animals, went in for education, and thereby entered business, then what would caste Hindus do?

7.4 The story of young girls: It was wedding time in the Bhangi colony, when a few youth from the Darbar community, fully drunk, entered the settlement and started making gestures at young girls. The host went to the Darbar elders to request them to restrain their boys from harassing the girls, especially when there were guests around.

Everyone thought the matter had been resolved until those youths returned at midnight. Requests from a very elderly person and his wife to have mercy on their people were ignored and they were beaten up. Such incidents are not new to the community in the village. A year ago, feudal lords took one of the girls away along with the cot on which she was fast asleep. She was returned almost after two days, saying that she had lost her way and they had found her.

7.5 Unemployed Bhangi primary teachers: The hope for a prompt job has pushed many Bhangi parents to invest everything they have to enable their children to study at the teachers' training college. In 1992, Navsarjan, organised a protest programme in Ahmedabad on August 15, the Independence Day. The demand was for a change in the existing reservation policy, which had rendered over a 1,000 Bhangi trained teachers unemployed.

This policy reserves 2 per cent seats for Bhangis at the teachers' college. This was done in the belief that due to all kinds of hardships Bhangi students would not succeed in securing a good percentage in the matriculation examinations. And so, when it came to jobs, selection was done on the basis of merit. Merit was drawn on the combined marks of the matriculation and college examinations. In the process, most Bhangi students never stood a chance as they had a lower percentage in matriculation as compared to others. Our demand to reserve 2 per cent of the jobs to balance the position was accepted but never implemented. The entire reservation policy has changed now.

The changed policy has made it compulsory for schools to advertise for all vacant posts. However, the schools have been given the liberty to fill up reserved posts if they do not find suitable candidates after three rounds of advertisements and personal interviews. The Bhangis or Dalits never prove to be 'suitable' in schools managed by caste Hindus and their organisations. One job, however, is reserved 100 per cent for Bhangis - scavenging.

To conclude, it is not enough to develop beautiful plans for the rehabilitation of scavengers. The moot question is whether the state in power recognises them as human beings.

14

Dalits, Violence and Health Concerns

Alex George

The Dalits of India who constituted 16.32 per cent of the population of India in 1991 (Census 1991) have resorted to violence as a means of achieving their social, economic and political rights. Such acts of violence were invariably against the oppressive caste system, supported in varying degrees by the colonial state and the princely states attached to them, and even by the post-colonial Indian state. Very often, peaceful assertions of rights by Dalits met with repression by the upper caste elite and the state, thus leading to violence on both sides. This is not to say that the Dalits did not take to violence on their own. The point is that institutionalised violence of the upper caste, who mostly constitute the ruling classes, and the violence of the state machinery, go relatively unnoticed, whereas violence by Dalits in challenging the unequal social system gets very often treated as just a law and order problem, leading to further violence by the state. The peaceful façade of an unequal caste relationship is achieved by the coercive power of the upper caste elite in various local situations, and by the fact, that the state machinery is by and large not recognized.

In relating the health concerns to caste violence, one needs to point out that the two major strands of thought on redemption from caste inequalities, which formed part of the freedom movement, viz., the Gandhian and the Ambedkarite, did not have the health rights of the Dalits as a major concern. They were at the same time concerned with various other social, economic, and political rights of the Dalits, which were perceived as more important concerns of the period. Thus, in the social sector the thrust of postcolonial policy on Dalits has been on education and employment in the government. sector, which were seen as sources of upward mobility. Together with this was the concern and efforts towards removal of untouchability. Sensitivity in the health sector turned to Scheduled Tribes, in whose case, due to their concentrated habitats, it was geographically feasible to address the issue of access, though rather too formally—by fixing lower population norms for setting up primay health centres (PHCs) and sub centres (SCs) in tribal areas (Basu S.K., 1990). Needless to add that, the functioning of these PHCs and SCs leaves much to be desired than their counterparts in the plains. It is by sensitising the government health sector to the issues arising from caste discrimination that a sensibility to caste violence can also be built in. This sensitisation is one of the issues involved in developing a perspective on caste violence and health concerns. A few examples from the history of early 20th century Kerala would illustrate this further.

When it was thought of officially in 1890 to start a ward for Dalit patients in the general hospital of Thiruvnanthapuram, the durbar physician objected to it on the grounds that it would keep away the Brahmins (Kabir & Krishnan, 1992). However, it was agreed to in 1894 to build a few cadjan sheds to accommodate Dalit patients who did not have any shelter from the rains. Yet, the situation did not improve considerably (Ibid) until further petitioning, and under the influence of the later Dalit struggles for travel on public roads and access to public places (George A., 1990). It was only in 1905 that an unused kitchen, far off from the main wards, was converted in the Women and Children Hospital for the use of Dalit women and their children (Kabeer & Krishnan op.cit). It was again pointed out in 1911 by P. Govinda Pillai, a reformist Nair who incidentally was the first Dalit representative in the Travancore Assembly, that in the hospitals Dalit patients were attended to only after the other patients, and that medicines were just thrown to them from a distance (Chentarassery, 1979).

Though not in the same form and degree, as in the early 20th century Kerala, caste discrimination in various forms is likely to be present even today in the provision for and delivery of health care in other states as well. The historical specialities of the regions and states will have a bearing on the nature of these discriminations, which in turn influence the response to caste violence. In this connection, it will be relevant to look into the nature of caste violence, the factors involved in it, and its manifestations through a case study. The case presented here is that of the Dalits of the south and central Travancore region of Kerala, from the second half of the 19th century to the 1940s. The first part is a caste movement of the Dalits, and the second part is an agricultural workers' movement in which the Dalits took part. Before going into this specific case study a brief note on the social history of Dalits is required.

Socio-historical Background

Romila Thapar observes that though the Varna system in ancient India did not function exactly as a superimposed hierarchical layer of social groups, the identity of the untouchable remained generally clear in the historical sources of that period (Thapar R., 1984). On the status of low castes during the Moghul period, Irfan Habib remarked, "Members of the low castes, assigned to the most menial and contemptible occupations could never aspire to the status of peasants, holding or cultivating the land on their own. It would not indeed be surprising if the actual status of many of them was semi-servile, involving a kind of bondage to a particular community of caste peasants or zamindars" (Habib I., 1963).

Dharma Kumar noted that one of the most striking peculiarities of the Indian forms of servitude was their close connection with the caste system. In general, the serfs and slaves belonged to thc lowest castes (Kumar, 1965). It is a situation that is reflected when Francis Buchnan, who toured Malabar in 1807, wrote that slaves or Churmar performed by far the greater part of the labour (Buchanan F., 1807). Churmar being a corrupted form of Cherumar, which was the most populous agrestic, slave caste in the Malbar region of Kerala. Kumar was also of the opinion that the lowest castes were probably prevented from owning and leasing land by powerful social sanctions (Kumar op. cit.). That this practice was followed in Kerala is clear when we find that the Malayala Manorama (MM) newspaper was arguing through its columns in 1909 that land should be leased out to Pulayas (MM 1909), the largest Dalit caste of the state. Though slavery was abolished in the Malabar region of the state in 1843, along with British India (Logan W., 1981), and later in 1855 in the Travancore and Cochin areas (Saradamani K., 1980), a veiled form of slavery persisted in the name of attached labour (George A., 1987). The slavery abolition laws and proclamations were not backed by measures to provide economic sustenance to the freed slaves, thus forcing them to continue as attached labour under the same owners (Logan W., Saradamani op. cit). However, the practice of slavery did ease to some extent, and the sale and transfer of slaves, which was a characteristic feature of slavery, seemed to have stopped. An indication of this was the emergence of the system of attached labour after slavery abolition. (George A., 1987 op. cit)

Disabilities of the Dalits

Not only were the Dalits of Kerala slaves, and later labourers, but they also suffered from a number of disabilities and infringements of basic civic rights. The slave castes were denied admission to markets and had to stand at a distance to make their purchases and sales. They were prohibited from wearing gold and silver ornaments, and allowed to wear only brass and lead jewellery (Mateer Samuel, 1883). They were not allowed to wear anything above their waists, which strictly applied to females also. They could not use chappals or umbrellas (Jose N.K., 1982). Till they won their right to walk on public roads through various struggles - right from the 1890s to the early decades of this century - they were not even allowed to do so. They could neither attend courts, nor go to other public places.

Dalits were not supposed to be seen anywhere near temples, educational institutions and public wells (Mateer S., op. cit). While they addressed the Namboothiri, Nair and Syrian Christian landlords as thampuran, derogatory expressions like "Eta" and "Nee" were used by the high castes to address them (Chentarassery 1979, Alexander K.C. 1968). They were not even allowed to use the first person singular "I" for ego references. While talking to upper castes they had to cover their mouth with their hand and refer to themselves as adiyan, a slave (Chentarassery, 1979).

The rules of distance-pollution prevented the Dalits from taking up any employment, which put them in direct contact with the upper castes. This forced them to take up wet- land agriculture, which was particularly unhealthy, and demanded hard labour compared to dry-land cultivation (George A., 1987). The nearness of dry lands to the houses of upper castes prevented them from working in these fields (Unni R.K., 1975). In those places where dry lands were few, there arose another kind of division of labour wherein the hardest and dirtiest tasks were assigned to the Dalits. Other labouring castes did relatively less hard and dirty tasks (George A., 1987). This was particularly so in the punja form of rice cultivation practiced in Kuttanad. The punja fields lay below the sea level and water from the rivers were diverted into them after each cultivating season. Until the beginning of this century, when the first mechanised pumps were used (MM, 1901), this water had to be drained out before the next season by using manually rotated water wheels. The ring bunds protecting the fields from the river and the lake around them also had to be replenished using clay dug up from the riverbeds.

Gathering clay from the riverbanks and riverbeds, which required spending long hours in cold water, and rotating the water wheel which again was a very heavy task, were done by the Dalits who worked as attached labourers. Other routine agricultural tasks, such as, ploughing, sprinkling limestone, hedging, sowing, manuring, transplanting and weeding were done by casual labourers belonging mainly to the Ezhavas, a backward caste. Dalits took part in these tasks as well in addition to the work in other areas (George A., 1987).

Violence and Resistance

In addition to the cultural conditioning of the Dalits, various violent means were also used by the upper castes to suppress them. The awakening among the Dalits not only challenged these violent means, but also the caste system which legistimised it. The means used in this challenge by the Dalits were sometimes violent as well. In this section, we deal with some specific instances of this nature pertaining to Travancore from the 1850s to the 1940s. Samuel Mateer an L.M.S. missionary who worked in Travancore mentioned in 1883, long after the slavery proclamation of 1855, that their masters subjected the Dalits to very severe forms of punishments. For petty crimes, they were cruelly confined to stocks or cages and beaten up. They were tied up and flogged for not attending work in the early hours of the morning. There were cases where Dalits were blinded by pouring lime into their eyes. In another instance, the master extracted the teeth of a Dalit caught eating his sugarcane (Mateer, op. cit. 1883).

In the mid-nineteenth century, when slavery was still in force, the slave owners had the right to flog the Dalits (who were slaves), tie them up, mutilate them, or even kill them (Chentarassery, 1979). One horrible way of killing them was by tying them to a post and driving a sharpened stick from the anus to the throat. The victim died a slow death in 2-3 days because of the bleeding and ruptures of the various organs of the body (Chentarassery, 1979). The murder of Dalits by powerful landlords of the Kuttanad region, and of throwing their bodies in various rivers and lakes of the area, is a part of the oral lore of Kuttanad (Shivshankarappilai T., 1985). The bodies of the victims were tied to heavy stones, or other weights, to ensure that they sank in the water and never surfaced. Another form of murder of the Dalits, widely known, was done as part of a belief that their blood and bodies gave strength to the ring bunds around the Kuttanad paddy fields. This would avoid breaches in the bunds and prevent the flooding of fields from the rivers and lakes around them. While filling up a major breach in the bund a Dalit was trapped in it by a group of workers, under the leadership of the landlord, and buried alive (Kamalasanan N., 1993). The belief that human blood and body strengthened the construction of bridges and big buildings is also a part of the oral tradition elsewhere in South India.

The violence perpetrated on Dalits in the name of caste was sometimes met with violence when they asserted their civic rights. In 1898, a padayatra was organised by the Dalits from Venganoor to Aralumoodu market to demand for their right to travel on public roads. The upper castes blocked this padyatra midway. The Dalits resisted, which led to a confrontation in which both the groups sustained injuries. This incident inspired the Dalits in other parts of Southern Travancore to clamour for this right (Chentarassery 1979, Gladstone 1984, Saradamoni 1980). In another similar incident, Dalits renewed their demand for this right by presenting their case to the King, when he made a public appearance for the pujayetuppu (Dasara) festival. The Dalits went in a procession carrying a portrait of the King as shield. However, they were attacked on their way back and had to change their route. They reached their places in safety, travelling by the sea in fishing craft (Centarassery 1979). A marriage procession of Dalit Christians of Agateeshwaram taluq, South Travancore was attacked by the Vellalas in 1909 (a caste of equal status as the Nairs in that area) when it passed through a lane in their street. An analysis of this case, which is profusely documented in the Judicial Department Documents of Travancore (JDDT), showed that barring stray cases of violence by individual officers the judiciary and the police did not consider the right of travel of the Dalits as a natural civic right, but only as a recently granted concession from the upper castes on which the Hindu shasthras still had a say (JDDT 1909, George A., 1990). The Dalits' right to walk through the road in the Vellala locality, and even to go in carts, which was regarded as an exercise of prestige, was upheld in a case in 1887 and agreed to by the latter. The question was regarding their passage in a procession, which the Vellalas objected to (JDDT 1909). A procession is not just a bunch of people, but an organised group brought together by a common purpose. The purpose in this case was an open and organised assertion of their right to travel, even if it was through a Vellala street in the celebrant mode of a marriage procession. It is this, which wounded the Vellala prestige, and it is precisely this, which the Dalits wanted to assert (George A., 1990). The view of the judiciary also coincided with that of the Vellalas. The district magistrate of Padmanabhapuram observed, "The people belonging to a particular caste or sect had, in their anxiety to maintain their exclusiveness, put up shelters and congregated together and established places of worship in the streets, occupied exclusively or for most part, by members of their own community. The roads in such streets; though maintained at public expense were not allowed to be used for purposes distasteful to the occupants of the streets" (DDT, 1909). The magistrate observed that, "this was the received notion on the subject", which he said was also according to the Hindu shasthras. He said, "This is a Hindu State and in the absence of statutory laws… the rules and principles in the shastras should guide the courts" (Ibid). The police view was also the same: the Dalits should have not passed through the Vellala street as the village pagodas and temples were situated there. (Ibid). In both these views, an attempt to camouflage an essentially caste-class issue into a communal one is evident, since the Dalits in this case had converted to Christianity (George A., 1990).

The right of admission of Dalit to all government-run schools was officially granted by the Travancore state in 1910, (EDDT 1910, George A., 1990) but it was not allowed by the upper castes until various struggles by the Dalits in this regard ensued. The Pulaya–Nair clashes, which took place in 1914, started off when Pulaya children were denied admission by the local upper castes in a school in Urοottambalam, in the Neyyattinkara taluq of South Travancore (EDDT1910, George A., 1990). Pulayas are the largest Dalit castes in Kerala. In 1914 the Nairs of Neyyattinkara taluq petitioned to the king of Travancore that over a thousand Pulayas, armed with guns, spears, axes, choppers, knives and such other lethal weapons, attacked two persons travelling on the road and were creating trouble in other parts of the taluq. The petition further argued that the Pulayas had the audacity to do so because their children were allowed to study with the Nair children in government-run schools, by a declaration to this effect in 1910 (JDDT 1914).

The Pulayas, however, had a different story to tell. In one of their petitions they pointed out that they had sent several petitions and complaints to the higher authorities about the riot that took place among Nairs and Pulayas in Neyyattinkara taluq, and which included robbery and destruction of Pulaya houses, and infliction of grievous injuries on them. They said that not a single police officer of the area had made an on the spot enquiry, or arrested any of the accused (Ibid). Another petition of the Pulayas rather starkly stated that there was a rumour that the riot was carried on with the permission of the government and that there were instructions that grievances of Pulayas need not be considered for three months (Ibid). The acts of violence against Pulayas, included, the infliction of grievous bodily harm on them, ill-treatment of their women, including rape, large scale destruction of their huts, the robbing of their meagre gold and silver ornaments, the stealing of their goats and poultry, and the destruction of their clothes – particularly the decorative ones (Ibid).

The social content of these acts of violence need to be looked into more closely. Most of these acts have a dual meaning. One that appears on the surface, and the other, that has a deeper socio-historical implication. The Nairs in this case were trying to re-establish some of their prestige and authority over the Pulayas and push them back by a stage in history. Thus, they tried to re-establish the authority of the upper castes over the bodies of Dalit women, by raping them, by destroying Dalit huts they were virtually exercising their right over that piece of land; by robbing their gold and silver ornaments they were threatening to push them to the past where they were permitted to wear only brass and lead. The same applies to their ire over the clothes of the Dalits, particularly the decorative ones.. The Dalits were previously not allowed to wear anything above their waist, and permitted to wear only soiled clothes. The robbing of their poultry and goats was probably the reassertion of the old slaveholders' rights, where slaves were not supposed to own anything or make an income out of it. In fact, this right partially continued even over the property and produce of the small hutments on which the Dalit labourers lived.

The civic freedoms of the Dalits of Kuttanad were won because of their struggles - sometimes violent - against the system of attached labour (George A., 1987). Through fraudulent accounting, through the social disabilities of castes, and through physical violence, the upper caste farmers of Kuttanad saw to it that the Dalits of the area (Kuttanad) were available for them as cheap, reserve labour force to do the hard and dirty tasks that were characteristic of punja cultivation (Ibid 1987). It was the casual labourers belonging to the backward Ezhava caste who first organised themselves with the help of the coir factory working class of Alappuzha in 1940. In 1941, this organised movement took the name of the Thiruvithamkoor Karshaka Thozhilali Union (TKTU), which was a part of the confederation of trade unions in the industrial and agrarian fronts of Alappuzha district (Ibid 1987). This strike, which took place in various parts of Alappuzha, Kottayam and Pathanamthitta districts, was taken serious note of by the Travancore administration, and also attracted the attention of the newspapers (Deepika, 1942). The Kuttanad Karshaka

Sangham (K.K.S - a Kuttanad farmers association) sent a delegation to the authorities at the divisional headquarters at Kollam. They said that that the workers on strike were going about in processions shouting socialist slogans and alleged that they were destroying standing crops. One newspaper asserted that strikes and other forms of protests, common with the workers of Alappuzha town was being put into operation among the agricultural labourers also (Deepika, 1942). Though the Travancore administration offered police support to the farmers, the latter had to concede to the demand for higher wages (Ibid). A frustrated farmer beat up the general secretary of the TKTU, when he approached him to stake the claim for a right to work on behalf of some pro-union workers. The workers took their revenge by beating up the farmer when he was passing by in a country boat (George A., 1987).

It was in 1943, as a result of the special efforts taken by a group of full-time activists of the Communist Party of Travancore (CPT), who were deputed to strengthen the agricultural workers movement (Das D.J., 1983), that the Dalit attached labourers also got organised. Until then they suffered from a self-negating sense of loyalty to their masters. They would even die for them. The farmers used some of the Dalits to terrorise CPT activists who tried to unionise the latter (George A., 1987). It was only after these activists could organise a successful strike of a group of Dalit labourers in Kavalam, the citadel of large farmers of the area, that the self-confidence of the rest of the Dalits grew and they could believe in what they could achieve. The demands of this strike, which were conceded by the farmers, included the correct settlement of the work accounts of the Dalit attached labourers, and an increase in their annual payment.. As a result of this strike attached labour came to be seen as a costly system by the farmers. They began to cut down on the number of attached labourers and eventually gave up the practice. (George A. 1987). During this strike several Dalits were attacked and evicted from their homesteads owned by the farmers, but after its success, they as a community started asserting themselves for the various civic freedoms denied them, and cast off the shackles of caste-based disabilities imposed on them.

Caste Violence and Health Concerns

Generations of literature dealing with forms and content of caste violence— The above case study of 19th to mid 20th century Kerala gave us the opportunity to look closely at caste violence by even using government documents. Though this access to government documents may not be available in the case of contemporary caste violence, but still more studies are required on this topic. Other informative sources, such as newspaper reports and oral sources, could be looked into with sufficient cross-checks. Such studies in various regions of the country should bring out the different forms of caste violence, the symbolisms in it and its social content. This will be useful in developing a health perspective on caste violence as well as bring about a better understanding on the subject. This paper was an attempt towards that.

Sensitisation of health sector and health professionals to caste issues in general, and caste violence in particular—While there are modernist attempt to ignore caste in some quarters, yet its presence in our daily lives is palpable, as it permeates the whole gamut of our living, from village settlement patterns to marriages. It has to be accepted as a reality of Indian life. Health professionals alone need not be blamed for not having this perspective for they are not the only ones lacking this view. That the various arms of the administration and social institutions are not much different comes out from this study. Without questioning our basic cultural conditioning and the class issues involved in caste, we will be going in to a "high living and low thinking" syndrome. There is a need to sensitise the profession to caste and communal violence. Sensitivity to Dalit issues in health planning would set the right note in this direction. As a first step it has to be ensured that Dalit and non-Dalit patients got the same kind of attention and treatment in the government health institutions. Given the class basis of this issue, it would not be an easy task. The various studies on the quality of care should also address questions on the quality of services available to Dalits.

15

Mass Violence in Non-Combat Situations: PTSD and Rehabilitation

V. Suresh

Preface

This paper is a rather tentative exploration of an issue, which, until recently, I had not paid much attention to. The writing of this paper represents a new endeavour on my part. Despite being associated with a mass organisation of the tribal for over six years, having completed a doctoral study on caste violence, and in spite of being actively involved in the last five years with a national level human rights organisation, the People's Union for Civil Liberties (PUCL), until recently I had not paid much attention to the health problems faced by surviving victims of violence, and their families in particular.

I was forced to grapple with the issue of health and mass violence when, as a member of two PUCL-appointed fact finding teams (FFT), I was compelled to respond to, and deal with the trauma experienced by victims and survivors (and their families) of widespread caste and communal violence in Tamil Nadu. The experience made me painfully aware of the fact that I had neglected to examine the broader issues of health problems and policy, and the role of the medical profession during caste and communal violence.

This paper attempts to redress this situation by exploring the subject of health problems of survivors of mass caste and communal violence. The subject of examining the effects of systemic (and endemic structural violence) is a topic of its own, requiring a very different frame of reference, and which will not be explored in this paper.

Introduction

On November 29, 1997, in Coimbatore, a Hindu police constable was killed by three Muslim youths over a minor traffic incident. The minority Muslim community handed over the three youths to the police. The communal problem, instead of subsiding, exploded. Over the next three days a major pogrom of the minority Muslims took place, led by communal elements in the local police force and a Hindu fundamentalist party. Over 20 people were killed, many dying gruesome deaths. The property of Muslims, worth Rs five hundred to a thousand crores, was reportedly looted or destroyed. One month after the incident, when the PUCI FFT visited the area, most people talked of three events, which evoked strong feelings of anger, resentment, helplessness, alienation, and vulnerability.

1. Soon after the outbreak of violence in the Muslim areas, injured Muslims, being transported to the nearby government hospital, were surrounded by a violent mob of armed policemen (in mufti, i.e., not in uniform) and majority community fundamentalists, and burnt alive right at the entrance of the hospital, and in front of the eyes of senior police officials who did nothing to prevent the killings.

   What shocked the minority community even more was the news that frenzied Hindutva mobs chasing fleeing Muslims inside the hospital did not spare even the morgue. Men with knives pulled out dead bodies from the freezer and stabbed randomly to ensure that there were no Muslims hiding in the morgue.

   This incident, more than any other black event that occurred on those three fateful days, inflicted such a deep psychological and emotional shock on the minority community that many complained of emotional and psychological feelings, such as, fear, distrust, anger and resentment while dealing with the Hindus.

2. There were heroic tales too of the role of doctors during the violence. An unnamed Hindu doctor helped two injured Muslim youth escape from a bloodthirsty mob bent on burning them alive by driving them away on his motorcycle. He not only took them to a nearby medical clinic, introduced them as Hindus, and provided life-saving first aid, but also gave them money to flee before the clinic staff discovered that they actually belonged to the minority community.

   This incident contrasts sharply with what occurred several days thereafter. As government hospitals were no longer safe for the injured Muslims, many of them sought medical aid from large private hospitals, far away from their areas, owned predominantly by members of the majority community. Within a short time, Hindu fundamentalist groups threatened to attack these hospitals unless they stopped providing medical assistance to the injured Muslims. Without a murmur of protest, almost all the hospitals complied with the threats and closed their doors to these injured people. Almost no hospital chose to complain to the authorities or sought state protection, to ensure that their professional duties were not thwarted.

The failure of the mainstream media to expose such bigotry, and the silent acquiescence of the medical profession to the threats, created such a sense of shock, dismay, and disappointment that attitudes towards doctors and medical institutions owned by the majority community have become tinged with bitterness, rancour, and suspicion.

3. Following continuing clashes between the Dalits and upper castes in the southern districts of Tamil Nadu over a period of almost two years, scores of Dalit youths have been arrested by the police and jailed for long periods. The fear of arrest, and implication in false cases has become so common among the Dalits that in many villages, most able-bodied youth and men have fled their homes. Continuous raids by policemen at the dead of night have resulted in many children and older people developing symptoms of neurosis, sleeplessness, anxiety and stress. The fear of the midnight knock has become so acute in some places that people have contracted many non-specific psychosomatic illnesses. Mere recounting of the experience of violence (experienced twice over, first at the hands of the upper castes and later, at the hands of the police) was sufficient to drive some people into a catatonic or trance-like state.

A similar experience was recounted in the village of Melavalavu in Madurai district on June 29, 1997. Six Dalits were killed by upper caste Thevars. Their main crime was that they belonged to the ex-untouchable castes and contested for the posts of president and vice-president to the village local body (called panchayats), which were reserved for members of their community under law. Since they did not heed the warnings of the upper castes not to stand for election for positions traditionally occupied by the upper castes alone, the elected president was beheaded in public in the middle of the day and his head thrown into the main drinking water well. The traumatic event produced serious medical and psychiatric problems amongst the scheduled castes of the village. As the first anniversary of the beheading and killing approached on June 29, 1998, many of the Dalit villagers complained of a variety of illnesses and exhibited signs of great emotional and psychological stress.

These issues, apart from the human rights angle, brought to the fore the issue of the role of the medical profession in the context of mass caste and communal violence. How equipped are ordinary doctors to deal with physical and emotional health issues produced as a result of such mass violence? How should the human rights movement address these issues? What should be the approach of the state health policy towards this problem? These, and other issues, call for serious attention from all sections concerned—the medical community, the human rights fraternity, legal experts, and the government. What creates a sense of urgency is the fact that incidents of mass violence in Indian society are showing signs of becoming more and more endemic, rooted, and recurring.

Mass Violence in Non-combat Situations: Caste and Communal Violence

A major proportion of the current literature on the impact of mass violence on individuals and communities seems to concentrate on issues of violence perpetrated during situations of internal or civil strife, or in warlike contexts like those, which exist, for example, in Bosnia or Rwanda. Fewer studies seem to exist which have examined the medical issues caused by events of mass violence in non-combat situations.

There are a number of crucial differences in both contexts. During events of internal and external war, the enemy or aggressor is clearly defined. The open recourse to armed warfare and the resultant physical injuries and trauma it produces are consequences, which are immediately visible, and are actually accepted as inevitable during such warfare or armed conflict. Most often, there is a breakdown of civil society, and the legal and administrative institutions. Hence, people cannot hope to take recourse to law to seek legal remedies for losses inflicted and injuries suffered.

The context of non-combat-based mass violence presents a totally different problem altogether. In India especially, caste and communal violence has claimed hundreds and thousands of lives in countless small and major incidents throughout the country. Actually, there are very few places in the country that have not witnessed some form of such violence in the last 20-30 years. While there are dissimilarities in the conditions underlying the outbreak of caste and communal violence, there are a few similarities as well.

Firstly, and most importantly, while the dominant caste or community invariably socially engineers mass violence, the role of the state is very ambiguous and prevaricating. On one hand, the state institutions and officials cannot, at all times, be very clearly identified. Equally important is the issue of social legitimacy accorded to acts of aggression perpetrated by members of the dominant community or caste.

What marks such violence is the fact that at the systemic/structural level itself, an enormous amount of violence underscores the lives of the Dalits or Muslims, which is most often not clearly visible as clear acts of violence that accompany mass killings, looting or rape. This component of systemic violence, in the view of the present author, is far more insidious and devastating on the victims. For, without recourse to bloodshed and overt violence, the system is able to traumatize the minority communities at the emotional and psychological levels, and prevent them from ever trying to challenge the status quo. It needs to be emphasized at this juncture, that one is not merely talking of the general effects of economic deprivation. The Dalits and the Muslims have to deal with problems of constant police surveillance and frequent arrests, as well social stigmatisation of being uncultured, uncivilized and violence prone! (Ironically, the victims of violence are very often characterized as being violent themselves!). Thus violent police action against these sections do not attract condemnation or opposition from mainstream society, who view the police or state action as warranted and necessary in order to deal with such unruly and violent communities.

Since there is no overt indication of the effect of systemic violence, large sections of the mainstream society remain blind to the issue of how at the structural level, the minorities have to experience a great amount of institutionalised violence. Thus, any attempt by these communities to claim equity and equal status in law and society is seen as unjust, unfair and unsupportable by the majority community (in caste context, the upper castes, and in communal context, the majority Hindu community). These sections, who most often also occupy important positions in bureaucracy, business and other professions, are by virtue of their position able to put forward an artificially engendered social consensus on the necessity of taking firm action against the subaltern sections. This becomes the rationale for violent suppression by state authorities of the minorities demanding social equity and equal status in society and polity.

What is put forward here is not a discussion on the sociological dimensions of caste and communal violence, but on the relatively poorly examined issue of health problems faced by these communities. What is striking is that they suffer at two levels. On the one hand, they are the victims of structural violence, which takes a toll on their psychological and emotional well being, while at the same time they have very poor access to health facilities. Firstly, these communities experience a different variety of health problems when they become victims of mass violence. As targets, they are the ones who suffer considerable physical trauma ranging from killings to mutilation and rape. As patients they have access to few infra-structural facilities for treatment. What is the sum effect of both these levels of violence is the moot question, which requires a systematic study. As remarked earlier, this paper addresses only the issue of the problems created by the outbreak of mass violence against members of the minority Dalit (or Scheduled Castes) and Muslim communities.

Ghettoisation, Access to Medical Assistance and Health Problems During Mass Violence

It needs to be emphasised that while in this paper we seek to examine in a common framework health issues vis-à-vis the outbreak of mass violence against Dalits and Muslims, it is not suggested that the causative reasons resulting in mass violence against both communities are similar. Actually, there is a great amount of complexity and diversity underlying the problem of caste and communal problems within various geographical areas of the same region, not to talk of the whole country. However, despite the vast differences in the economic and social contexts, there are a few common aspects marking the lives of the Dalits and Muslims in India.

In many parts of the Indian countryside, Dalits are socially forced to live in ghettoes outside the main village into which no non-Dalit would generally enter. In the towns, Dalits are refused rental accommodation in upper caste localities, and are perforce made to live in economically run-down areas, which then become socially marked. The situation in big cities is not so marked by geographical stigmatisation, but the sheer impoverished economic condition of large sections of the Dalits results in them living in geographical concentrations, generally in the poorer or middle-income areas. Very seldom, have Dalits managed to buy properties in elite or upper class areas. Even if they have, such Dalit families would seek to hide their social origins.

A similar situation prevails among the Muslims. Generally, Muslims are concentrated in towns and cities and live in clearly marked out geographical locations. By and large, Muslim areas of the city are distinct in appearance, and during communal unrest can be easily targeted. Though in some cities some wealthy Muslim families own large mansions or estates in wealthy sections of the city, and are involved in business, their numbers remain small in proportion to both the overall Muslim population as also the general population. The bulk of the Muslims across the country are economically deprived.

Another common aspect is the fact that generally the areas where Dalits and Muslims live are distinguishable by the economic levels of the people. Overcrowding, poor water, drainage and sanitary facilities, and lack of public facilities characterise these places. Both Dalits and Muslims have to travel to other areas of the village or town to access public facilities like municipal offices, colleges, big hospitals, banks and so on. (Here we need to clarify that in some mega cities like Mumbai, Muslims live in such concentration that they occupy major areas of the city, and since a considerable section is involved in economic enterprises, there are relatively better infra-structural facilities present there. However, when viewed in the national context, such situations are exceptions than the rule.)

Ironically, whether proper infra-structural facilities exist or not, a ubiquitous institution always to be found there is the police station! In sharp contrast, in most towns and cities most of the higher- level medical institutions are located in non-minority areas, i.e., in the midst of the majority caste/community localities.

The spatial locations of both Dalit and Muslim habitations, which in many situations resemble ghettoes, clearly identifiable and distinguishable from other areas of the village, town or city, play an important role during the outbreak of mass violence. The very fact that these minority sections live in geographically distinct areas makes it easy for the perpetrators of violence to target them. The Dalits and Muslims, in most instances, become sitting ducks for the aggressors.

The ghettoised living also has another dimension. It becomes easy to localise the problem and deal with it by sealing the living areas of the Dalits and Muslims. It is easy to pour in police forces into the areas to suppress quickly any reaction or backlash from the victimized communities. In sharp contrast, the upper caste or majority community aggressors come from a much more geographically dispersed area, which makes both localization and identification difficult.

During such periods of mass violence, the minimal medical facilities existing in the areas prove insufficient to deal with the problems of the injured. What causes the problem to become more acute is the fact that to access higher medical institutions injured Dalits and Muslims have to travel to other localities of the city, thereby making them more vulnerable to attacks by the majority community. Additionally, since state (meaning police) response also invariably victimizes the victims by accusing them of being the originators of the trouble, there is the fear of arrest and apprehension if Dalits or Muslims travel outside their living areas, and which inhibits them from immediately trying to access medical facilities outside. Finally, as the recent Coimbatore incident reveals, if the injured end up becoming targets of mob attacks in hospitals meant to provide them medical succour and relief, then fewer people will access government hospitals - invariably situated in the majority-dominated localities - for medical assistance.

Impact of Inadequate Health Professionals and Medical Facilities

Similar to the issue of spatial location, both Dalits and Muslim communities share another common characteristic. In both communities, the number of medical professionals is inadequate and pitifully small in proportion to their population. While there are historical and sociological reasons as to why there are fewer professionals amongst these communities, the reality is that there are fewer people from among the minorities themselves serving their own people.

The situation has been redressed somewhat in the context of the Dalits because of the reservation of seats in educational institutions and jobs through a Constitutional provision. The numbers of health professionals amongst Muslims are far fewer in contrast. However, even though there are more Dalit doctors today, than, say two to three decades back, the reality is that for economic survival most of them have to seek employment in government.

There are very few instances of Dalit doctors becoming successful private practitioners. There are even fewer cases of Dalit doctors setting up big medical institutions. If at all they are successful, Dalit doctors have to rely on their own brethren concentrated in the Dalit areas of the town.

Socially, there is a caste and communal dimension to this problem. In the case of Dalit doctors, very few among the non-Dalit sections of the populace will approach them for medical care or assistance if they know the caste background of the doctor. While the problem with regard to Muslim doctors is not so acutely exhibited, apart from the fact that there are fewer Muslim doctors, the truth is that the practice of these doctors is concentrated in areas where their own people live. In both situations, the lack of an adequate number of medical professionals among Dalits and Muslims becomes one more factor inhibiting the reach of medical services at the time when violence has broken out.

Rehabilitation Policy, State Action and Post-traumatic Stress Disorder (PTSD)

An unfortunate aspect of the state health policy is that during mass violence the state provides only immediate medical relief. This invariably covers only those victims who have suffered physical injuries. However, the fact that victims include not only those who have been physically traumatized, is not acknowledged, let alone accepted by the state.

As discussed earlier, victims are not just those physically affected. There are a whole lot of others, equally affected. The following is a listing of different types of situations that can be witnessed soon after mass violence, and which produces different types of trauma among people, as has been witnessed during various fact-finding missions of the People's Union for Civil Liberties.

1. The psychological trauma of having near relatives and/or friends becoming victims of mass violence either in terms of being killed, injured, mutilated, or in other ways, physically traumatized.
2. The mental and emotional trauma of having personal belongings and property vandalized, destroyed, looted, and burnt by attacking mobs.
3. The practice of immediate and random arrest of persons from among the Dalits or Muslims living in isolated pockets in the city or town, on the premise that they are the ones responsible

for triggering the violence. The resultant torture, the illegal detention and the psychological trauma experienced by those arrested is matched by the trauma of the entire extended family and the community at large.

The stultified attitude of the state is more explicitly revealed when we consider that it extends compensation to only those victims of mass violence who bear physical injuries. The main emphasis is on those killed, followed by those who suffer, in what is known in bureaucratic and legal parlance, grievous injuries—meaning injuries to limbs, which cause drastic physical impairment. All other injuries, which do not strictly fall in the legal definition of grievous, are treated as simple, and for which no compensation is provided. Therefore, in such a scheme of things there is no place for the state to provide any assistance to persons who physically bear no outward symptom of injury, but nevertheless, are psychologically scarred for life because of their experiences.

In fact, it would not be untrue to state that the state in India does not perceive psychological trauma and psychosomatic illnesses as health issues. The whole gamut of issues ranging from somatic illnesses to psycho-somatic illnesses, including the prevalence of 'post traumatic stress disorder' (PTSD), find no place in state rehabilitation policies, or activities, in relation to victims of caste violations.

Ironically, it took more than 45 years for the international community to accept PTSD as a discrete psychiatric disorder with unusual medical, psychological and physiological features. Much slower has been the development of legal principles to cover the issue of liability and compensation in cases of victims and survivors traumatised by mass violence. Thus, in the absence of a clear-cut health policy to enable provisions of appropriate treatment facilities for victims suffering from PTSD, and with no legal principle to enable us to demand for the provision of such facilities, there is a great need for a forceful campaign from among health professionals, human rights activists, advocates, policy planners and others demanding re-examination of state health policy vis-à-vis victims of mass caste and communal violence.

Role of Medical Profession

At this juncture it may be instructive to briefly consider the response of the medical community to the prevalence of PTSD among victims and survivors of mass violence. A noticeable feature is the general lack of awareness about the nature of PTSD or the type of integrated, multi-disciplinary medical treatment required for victims suffering from it. There is also not much knowledge about the various international conventions that have evolved from time to time calling upon the medical profession to maintain the highest ethical standards in the practice of their profession. The Geneva Convention (1948, 1968, 1983), the Tokyo Declaration (1975) and the Declaration of Hawaii (Worlds Psychiatric Association, 1977, 1983), which called upon doctors not to countenance, condone or participate in the practice of torture and other cruel, inhuman or degrading procedures, exist more in the books rather than in the knowledge base of the general medical practitioner.

The illustrations given in the introduction of this paper clearly points out that there are good doctors and bad doctors. There are doctors, who enable the police and other aggressors to literally get away with murder, by doctoring medical records and post-mortem reports. There are yet others, who under no condition would betray the oath they have taken to maintain the highest standards of the profession. What worries one is that the latter type of doctors is dwindling in numbers as compared to those who seem to be willing to bend the rules for a consideration.

There are thus two types of issues, which crop up in the context of treating violence victims. On one hand we are faced with the lack of expertise or knowledge to treat patients afflicted by PTSD and related illness and that is a serious handicap in ameliorative services. On the other hand, we are faced with the issue of unethical medical practice that sides with the perpetrators of violence, both directly by covering up medical symptoms of violence, and indirectly by refusing to extend medical assistance to the victims, either wilfully or due to coercion.

Issues before the Larger Medical, Human Rights, and Legal Community

It is under these circumstances that we have to visualise the type of policy shifts that we have to aim for so as to bring about a more comprehensive policy regime to treat the problems of the victims of mass violence.

1. First, and foremost, the state health and rehabilitation policies should acknowledge and accord importance to the phenomenon of PTSD and make it a part of the policy framework, both the health, as also other related departments that provide other support services.

2. Special training should be given to medical personal belonging to government services on the various dimensions of the problems of victims of mass violence, and the psychological and emotional trauma they undergo. Multi-disciplinary treatment should become the norm.
3. Core courses on PTSD should become part of the regular syllabi of medical colleges throughout the country.
4. Emphasis should be on recognising the fact that the problems of PTSD are not merely clinical, and that mere clinical or medicine-based treatment will not suffice, and that there is a need for more supportive treatment and response from immediate family members of the victims of PTSD, as also friends and the general community as well. Community involvement in the treatment of those suffering from PTSD is crucial to tackling the problem in the long run.
5. There should be widespread dissemination of information about various medical conventions and the ethical and moral duties of doctors. It is only by involving a greater number of general practitioners and conscientising them about the prevalence of new forms of treatment for the victims of mass violence that there can be any sustained basis for such efforts.
6. To educate more NGOs about the prevalence of PTSD and launch rehabilitation campaigns to treat such victims.

Finally, what is required is a sustained discussion among various professionals who by the nature of their work come into contact with victims of mass violence. Through this alone can the issue be studied and understood, but would require greater campaigning to make people aware of the fact that the mental problems of these individuals is a manifestation of an extremely harmful and debilitating process.

Epilogue

At the personal level, the process of writing this paper has helped in strengthening the resolve to launch a comprehensive study of the health problems of victims and survivors of mass caste and communal violence in Tamil Nadu. I hope that by the time the next conference is held, there would be a larger database to share with other concerned people. It is through this shared concern that we can provide meaningful alternatives in a world becoming more and more individualized, selfish, and impersonal.

The shared concern is also a source of common strength, and forms the basis of sustaining our endeavour to make the world a better place to live in.

Acknowledgements

This paper owes much to two very concerned doctors, who literally opened my eyes to the prevalence of PTSD. They are Dr Yonas Geda, of the Mavo Institute, USA, who was himself a torture victim and jailed for seven years in Ethiopa, and Dr Mathiharan from the Forensic Science Department, Chennai Medical College, Chennai, who guided me through the subject and patiently explained every doubt. There are two other doctors whose promptings pushed me to put on paper my experiences and thoughts on the subject—Dr Madhukar Pai, of the Sundaram Medical Foundation, was the one who informed me and motivated me to write, and Dr Amar Jesani who readily agreed to include my paper as part of the proceedings. Finally, my wife, and fellow advocate and human rights activist, Nagasaila, critically edited my confused ramblings and added many relevant portions, especially on the subject of state health policy. Needless to say, the shortcomings are entirely mine.

16

Impact of Communal Riots on Children

H. S. Dhavale
Leena Damani
Jhanavi Kedare
Shanu Jethani

Introduction

The WHO slogan for 1993 was 'Handle life with care. Prevent violence and negligence'. This aptly states the importance of violence on the physical and mental health of human beings.

Mumbai, the Urban Prima and financial capital of India, with a population of almost one crore drawn from all over the country, was regarded as a peaceful, disciplined, well-managed cosmopolitan city. Indira Gandhi was killed, Rajiv Gandhi was killed, and violence erupted in many parts of the country, but Mumbai remained peaceful on both occasions. Then suddenly in December 1992 and January 1993, communal riots erupted and threw the entire city into confusion. People witnessed large-scale violence unknown to this city. There were dead bodies on the road; hospitals were full of them, and many of the injured suffered stab injuries, bullet injuries, etc. As if this was not enough, when Mumbai was limping back to normalcy, on March 12 a barrage of bomb-blasts took place in the city resulting in house collapse, massive fires, and loss of lives.

The riots were much discussed. Newspapers had them on their headlines; the TV was full of them. Horrifying pictures got splashed all over the newspaper pages and violent scenes got constantly telecast. The focus in all this was death, destruction, and the injured. This was in keeping with most newspapers of the world that sensationalize news, especially crime news. Studies, however, point to the negative effects of such coverage. Distrust grows to the extent of paranoia. Long acquaintances and friends from the other community are looked upon with suspicion—in fact, very few can distinguish between friends and foes. Under such circumstances the social fabric is shattered, and succour and support comes from no quarter. If this can happen to adults, one can imagine what must have happened to the children! In one college, good friends from two communities stopped talking to each other. A 7-year-old child of an anaesthetist asked her, "Why do you ventilate patients from the other community?" One 10-year-old boy admitted in the paediatric ward of a general hospital was so scared of bombs that he checked the pockets of anyone entering the ward. As it always happens in such cases, it is the children who are the worst affected in a variety of ways, ranging from immediate physical loss to emotional and mental trauma that could have long-term consequences.

Some schools tried to purge this emotional trauma out of the students' system by asking them to write essays, poems, or indulge in drawing. For example: an 8-year-old girl wrote, "I don't know why people hate us. Aren't we all God's children?" One 11-year-old girl wrote in her poem.

Blood, blood all around
Blood, blood on the ground
Bang, bang and a cry
Blood, blood I don't know why?

After reading and listening to this our department decided to conduct a study on the 'Impact of riots or violence on children's mental health'.

Materials and Method

Our mental health clinics for schools were being conducted in nearby municipal schools. First, we decided to use Children's Apperception Test (CAT) cards. However, we were disappointed, since we realised that the children ended up writing the same stereotyped stories, and could not pinpoint their disquiet related to the riots. Therefore, we designed a special questionnaire where some questions measuring anxiety and fear were intermingled with specific questions related to the riots. We decided to give these to 3rd and 4th standard students of two municipal schools at Agripada and Aryanagar (Tulsiwadi), which were riot-affected areas and are near B.Y.L Nair Hospital, a municipal hospital. Each question had thee components. A 'no' response was scored as zero. If the response was 'yes to some extent' it was given a score of one, and to a large extent was given a score of two.

Psychiatry residents, social workers and psychologists from our department gave questionnaire to each of the students. We started a interviews in February 1993, but it went on till March end, and those interviewed after the bomb-blasts could not differentiate between a riot and a bomb-blast. 515 students were interviewed, but we could analyse only 495 cases.

Results and Discussions

The age of the study group ranged between 7 and 12 years. There were 51.51 per cent males and 48.49 per cent females. There was no significant difference in the total score for boys and girls.

Among those interviewed 54.74 per cent were Hindus, 8.89 per cent Muslims, 0.4 per cent Christians, 15.15 per cent Buddhists, and 20.80 per cent said they were in the 'don't know' category. We really do not know whether the last mentioned category is a good sign or not, and whether parents and teachers should encourage such things, rather than build watertight compartments of religion. However, such thought would surely help maintain the country's unity and integrity. Many students reported disturbed sleep; and 62.62 per cent of them reported of dreams and nightmares, which was significant. Contents of the dreams were frightening, and they re-visualised the scenes seen in the neighbourhood during the day. Re-experiencing the traumatic event through nightmares is one of the essential features of post-traumatic stress disorder. According to Paul Vaz, director of Seva Niketan, the healing process in these cases would be much more difficult than in normal cases where children have persistent nightmares. This was because the pursuers in the dreams had identifiable faces, had other qualities that were very real to the children, even during their waking hours. The enemy was hardly an ill-defined phantom.

Physical symptoms like headaches and stomach-aches were present in 40.21 per cent of the cases. Anxiety symptoms like fearfulness, worry, tenseness, tiredness, nervousness and breath-less-ness were present in 33.53 per cent of the cases, which was very high. The symptoms shown in the two tables were associative features to diagnose PTSD. The exposure to violence fosters fear, which is out of proportion with reality, and this was proved in our study.

Fear of destruction of house and property, like burning and looting, was present in 60.80 per cent of the cases. Fear of injury, illness or death of self or family member was present in 42.82 per cent of the students. Fear of going out on the street was present in 39.39 per cent of the students. Fear had even prevented children from attending school. In fact, newspaper reports of that period too corroborated this. For example, only one girl in a class of 70 came to school. Third and fourth standard students were combined in a class, and still the total number did not exceed seven. Students were scared to go to school alone, so either they went in a group or insisted that adults accompany them. Nobody loitered around the school or on the way back home, which students normally like to do. Fear of playing with other community children was present in 64.24 per cent of the students. As mentioned earlier, children were unable to differentiate between the good and the bad, and therefore were scared of the whole community. It also could be that they were just imitating the behaviour of their parents.

Regarding the total score, 11.72 per cent had scores above 10, and 9.89 per cent had a zero score. There were 76 victims whose houses were burnt or looted, a family member was dead or injured, or taken to jail. If we compare the score of the victims to the total study population, this was very high. For example, in victims, 23.69 per cent had scores above 10 as compared to 11.72 per cent in the total study population. This was expected because the child who suffered directly was going to feel more insecure than the others, and suffer from greater anxiety than others. An interesting finding was that low scores or zero scores could be explained on the basis of psychic numbing or emotional anaesthesia. Numbing of responsiveness to or involvement with the external world by a marked constriction of emotional responsiveness is one of the essential features in diagnosing PTSD. Another reason for this zero score could be their denial to accept the facts, or they were discouraged to talk about the riots by their parents and teachers. 10 per cent of the students were evacuated from their houses and 13 per cent of them had a high score.

Teachers and principals too refused to accept reality. They were reluctant to discuss anything related to this sensitive issue. When we approached the school, their instantaneous reply was, "There is no problem with our children." If they thought that their students were not aware of the reality, or that the riots had not really registered in their minds, they were mistaken. This was proved by our study. The fact is that if teachers refuse to discuss the issue with their students or parents with their children, then they will live on with a host of unanswered questions.

When we queried the students about their feelings during the riots, more than 90 per cent said they were scared, and which was a normally accepted reaction. However, 8–10 of them said they were happy. This response was, unexpected and shocking. How could anybody be happy in such circumstances? We do not know whether they would turn out to be psychopaths in the future. Because children affected by riots could well nurture hatred for each other at this tender age. This feeling could become deeply entrenched if not dealt with at an early age, since watching other people behave aggressively encourages aggression. Three or four boys were drawn into some sort of participation in the violence, and studies show that frustrated individuals who watch aggressive films, or who participate in aggressive plays, usually become more aggressive. Even if violent scenes are repeated frequently, the ability to tolerate aggression is bound to give away and may give rise to crime or delinquency.

On the probability of recurrence of riots, 52.32 per cent of the respondents said it was definitely going to recur, and the days they predicted were related to some religious festival or the other. On probing, they were unable to give an explanation. It could be that they were repeating - parrot-like, all that they had heard in their homes, and around them. 29.49 per cent felt there wouldn't be any more riots—at least a few thought positively. 18.18 per cent were not included in any group because they either did not reply or answered, 'Can't say'.

The idea was to screen and identify students who were badly affected, because detection was not easy, as teachers were unable to read the signs, or it could be that at that time everybody accepted their behaviour as normal. The common behaviour pattern following a catastrophic event is called a disaster syndrome. This may not happen immediately after the trauma but may get triggered by some minor stress, several weeks or even months later. That is why we decided to do a follow-up of the students who were either victims, or where the score was more than 10.

The follow-up was done with the help of the same questionnaire. There were 104 such students, but we could interview only 59. This was because 12 students had dropped out of the school, 20 were chronically absent and we did not know whether they would continue or eventually dropout, and 13 had left school after passing the 4th standard. The Education Officer of the BMC had stated to the media that there were

30,000 dropouts in municipal schools that year. In municipal schools a dropout is not a rare instance, but such large-scale dropouts were something to worry about.

We tried to compare the score of 59 students in March and July. We found that the proportion of those with a high score had definitely come down from 57.62 per cent to 11.88 per cent, which meant that the impact had reduced. (However, if we took the total study population, the score above 10 had remained exactly the same, 11.88 per cent in place of 11.72 per cent. The problem, therefore, still persisted).

Fear of destruction to property, fear of harm to self or family member, dreams and nightmares still persisted in a majority of the cases. When they spoke of the riots they could convey their anxiety. They knew everything about the riots, they knew that questions were repeated, but the answers were different.

Conclusions

Psychiatric morbidity was high in the study population. The score was high on riot-related questions in the beginning, as well as in the follow-up study, later. The riot victims had very high scores, followed by students who had witnessed the violence, followed by those who had only heard about it because they were not directly exposed to it, or had minimal exposure because they had been shifted to safer places.

The scale of the score also reflects the degree and type of violence witnessed, e.g., firing, stabbing, taxies burning, houses burning, throwing stones, soda water bottles, fireballs, etc. That is why there was a significant difference in the total score of the two schools. The score varied with the type of accommodation: children staying in hutments suffered from greater insecurity and recorded a higher score than those staying in chawls.

Outcome

Time is going to decide what happens to these children in the future. Therefore, a long-term follow-up is necessary. The various possible scenarios in the future could be:

As time passes by, they may forget the whole episode. Now, it may affect their studies and influence their personality. Over-exposure to violence may change their attitude. They may realise that indulgence in such violence does not necessarily lead them anywhere, so they may become passive observers, who are less likely to participate in violence.

There is a possibility that the element of revenge may get nurtured in these children, and which will mainly depend on the social environment, especially the attitude towards violence of parents and elders in the society. Any stress ultimately ends in returning back to the normal in a more matured way. The victims may have psychosomatic problems or emotional ones, but it is the duty of mental health professionals to help them return to the normal. In such cases, they do not require medicines but counselling, especially group counselling. Supportive psychotherapy, catharsis and abreaction may help them, or may bring about behavioural modification in them with the help of relaxation. We are planning to do a detailed workup of the students whose scores were high even on follow up.

We would like to end with Mahatma Gandhi's words: "I hold that the more helpless the creature, the more entitled it is to protection by man from the cruelty of man."

Demography

Age	**7 to 12 years**	
Sex	Boys	51.51%
	Girls	48.49%
Religion	Hindus	54.74%
	Muslims	8.89%
	Christians	0.40%
	Bauddh	15.15%
	Not aware of religion	20.80%

Somatic symptoms

	Number	**Percentage**
Any symptom	199	40.20%
Headache	148	29.89%
Stomachache	90	18.18%

Sleep disturbances

Sleep disturbances with frightening dreams and nightmares with revisualisation of the scenes seen in the neighbourhood, or on TV, were present in 310 cases, that is, 62.62 per cent.

Anxiety Symptoms

	Number	Percentage
Feeling scared, tense, worrying	166	33.53%
Fear of destruction of house	301	60.80%
Fear of injury, illness or death	212	42.82%
Fear of going out	195	39.39%
Fear of playing with other community	318	64.24%

17

Response of Doctors to Communal Conflict

Ali Asghar

This presentation is based on our experiences, working in the communally sensitive areas of Hyderabad - mostly the old city. The old city is congested and is with very few basic amenities. Mostly the poor, uneducated masses and frustrated youth - both from the Muslim and Hindu communities - inhabit it. It also provides cannon fodder for vested interests who at the slightest opportunity; stoke communal fires to achieve their dubious ends. The common man has come to view the people's representatives, the government and the administration with suspicion. Everything is "they or we"; "theirs or ours"; "them or us"; the government and the administration usually belong to "them" and work for "their" good. The mutual suspicions of the Muslims and Hindus are based on the perceived well being of the other communities, and on the false premise that the government and the elected representatives always work for the benefit of the other community.

The influence of political and religious groups on the students, through their respective students and youth wings, is well known. All major educational institutions have students unions, which are affiliated to different political and religious groups. These groups make no bones about using the student unions to propagate their ideologies and influence the young minds. Medical colleges and medicos are no exception to this influence. The cleverly designed propaganda of the political parties percolates into the subconscious of the people. A few who are aware of this remain immune. The rest, who are more occupied about the routine, mundane things of life, get swayed and accept the stereotypes created by the communal forces. This, in the long run, dictates all their actions - both professional and personnel. Doctors, after all, are human beings - can they be free of such influence?

The doctor, during a conflict, is in a very unique situation. The doctor-patient relationship at such times is a very delicate one. For the patient, who is undergoing severe mental and physical trauma, the doctor is the only person who can save his life. He views the doctor as one notch above everybody else—close to the super human who has the power to restore life to the dying. One of the other hand, he is also convinced that he has suffered because of his identity. That 'they' have made him suffer in the hospital shatters this image of the demi-god, and every act of the doctor or his associates, if they happen to be from the other community, is seen as an attempt to inflict more suffering on him. For the doctor the patient is one more numeral, and hardly any effort is made to regard him as an individual in need of care, counselling, treatment and rehabilitation. This is not supposed to be the work of the doctor.

Information sought by anxious family members is seldom readily given. A young 10th standard student, Afroze, was injured in police firing when he ventured out to fetch tea for his uncle. He was operated upon 12 hours after he was admitted to the hospital. The blood procured on the doctor's prescription was not infused for more than two days. Anxious inquiries by his father were met either by stoic silence, or with remarks like, "Doctors know what they are doing" Finally, after two days, a doctor cared to explain that since the blood had not been screened properly, and since the patient was young, they did not want to risk infecting him with unscreened blood. During my work among riot victims, such instances, where doctors really took the trouble of explaining the line of treatment to relatives, were rarely found. Doctors on other hand feel that the sheer number of patients during riots makes it impossible for them to satisfy every query. Interference from political activists, who demand immediate attention for their supporters, or for the victims of one particular community, adds to the pressures on the doctors. Instances of doctors being threatened and manhandled are many.

Communal riots do not erupt all at once. There is usually a build up for days before the actual riot takes place. Even a common person on the street feels the riot coming. But surprisingly, no government hospital has any contingency plan. As a result, the hospitals are ill equipped to handle the huge influx of riot victims. Victims are asked to get medicines from outside. One fails to understand how a riot victim, who has been brought to the hospital either by the police or some Good Samaritan, will have sufficient money on his person, and more shockingly, is expected to go out and purchase medicines when the whole city is up in flames. The hospital authorities cite 'no funds' as the reason for not stocking even life saving drugs. Indeed, the budget allocations for health services do not increase proportionately to the increase in the number of people utilising the services. Meagre budget allocations reduce the utility of hospitals in more than one way.

- Since the hospital cannot provide transportation, doctors are unable to reach their workplace during riots. An overworked police force makes matters worse by not recognizing their identity cards and insisting upon a curfew pass. As a consequence, doctors 'caught' inside the hospital are forced to work non-stop—sometimes for days together.
- Lack of funds is frequently cited for not filling up vacant posts. In the Osmania General Hospital a number of posts have been vacant for almost a decade now.
- Life saving equipment is usually in a state of disrepair. Even an ordinary x-ray has to be taken outside.
- Drugs, saline solutions, even syringes and needles, have to be procured from the market.

Co-ordination between different government departments, especially between the police and the health department, can help solve the problems to a certain extent. In fact, the sharing of police intelligence reports with hospital authorities will enable the hospitals to prepare themselves for a huge influx of riot victims.

Instances of riot victims being turned away from private hospitals abound. Private practitioners to keep away helpless victims quote laws relating to medico-legal cases. Under Section 39 of the Criminal Procedure Code, a medical practitioner is not legally obliged to give information to the police officer or magistrate of the commission or the intention to commit an offence by any person. Yet the private practitioners resort to the plea of police harassment to avoid treating poor patients. The Supreme Court has also directed private practitioners to attend to the victims of accidents or disasters, if they are called upon to do so. Most of the affected people I spoke to said that private practitioners feared that the riot victims, since they were usually from the poorer sections, might not be able to pay the hospital bills.

It is important that riot victims be attended to at the nearest hospital. This will save lives, which are needlessly lost. This will also help reduce pressure on the over-burdened, ill equipped and under-staffed government hospitals. It is essential that doctors, especially medical students, be sensitised on issues relating to victims of communal violence.

Although prevention of communal conflict is of prime importance, the response of doctors to communal violence should be necessarily curative in nature. It is therefore imperative that legislative reforms for treatment of victims at private hospitals be brought in, contingency plans drawn up, life saving drugs stocked, steps taken to make hospitals free of political interference, and co-ordination with other government agencies be made. Lastly, sensitisation of doctors and paramedical staff on issues relating to communalism is needed not only at medical colleges, but also in the hospitals at periodic intervals.

18

Communal Violence in Mumbai: A Community Perspective

Nasreen Contractor

Introduction

This presentation describes the context of violence, its manifestations and the response of the health profession and services as experienced in a slum community located in Jogeshwari East, a suburb of Mumbai. The population of this community is about 40,0000 with the majority being Muslim households. This community is unique in the sense that over a span of three decades this community has experienced periodic riots that have impacted the social, economic and political fabric of the community.

Demographic and physical profile—The area referred to in this presentation is a community of about 3,50,000 people living in slum settlements over 6 sq. km in Jogeshwari East, Mumbai. The community lies approximately 2 kms east of the railway line dissecting Jogeshwari, a suburb situated about 30 kms north of the Mumbai's commercial and political centre. The population consists primarily of Hindus (about 60 per cent) with a large concentration of Muslims (about 35 per cent). Other religious groups like Christians and Sikhs comprise the rest (about 5 per cent). More than half of the Hindu population falls under the category of Backward Castes.

Living in small one/two room tenements, the majority of residents belong to the poor working class. While some are employed in the formal sector as clerical staff in government offices, or private businesses, or as factory workers, the majority form part of the informal and unorganised sector, being carpenters, masons, painters, artisans, hawkers or labourers in small manufacturing units. A few are involved in business, trade or own shops. Women work in home-based industries or as domestic help in middle and upper class neighbourhoods.

The settlements are located on and around a hillock. Whereas earlier residents from diverse religions lived in interspersed clusters, today there is a clear divide in the geographical location of the Hindu and Muslim residents. The Hindu settlements are located at the base and around the slopes of the hillock with a dense concentration of Muslim residents at the top of the hill. Over the years there has been a phenomenal increase in the population of the entire community. Jogeshwari East has drawn several migrants to it in the last 15-20 years. Increase in the density of population stands higher in the Muslim settlements than in the other settlements.

Housing and living conditions—The settlements of the slum community of Jogeshwari East are located on lands owned by the municipality, the state housing board, private trusts or individuals. Each of these is governed by differing legislations. The extent of security and amenities enjoyed by the residents; is determined by these laws as well as the duration of their existence on the land. For instance, some of the settlements are declared as 'slums' under the Maharashtra Slum Areas Improvement Act and enjoy certain basic amenities, whereas other settlements within the same area are more deprived. The process of securing amenities is usually through people's initiative and struggle. For instance, the settlements of Indiranagar and Shivtekdi had a perpetual water problem, as they are located at a height. The municipality made no attempt to manage the water pressure so that water could reach these areas. People were told to purchase their own pipelines, which they did, only to be left frustrated at the continued absence of water. The availability of civic amenities is very often determined by the negotiating power of the residents or their connections with local politicians, officials, and even goons. As the amenities are not granted as a right to all residents, they become opportunities for speculation by the goons.

Toilets, drainage and sanitation are also in a severe state of disrepair, or prove inadequate. Residents are not permitted to build their own toilets. It is only recently that the municipality in certain areas have entered into contracts with private welfare groups to construct toilets. While civic amenities, in terms of toilets, drainage, water, electricity are generally inadequate in all the settlements, schools, banks, post boxes and other government welfare services are almost nonexistent in the Muslim settlement. While most tenements are constructed with formal building materials like bricks, cement and concrete, approximately 20 per cent of the structures are built of informal materials like plastics, bamboo, tin and jute sheets. A maze of narrow lanes, open drainage, queues at water taps and ration shops–these are some of the most vivid descriptors of the community and its living environment.

In terms of transport, it has again been only very recently that more than one bus route goes through the entire community. There is no public transport to the centre of the area, and even auto rickshaws can ply only up to a point. This leaves certain settlements completely cut off, confined within a maze of intricate lanes and gullies that are accessible only by foot.

With regard to educational facilities, there are only three municipal-run primary schools and no state-run secondary schools. The few secondary schools that exist are private and unaffordable for several of the poor residents. Health facilities are also poor. The closest municipal-run general hospital is located at least 5 km away. There is only one maternity home and one municipal-run dispensary in the entire community. Residents are compelled to depend on private doctors, and even quacks.

Profile of Riots

As a site of communal violence, the slum community of Jogeshwari East is both unique (there have been riots here alone while rest of the city was peaceful) and illustrative of the general characteristics of riots all over the country. There have been five riots during the last two decades: in 1964, 1974-75, 1984, 1990-91, 1992-93.

The most important pattern that has emerged through the trajectory of riots is the alarming demographic alteration of space within communities caused due to eviction and uprooting. The demographic profile of Jogeshwari has been radically altered from one of religion-wise interspersed population clusters to polarized population clusters. Since the population of Muslims in Jogeshwari is in a minority in the area the physical polarization has lead to these families being huddled together into one geographical pocket. The peculiarity of the pattern in which the community has developed is such that this pocket lies in the centre of the community, which is at the top of the hill, surrounded by settlements of Hindu families all around. All access routes out of the community, except one, which leads directly to the highway, are through the Hindu settlements. At times of crisis, such as communal riots, this pocket, which was described above, is starved of public health facilities, and faces a particularly vulnerable situation.

Impact and Manifestations

The consequences of the riots have been both immediate and long term. The immediate consequences relate to: threat to life/evictions, the trauma of relief camps, damage and destruction of homes, impact on work and income, effect on women, impact on children's education, impact on mental health. The long-term impacts relate to: uprooting and dispossession, decline in economic status, loss of educational opportunities, break up of families, impact on women and criminalisation. These manifestations have been defined on the basis of a survey of 78 families that was conducted in the post 1992-1993 period.

Threat to life/evictions—Most people experience immense fear and insecurity and threat to their lives on the outbreak of a riot. Of the 78 uprooted families interviewed, 71 families had to flee from their homes though only 13 reported that they were actually injured. Seven did not flee but later shifted residence.

The Trauma of Relief Camps—The difficulty and discomfort of temporary stay is yet another important impact to be considered. The feelings of anxiety about one's home, of being unsettled, the dependence on outsiders on all basic necessities like food and clothing, the feeling of being a burden on relatives, overcrowding and lack of privacy are conditions of being nothing more than refugees, and the trauma of this experience must be considered so.

Damage and Destruction of H omes—Another very real impact of the riots and evictions is the physical damage caused to homes. Besides, families have lost valuable documents pertaining to the legal security of their homes, ration cards, birth certificates, medical papers and education certificates. During the period between the riot and resumption of normalcy, people are unable to work, be it at their workplace or at their homes. Being unable to move out during the periods of rioting and curfew, and the subsequent time spent in resettling, remaking documents, medical treatment and arrests have all resulted in loss of valuable workdays.

Effect on Women—Riots are a period of great insecurity and vulnerability for women. They become targets of male sexual abuse, and sometimes even assault, to symbolize the attack on the particular community, which they represent. Taunts, abusive language, and eve teasing have been used freely. Besides this, the trauma of fleeing, feeling unsettled, fall in diet patterns, illness, or arrests of family members are particularly severe on women as their role of nurturers and housekeepers undergo stress. The experience of witnessing their husbands, sons or brothers rioting, or being attacked and injured, is traumatic and debilitating. An alarming trend that was observed after the 1992-93 riots was a spate of suicides among women. Five to six suicides occurred within a span of a couple of months. While a direct link between these incidents and the riots cannot be established, a weakened coping capacity leading to depression was definitely observed among women.

Impact on Children's Education—Just as adults are unable to go to their workplaces, children are compelled to absent themselves from school. If the riot period corresponds with examinations then it might lead to the loss of an entire academic year. This leads to dropouts. Girls are kept back at home due to the sense of insecurity and unwillingness to send them to schools outside the community.

Break up of Families—As a result of dispossession, families that were once joint families, are unable to find similar kind of accommodation that they enjoyed earlier, and are hence forced to become nuclear. This disintegration has led to a loss of physical and emotional support.

Impact on Mental Health—Forty-two persons from the 78 interviewed, mentioned loss of sleep due to fear and shock. 12 spoke of having nightmares. In 24 families the children/elders suffered fever. Three persons spoke of temporary loss of mental balance due to the trauma of the riots.

Uprooting and Dispossession—One of the most significant, long-term impact of evictions has been the overnight uprooting and dispossession of people from homes in which they have lived in peace and harmony for 20-30 years, to seek shelter in places where they feel more safe and secure.

Deadline in economic status—The economic status of riot-affected families has fallen sharply. This is a result of loss of capital assets, fall in income, loss of ownership of one's house, change in quality of house, reduction in size of house, indebtedness.

Criminalisation—The youth have taken to anti-social and even criminal activities. Bitter experience, and frustration have pushed these youth to the brink.

Hence the impact of riots is not just physical injury and destruction of homes, but impacts on people's lives, livelihood, and productivity, ultimately impacting mental health.

Experience of the role played by health professionals and services

Residents of the community reported that the experience with injuries that were comparatively small and those that were more serious were completely different. Families whose members had suffered from small injuries were just not willing to have these treated, as they feared that if they did so they would be faced with a police case. Major injuries had to be rushed to the nearby hospital. But given the ghettoised condition of the community and the tense situation patients could just not be taken to hospitals. The area was heavily guarded and families could not respond to their injured. Many a times, victims were just lying on the road and when the police came they would be taken to hospitals. The residents of one community attacked ambulances driven by residents of another community, and the police and people had stories to tell of heroic attempts to drive through all odds to rush victims to hospitals. At hospitals, till the panchnama was not done, medical attention was not given. There are even instances of preferences being given to patients of one community over another. Victims have even been refused medical attention. In this case, the local politician took out a demonstration to the hospital to ensure that members of one community were taken even over and above the urgent attention required by others.

Hence in a riot situation, this community becomes completely fortressed with all exit routes cut off due to heavy security and violence. In the absence of any health facilities in the community, residents are left to the mercy of the police to take them to hospitals. Doctors are unable to enter the area, and the few doctors who reside locally are afraid to work openly. Medicines are unavailable. Such a situation is particularly dangerous for pregnant mothers and patients suffering from high-risk medical disorders, as during such a crisis there is no possibility of treating any emergencies of this kind.

Thus the inadequacy of facilities is true to several other communities in Mumbai and is indeed the case for the entire city. But what this presentation highlights are serious consequences of inadequacy of services coupled with inaccessibility at the time of crisis that the residents of this community face.

(Acknowledgement: The material for this presentation is drawn from the experience of YUVA working in the slum community of Jogeshwari East, Mumbai, for the last 14 years, and from a research study that was conducted during the period, 1993 to 1995. For more information see "Planned Segregation: Riots, Evictions and Dispossession in Jogeshwari East, Mumbai, India", Mumbai:YUVA, COHRE, 1996)

Part-V
Violence against Women : Domestic Violence and Sexual Assault

19

An Investigation of Domestic Violence Using Hospital Casualty Records

Achala S. Daga
Shireen J. Jejeebhoy
Shantha Rajgopal

Introduction and objectives

Domestic violence against women is increasingly recognised as a major health and social problem in India. It is also a concern for public health. Not only is violence against women widespread, deeply entrenched, silently borne, and relatively impervious to social change. Attitudes uniformly justify wife beating; and few women would opt out of an abusive marriage (Jejeebhoy, 1998, Jejeebhoy and Cook, 1997). At the same time, there is a dearth of information on the magnitude and patterns of domestic violence against women in India, particularly by way of community-based data. Facility-based data from police, court, hospital, and NGO records do exist, but these remain scattered, poorly maintained, and seldom used.

The objective of the paper is to explore faculty-based data from one source, the casualty department of one public hospital in Mumbai city (J.J. Hospital) for insights into possible domestic violence. The intention is to draw up a profile—limited though it might be—of the patterns and determinants of violence against women, as assessed from routine hospital records. The aim is also to demonstrate that a scrutiny of casualty registers can throw up insights into domestic violence against women, and to challenge health facilities; to use (or supplement) these data to detect, and provide appropriate counselling and other services to women victims of domestic violence.

Studies based on emergency department admissions have been carried out in other settings. One study was conducted among female trauma patients at an emergency room in Philadelphia (McLeer and Anwar, 1989). Routine records in this study suggest that some 6 per cent women trauma patients had been battered; this proportion increased to 30 per cent after an intervention in which the staff were sensitised, and new protocols instituted for identifying battered women. In another such study in Denver, injuries of 12 per cent of women inflicted by a current male partner were attributed to domestic violence (Abbott and others, 1996). A similar study in Australia whose sample comprised women attending the emergency department only between 8 a.m. and midnight, observed that only two per cent of women attended the hospital as a direct result of an incident of domestic violence, although one quarter of them admitted to having experienced domestic violence in the past (Bates and others, 1995).

Major, and well known limitations of such a design (applicable to any facility-based study), are evident in all facility-based studies. For example, such studies are handicapped by the absence of a denominator, and hence an inability to indicate the proportion of women in any community who suffer domestic violence. Nor do they enable attention to community norms regarding domestic violence against women. Such studies also omit the large majority of women who suffer violence in some form, but are not compelled by injury or desperation to seek help; in other words, these studies are restricted to women who represent "the tip of the iceberg" only. For example, one study observes that while the injuries suffered by 12 per cent of women visiting the emergency room related to domestic violence, over half the women attending the emergency room reported that they had experienced domestic violence at some point in their lives (Abbott and others, 1996). Another concern is the limited scope and quality of data. On the one hand, few women are willing to admit that their injuries resulted from domestic violence. On the other hand, neither recording systems nor physicians recording routine admissions are sensitive enough to probe and elicit data on domestic violence. Concerted efforts at developing sensitive reporting protocols, for example, effected a six-fold increase in reported cases of wife battering (McLeer and Anwar, 1989).

Data

Recognising these inherent limitations, this study examines evidence from existing data from one public hospital in Mumbai, the J.J. Hospital. The hospital is medium sized, situated in south central Mumbai, and caters to the relatively low income, largely mixed Hindu and Muslim populations residing in its vicinity.

Typically, the point of entry for all emergency cases arriving at any hospital is the casualty department. Details of all accident, injury, burn, or poison cases are, moreover, maintained in a separate register, known as the Emergency Police Register (EPR). This register records both life-threatening and relatively less serious injuries, and the patients whose information is recorded in these registers are either treated in the casualty department, or in other departments as out-patients and then allowed to return home, or if warranted, admitted as in-patients, usually to such departments as surgical, trauma, burns and obstetrics and gynaecology.

Data collected in this study refer to all women whose cases were recorded in the EPR of the J.J. Hospital during 1996. Data drawn thus are typical of all public hospitals in the city that serve casualty cases. Only existing records have been analysed; no attempt has been made to interview women, or their families.

A well-known limitation of facility-based studies is the paucity of appropriate data available from them. EPR registers typically do not contain much socio-economic data, aside from age, religion, and area of residence. But they are rich in such other information as the time of the incident, and the time of admission, the kind of assault and type of instrument used, part of the body injured, and it's severity, and the kinds of treatment received. On occasion, supplementary information—pregnancy status, or information on who accompanied the woman to the hospital—is also recorded.

Classification of Injured Women

833 women visited the casualty department during 1996 with a variety of injuries: assault, accidental falls, burns, and attempted suicides. This paper deals with 745 of these women who were aged 15 or more. Table 1 classifies women by cause of injury, as specified in the registers. As Panel 1 shows 15 per cent had consumed poison, 11 per cent had suffered burns, and 9 per cent had suffered a fall. The remaining 21 per cent had suffered traffic and other accidents, the largest proportion of women had suffered assault – 45 per cent. Not surprisingly, few women would, without sensitive probing and counselling, implicate their husbands or other family members as perpetrators of the violent incident. Hence, this paper has had to adopt a fairly liberal definition, on the basis of supplementary information available in the casualty registers. Domestic violence is classified now as (a) definite, (b) possible & (c) unlikely as seen in Table 1.

Table 1: Types of injuries reported, adult women 15+ attending the casualty department of J.J. Hospital, 1996.

		Number	%
I	**Classification of casualty attendance**		
	Assault	332	44.6
	Falls	67	9
	Burns	79	10.6
	Consumption of poison	112	15
	Vehicle, other accidents	155	20.8
	Total	745	
II	**Classification by domestic violence status**		
1	Definite case of domestic violence: perpetrator reported	167	22.4
a	Assault by husband, other family member, or "known" person	164	22
b	Set on fire by husband	3	0.4
2	*Possible cases of domestic violence*	330	44.3
a	Assault; no information on perpetrator	138	18.5
b	Burn; stove burst or other cause	70	9.4
c	Attempted suicide	122	16.4
	Consumption of poison	112	15
	Assault on self	4	0.5
	Set herself on fire	6	0.8
3	*Unlikely case of domestic violence*	67	9
	All falls, reportedly accidental	67	9
4	*Definitely not cases of domestic violence*	181	24.3
a	Assault by outsiders	26	3.5
b	Vehicle and other accidents	155	20.8
	TOTAL	**745**	**100**

Definitely domestic violence—A definite case of domestic violence is one in which the injury is clearly attributed to the husband, other family members, or a "known" person. Over one in five women (22.4 per cent) fell into this category: 164 women were assaulted by their husbands, other family members, or a "known" person, and three women reported that their husbands had set them on fire.

Possibly domestic violence—A possible case of domestic violence includes women who refused to report the name of the perpetrator of the incident, whether assault, or burn. Also classified as possible cases of domestic violence are women who have attempted suicide, since much of this relates to harassment and abuse. Almost half of all women (44 per cent) fell in this category. They included, (a) 138 women who had suffered assault, but refused to give the name of the perpetrator, (b) 70 women who suffered "accidental" burns, and (c) 122 women who were recorded as having attempted to kill themselves, 112 by consuming poison, six by setting themselves on fire, and 4 by wounding themselves.

Unlikely cases of domestic violence— Falls were difficult to classify: all were reported as accidental, and hence we have classified them separately as unlikely cases of domestic violence. A total of 67 women, or 9 per cent of all women who reported accidentally falling down stairs, tripping, and so on.

Definitely unrelated to domestic violence— Finally, traffic and train accidents, accidents occurring in the workplace, as well as assaults reported to have been committed by outsiders have been distinguished as clearly lying outside the realm of domestic violence. About one quarter of all women fell in this category: 21 per cent for vehicle and other traffic accidents, and four per cent as a result of assault by outsiders.

In contrast to women, not only do more men visit the casualty department for injuries, but also, they visit for a quite distinct set of injuries. Table 2 reports on data drawn from one register, randomly representing the first quarter of 1996. Information on 159 men, aged 15 or more, is available. Data are classified by cause of injury, as specified in the registers. The leading cause of injury was assault by an outsider, experienced by almost two in five cases (38 per cent). One quarter was treated in the casualty department for alcohol abuse. And almost one-third of the cases (31per cent) were treated for various accidents–largely traffic (18 per cent) and falls (9 per cent). Only 4 per cent, compared to 16 per cent among women, visited as a consequence of attempted suicide.

Table 2: Types of Injuries Reported by Adult Men 15+, attending the Casualty Department of the J.J. Hospital—first quarter, 1996 (a)

	Number	%
Alcohol consumption	**41**	**25.8**
Attempted suicide	**6**	**3.8**
Consumption of poison, assault on self (b)		
Assaults	**62**	**39**
Assault by outsider	61	38.4
Assault by family member	1	0.6
Accidents	**50**	**31.4**
At home (burn, other)	2	1.3
Fall	14	8.8
Vehicle/ train/ road accidents	28	17.6
Injury or accident at work	6	3.8
TOTAL	**159**	**100**

Note: Data are drawn from one of the four registers covering this period. The register was randomly selected. Consumption of poison: 5, assault on self: 1, accidents at home: burn: 1, other: 1.

Profile of injured women

Little data is available in the EPR on socio-economic or demographic characteristics of patients treated in the casualty department. Information on gender, religion, and age is almost always available. Other data, such as, pregnancy status, and person accompanying the injured, are less uniformly recorded, and hence cannot be analysed.

Table 3 presents a profile of injured women. The J.J. Hospital serves a population of roughly 4 lakhs residing in the areas of Nagpada, Kamathipura, and Byculla. These areas have a large concentration of Muslim residents, and hence, it is no surprise that Muslims constitute 44 per cent of the women treated in the casualty department over the year, 1996. What is mildly notable is that Muslims are somewhat more likely to fall in the category of deliberate assault than Hindus, suggesting either that they are somewhat more likely to suffer domestic violence, or that they are more likely than Hindus to identify the perpetrator. In contrast, burn victims are predominantly Hindus (7 6 per cent).

Table 5: Profile of Women aged 15+ presenting in Casualty Department (EPR) by likely domestic violence status, women attending the casualty department of JJ Hospital, 1996

		All	Definite	Possible				Unlikely	Not domestic violence
			Assault & burn	Total	Assault	Burn	Attempted suicide	Falls	Accident assault by outsider
	NUMBER	745	167	330	138	70	122	67	181
1	Religion								
	Hindus	52.9	41.9	57.6	50.0	75.7	55.7	67.2	49.2
	Muslims	44.0	52.7	40.9	49.3	22.9	41.8	28.4	47.5
	Christians, others	3.1	5.4	1.5	0.7	1.4	2.5	4.5	3.3
2	Age								
	15-19	10.1	7.2	12.4	8.7	11.4	17.2	10.4	8.3
	20-24	20.9	19.8	24.2	12.3	31.4	33.6	16.4	17.7
	25-29	18.0	25.1	17.3	20.3	11.4	17.2	9.0	16.0
	30-34	14.9	16.2	16.1	16.7	20.0	13.1	13.4	12.2
	35-39	11.1	12.0	12.7	18.8	14.3	4.9	9.0	8.3
	40-44	6.8	9.6	5.8	8.7	0.0	5.7	1.5	8.3
	45-49	4.4	3.6	3.9	2.9	5.7	4.1	4.5	6.1
	50-59	5.5	2.4	2.7	3.6	2.9	1.6	13.4	10.5
	60 and above	7.1	3.6	3.3	5.1	2.9	1.6	20.9	12.2
	N/A	1.1	0.6	1.5	2.9	0.0	0.8	1.5	0.6
3	Admission time								
	2100 – 2259	14.4	15.6	14.8	18.8	11.4	12.3	11.9	13.3
	2300 – 0359	18.3	18.6	20.0	18.1	20.0	22.1	13.4	16.6
	0400 – 0559	1.5	2.4	.06	0.0	2.9	0.0	1.5	2.2
	0600 – 1159	14.1	15.6	11.8	12.3	12.9	10.7	25.4	12.7
	1200 – 1759	34.8	34.1	34.2	38.4	34.3	29.5	32.8	37.0
	1800 – 2059	15.7	11.4	17.3	11.6	17.1	23.8	14.9	17.1
	NR	1.3	2.4	1.2	0.7	1.4	1.6	0.0	1.1

Note: Percentages are column percentages

The age profile shows clearly that 80 per cent cases, of both definite and possible domestic violence, tend to fall in the age group of 15 to 39. Well over 40 per cent fall in the age group of 20 to 29 (45 per cent and 42 per cent, respectively), and this proportion goes up to 51 per cent of all women who attempted suicide. In contrast, women who reported falls are considerably older: 58 per cent are aged between 15 and 39, and 34 per cent are aged 50 or more. Women, whose injuries were clearly unrelated to domestic violence, a relatively similar age distribution is reported.

Timing of the violent incident

Also recorded in the EPR is the time of the incident and admission. In about one third of the cases, the time that the incident occurred has not been reported; hence we rely here on the timing of the admission to shed light on average, a delay of up to one hour, between the time of the incident and that of the admission. Hence, we may assume that all incidents that occurred between the 10 p.m. and 5 a.m. will be admitted to the casualty department between 11 p.m and 6 a.m. Results suggest that over one in five (21 per cent) cases of both definite and possible domestic violence occur at night, between 11 p.m and 5 a.m. Falls, in contrast, are less likely to occur in these hours (15 per cent).

Description of injuries

Data recorded in the EPRs gives some idea of the extent of injuries suffered, and the ways in which injuries occurred. Table 4 describes the injuries women have suffered. Among the definite cases of domestic violence, the majority (44 per cent) were kicked, beaten, punched, bitten, choked or strangled; 19 per cent were assaulted with a stick, rod, or other blunt instrument, and 16 per cent with a knife or blade. Only four per cent admitted deliberate burning.

Among the possible cases of domestic violence, the prominent causes of injury included, beating, kicking, etc (34 per cent), assault with a stick, rod, etc (23 per cent), consumption of various poisonous substances (28 per cent), including pesticides (12 per cent), rat poison (8 per cent) chemicals and sleeping pills (8 per cent), and stove burst (15 per cent).

Information on falls once again gave few clues that would suggest deliberate violence. The large majority reported that they fell down stairs, or some other height (27 per cent), or tripped, or fell in the bathroom, etc (58 per cent) - given the housing conditions in which many chawl and slum dwellers reside, these figures are not, on the face of it, surprising.

Table 4: Description of injuries, women aged 15+, by likely deomestic violence status, Women attending the casualty department of JJ Hospital, 1996.

		Definite	Possible				Unlikely
		Assault & burn	Total	Assault	Burn	Attempted suicide	Falls
	Number	171	326	138	66	122	67
1	**Part of body injured**		(a)			(a)	
	Head, face, eyes, nose, neck	55.6	62.1	65.2	59.1	40.0	47.8
	Head	18.7	12.6	16.7	22.7	30.0	23.9
	Face	29.2	23.6	35.5	37.9	30.0	29.9
	Eyes	10.5	6.1	12.3	3.0	10.0	4.5
	Nose	4.1	4.3	6.5	4.5	20.0	3.0
	Neck	5.3	11.3	9.4	31.8	30.0	0.0
	Chest, back, abdomen	22.8	26.4	21.7	77.3	50.0	3.0
	Chest	12.9	17.8	8.0	65.2	40.0	0.0
	Back	6.4	11.0	8.0	30.3	50.0	1.5
	Abdomen	9.9	15.3	8.0	53.0	40.0	1.5
	Arms or legs	41.5	36.8	37.0	89.4	100.0	31.3
	Arms	33.3	29.1	29.0	71.2	80.0	16.4
	Legs	12.3	19.3	8.7	66.7	70.0	17.9
2	**How injured**						
	Blunt instrument, stick, iron rod, belt, etc	19.3	10.1	23.1	N/A	0.0	n.a
	Sharp instrument, knife, blade	16.4	9.2	18.2	n.a	3.3	n.a
	Slapped, kicked, strangled, bitten, choked	43.9	14.7	33.6	n.a	0.0	n.a
	Fell from height	n.a	0.0	n.a	n.a	0.0	26.9

		Definite	Possible				Unlikely
		Assault & burn	Total	Assault	Burn	Attempted suicide	Falls
	Tripped, fell over	n.a	0.0	n.a	n.a	0.0	58.2
	Deliberately set on fire, acid burn	4.1	1.8	n.a	0.0	4.9	n.a
	Stove burst, gas cylinder burst, accident	n.a	14.7	n.a	72.7	0.0	n.a
	Consumed rat poison	n.a	7.7	n.a	n.a	20.5	n.a
	Consumed sleeping pills, overdose	n.a	4.0	n.a	n.a	10.7	n.a
	Consumed chemicals poison	n.a	3.7	n.a	n.a	9.8	n.a
	Consumed pesticide poison	n.a	12.3	n.a	n.a	32.8	n.a
	No answer	20.5	23.3	25.2	27.3	18.0	14.9
3	**Type of injury**						
	Abrasion	25.7	14.4	33.3	0.0	0.8	16.4
	Contusion	35.7	15.6	37.0	0.0	0.0	22.4
	Laceration	3.5	2.1	4.3	0.0	0.8	1.5
	Contusion and laceration	24.0	8.9	19.6	0.0	1.6	28.4
	Fracture	1.2	0.9	2.2	0.0	0.0	7.5
	Profuse bleeding	7.6	5.2	11.6	0.0	0.8	6.0
	Semi-conscious	0.0	4.3	0.0	3.0	9.8	0.0
	Unconscious	0.0	8.3	0.7	19.7	10.7	7.5
	If burn < 40%	(b)	n.a	n.a	31.8	(c)	n.a
	If burn 41 – 60%	(b)	n.a	n.a	27.3	(c)	n.a
	If burn 61 – 80%	(b)	n.a	n.a	16.7	(c)	n.a
	If burn 81 – 100%	(b)	n.a	n.a	16.7	(c)	n.a
4	**Extent of injury**						
	Medium or serious (d)	12.8	43.4	9.4	60.6	24.6	11.9

Notes: (a) Excludes poison cases. (b) Of the seven cases of wife-burning, three received burns on more than 80 per cent of their bodies, one on 60 per cent-80 per cent, and one under 40 per cent; information on the remaining two was not available. (c) Of the six cases of attempted suicide by self-immolation, four received burns on more than 80 per cent of their bodies, and one on 60 per cent-80 per cent; information on the remaining case was not available. (d) For poison cases, all who were semi- or unconscious; for burn cases all whose burns exceeded 33 per cent of their bodies.

The head and the face were prime targets of abuse for about three in five victims of definite domestic violence; about two in five reported injuries to the legs or arms, and only about one quarter to the body. In contrast to these findings, in-depth studies on women suggest that a prime target for domestic violence is the abdomen and chest—parts of the body on which injuries are less likely to be visible. It is possible then that there is a disproportionate concentration among women who present themselves to the casualty department with clearly visible injuries - most likely on the face. In contrast, burn victims are most likely to suffer burns on their limbs and bodies than on their faces.

The types of injuries suffered were largely abrasions, contusions, and contusions with laceration among women who had suffered from assault. Profuse bleeding was noted in quite a number of women, including 8 per cent of the definite cases of domestic violence, and 12 per cent who suffered from an assault but did not name the perpetrator. Of interest also is that while 13 per cent of the possible cases of domestic violence were found to be in semi or unconscious states, not a single one of the definite cases were so—this may well suggest that if brought in a semi or unconscious condition the statements may more likely under-report family violence.

A measure of the severity of the injuries comes from the assessment of the physicians. As many as 13 per cent of the victims of definite domestic violence; had suffered a serious injury. In contrast, among the possible victims of domestic violence, as many as 25 per cent of the attempted suicide cases, and as many as 61 per cent of the "accidental stove burst" cases were assessed to be in serious condition.

Summary and Conclusions

Although incomplete, inadequate, and inconclusive, data collected in the EPR argues strongly for greater sensitivity in recording information on domestic violence against women, and in recognising and providing sensitive counselling and referral to potential victims of domestic violence.

The results suggest that as many as 23 per cent - almost one in four - women can be classified as definite cases of domestic violence. They have either suffered an assault by a family member or "known person", or, in a minority of the cases, attribute the burns they have suffered to their husbands or other family members. Another 44 per cent of all women appear to be possible victims of violence: they have either refused to name the perpetrator of the assault (19 per cent), or attributed the burns they have suffered to accidental stove burst, etc (9 per cent), or were clear cases of attempted suicide - a measure to which women who have suffered violence and harassment are likely to resort (16 per cent). Hence, certainly one quarter and up to two-thirds of all women reporting to the casualty department may have suffered domestic violence.

Other points that corroborate this suggestion on domestic violence include the fact that disturbing proportions - over one fifth - have suffered the injury in the late hours of the night (roughly between 10 p.m. and 5 a.m.) raising further doubts about their accidental status. The age distributions of women who attended the casualty department suggest, moreover, that large proportions of these women were in the peak reproductive ages, 20 to34 years - a period during which women have little say in their own lives.

Most of the definite cases of domestic violence occurred as a result of beating, either by slaps, punches, and kicks, or with a stick or belt; or knife or blade wounds, or, in a small proportion of confirmed cases, as a result of wife-burning. Attempted suicide claimed 16 per cent of all cases, and these may well have been attenuated by domestic violence and harassment. Most burn victims claimed the burn occurred accidentally while cooking; and a large proportion of women who suffered from assault refused to identify the perpetrator; undoubtedly some in both these groups have concealed the fact that they were deliberately set on fire.

While cuts and bruises dominated, profuse bleeding, and fractures were also evident among assault cases. A disturbing proportion of women had received serious and life-threatening injuries—one in eight women whose injuries had definitely resulted from domestic violence, one quarter of the attempted suicide cases, and three in five of the "accidental" burn cases, with burns over more than half their bodies.

The results clearly suggest that domestic violence is a serious, but still invisible, public health threat. Data that is routinely collected in casualty registers may merely scratch the surface, but remain at present, one of the only sources of information on the subject. Yet, this data remains obscure, only to be utilised in rare medico-legal cases. Data recorded in registers tend, moreover, to be superficial and incomplete. And practitioners who record this data are not even trained to recognise symptoms of abuse, let alone provide sensitive counselling or referral. What is needed is for practitioners to routinely ask all women direct questions about abuse (see, for example, Richardson and Feder, 1996). Modification of recording formats has enabled considerable improvement in the identification of battered women in at least two studies (Olson and others, 1996; McLeer and Anwar, 1989). The results of this study, while admittedly somewhat speculative, highlight the enormity of the problem, the need to review data collection systems and protocols, and the training of providers, and indeed, the urgent need for domestic violence to become integrated into the city's public health system.

Acknowledgments—We are grateful to Dr. Dongaonkar, Dean, J.J. Group of Hospitals, for permission to peruse data from EPR registers, and for his support and commitment to this project.

20

Deaths of Women Due to Burns:An Analysis of Hospital Data

Kamala Ganesh

Introduction

The causes of maternal mortality and the various interventions that can bring down maternal deaths have been highlighted and discussed at various forums in the past few years. Awareness about these factors is on the increase amongst health care providers, health agencies, and the community. All these have created an impression amongst health care providers that the major cause of death of women in the reproductive age group is pregnancy related.

Health information data of 1992 were analysed for demographic indicators of women's health. One of the indicators analysed was cause of death among women in the age group of 15 to 44. The data revealed that the impression of pregnancy-related deaths being the major cause of death in this group was wrong, and injuries and accidents, i.e., non-medical causes were actually topping the list (Table 1). Interaction with friends and colleagues from obstetrics and gynaecology, as well as from other medical and surgical specialities, further confirmed that many medical professionals were not aware of the above facts. To satisfy the urge for further information, hospital data was analysed.

Table 1 – Cause of Death in Women (15-44 yrs)

	15-24 Yrs	25-44 Yrs
Injuries and accidents	30.90%	19.90%
Infections and parasite	17.40%	19.90%
Pregnancy related	12.70%	8.90%
Ill defined	9.50%	9.40%

Source: Health Information of India 1992.

Collection of Data

Data from the death register of Lok Nayak Hospital was collected for three months (May – July 1997). The register contained entries of those who were admitted and died in the hospital. Those brought dead on arrival at the casualty were not entered in this register. Deaths due to injuries and accidents were analysed. Since burn deaths dominated the picture, data for burn deaths was collected for the preceding three months also. An informal discussion was sought with a specialist from the burns unit regarding these deaths on whether they were homicidal, suicidal, or accidental.

Analysis of Data

Deaths in Lok Nayak Hospital for a three—month period, and deaths due to injury and accidents are shown in Table 2.

Table: 2-Deaths due to injury and poisoning (15-44 years)

	Females			Males		
	15-30ys	**31-44ys**	**Total**	**15-30ys**	**31-44ys**	**Total**
Burns	82	12	94	18	11	29
Accidents	3	2	5	26	10	36
Poisoning	3	3	6	2	5	7
Total due to injury & poisoning	88	17	105	46	26	72
Total deaths due to all causes	162	68	230	124	82	206

Table : 3 Deaths due to Burns (February-July, 1997)

	<14 yrs	**15-30 yrs**	**31-44 yrs**	**Total**	**>45 yrs**	**Grand Total**
Female	j	153	25	178	19	215
Male	17	46	17	63	13	93

Total death = 2030 15-44 years = 829

Total burns death = 308 15-44 years = 241

Female = 73.85%, Male = 26.2%

Analysis of deaths due to burns is shown in Table 3. Women in the age group of 15 to 30 were the major victims, and 153 deaths were recorded among women as against 46 among men (4 times higher); this shows a strong female predilection. Interaction with a specialist from the burns unit indicated that more than half of these deaths were due to accidents, such as bursting of kerosene stove or kerosene spilling, and clothes catching fire. As to the social implications of homicide, suicide or abetment to suicide, the specialist said that these deaths were already registered as medico-legal cases and police would have collected the details and dealt with them.

Discussion

An analysis of the data revealed that a large number of young women in the 15 to 30 years group were dying due to injuries and accidents, mainly burns. Currently, the medical community is either unaware or feels that prevention of such deaths are not in their domain.

Malini Karkal (1985) after analysing data from urban Maharashtra has reported that in the age group of 15 to 44, one in four deaths were recorded as accidents and one in five due to burns. For the age group of 15 to 24 the figures quoted were one in three and one in four, respectively. She has said that in any industry even one tenth of this figure would have attracted greater attention and a search for some remedial measures would be on. Since the victims were women, such large number of deaths went unnoticed. Also, those who did not die, but were maimed or disfigured, were left to face the social and psychological consequences.

Ranjana Kumari (1989) reported that 25.3 per cent of the dowry victims were dead: others were physically and mentally harassed, deserted by husband and family, etc. She has also mentioned in her survey, that in hospital and police records, only 8 out of the 38 cases were registered under murder, 29 under suicide and one under abetment to suicide. But the survey of victims' parents showed that all the 38 cases were either murder or abetment to suicide. All the deaths were due to burns. The number of dowry deaths due to burns in Delhi (Ranjana Kumari 1989) is shown in Table 4.

Table 4: No. of dowry deaths due to burn in Delhi

Year	Number
1980-81	421
1981-82	568
1982-83	610
1983-84	690
1984-85	558

The present analysis of a single hospital in Delhi for a six-month period has shown 178 deaths of women in the age group of 15 to 44. Which raise a serious question - are the number of burn deaths in Delhi increasing?

Issues

- Are these deaths homicidal, suicidal, abetment to suicide or accidental?
- If these were due to accidents, as is presently felt by medical professionals, what were the causes of these accidents? Why and how such accidents happened more commonly in this age group?
- Would it help to record the type of the stove, the manufacturers' name, and the cause of the accidents? Could the victim's family go to the consumer court against the manufacturers' of these stoves?
- If girls are educated regarding the safe use of gloves, could such accidents be prevented?
- How could the medical community help prevent deaths due to burns in the future, especially among women in the age group of 15 to 44?
- Is there any guideline for health care professionals to record these deaths and help these victims get justice?

There may be many such issues. All of them need to be addressed in order to create awareness among medical professionals.

21

Sexual Coercion and PID in Slum Women of Mumbai: Role of the Health Care Provider

Renu Khanna
Korrie de Koning
Swati Pongurlekar
Usha Ubale
Manjiri S.

The problem of family violence, especially violence against women, is not a new one and evidence of such violations can be found throughout history in recorded documents. Abuse of female partners is referred to in the Bible and condoned in the Koran. Manu's patriarchal laws which dictated that a woman had to be under her father's guardianship in childhood, husband's in youth, and son's in old age, resulted in the 'deviant' woman being beaten and abused. Although violence against women is an age-old problem, it has only recently been positioned in the international public policy sphere as a human rights issue. This position has grown out of the work of pro-democracy movements in Latin America and parts of Asia. Women who were part of these movements realised that the violence they faced often in private spheres, was completely invisible in the mainstream framework of human rights, which had till then concentrated on civil and political rights. This catalysed the international women's movement to broaden the definition of human rights to include gender-based forms of violence, such as domestic and sexual violence.

Through the early 1990s, preliminary data began suggesting that violence against women was also a health issue. Amartya Sen's work on the 'missing females' and declining sex ratios in countries where females are discriminated against indicated that the 'missing' females were victims of female foeticide, selective malnourishment of girls, lack of investment in women's health, and various forms of violence. Subsequent work in the early 1990s on gynaecological morbidities also began to be related, in some part, to violence against women. And in 1994 the ICPD at Cairo in its Programme of Action placed violence against women fully on the reproductive health agenda.

Box 1: Impacts of Violence on Women's Sexual and Reproductive Lives

- STDs HIV
- Unwanted Pregnancy
- Abortion -related injury
- Fear of sex / loss of pleasure
- Miscarriage and low birth weight from battering during pregnancy
- Violent sexual initiation
- Premature labour
- Gynaecological problems
- Inability to use condoms
- Genital mutilation
- Forced abortion of female foetuses
- Suicide or homicide related to stigma of sexual violence

Source: Lori Heise et al (1995)

As Box 1 shows, gender-based violence is a profound health problem. At the most basic level, violence affects women's bodies and psyche throughout their life cycle. Ill health is a direct consequence of violence. Thus violence, in addition to being human rights, is also a health issue. Violence is an issue of power relations between men and women. It can be conceptualised as an issue of control of women, each of the forms in which it is seen serves to keep individual women within the control of individual men. Collectively, the sum total of violence against women can be viewed as one of the many forms of patriarchal social control. If reproductive health aims to empower women, programmes must address violence against women. Violence takes away control of the body. The reproductive health concept includes the notion of reclaiming control over the body, thus violence against women must be incorporated into its definition.

This paper looks at one aspect of gender violence—sexual coercion in consensual relationships. The paper examines data from a research study on pelvic inflammatory disease among slum women in Mumbai, in order to define what the role of health care providers can be.

The Study

The study was undertaken in Mumbai between October 1993 and December 1995. It was collaboration between the Brihanmumbai Municipal Corporation (BMC) and the Liverpool School of Tropical Medicine, U.K., and was funded by the Overseas Development Administration of the U.K. The data was primarily of women who approached the health care facilities of the BMC for mainly curative services. The study women were recruited at three centres located in three neighboring wards. Most cases were recruited at Lokmanya Tilak Municipal General Hospital (ward F/N), and most controls from Mahim Maternity Home (Ward G/N) and Ward F/South Post Partum Centre.

Women were defined as cases if they presented for gynaecologic investigations, either with symptoms of acute pelvic infection (suspected PID) or a history of infertility. Such women were suspected to have a reproductive tract infection. Controls were fertile women seeking tubal ligation and having no symptoms of gynaecological disease.

A total of 3,588 women were screened. A social questionnaire containing socio-demographic information (marital status, religion, migrant, history, education, and income) contraceptive use, and sexual history of the woman and her partner was the first instrument to be used. This was followed by a clinical questionnaire, gynaecological examination, and microbiological assessments. In-depth interviews of 240 women were done. Around 23 group discussions were also held.

A total of 30 Auxiliary Nurse Midwives (ANMs) were seconded by the BMC to the research project and trained to enhance their skills in questioning women on their sexual behaviour. The social questionnaire was developed with the ANMs through a process of careful piloting, asking open-ended questions on pre-determined issues, until closed questions with meaningful response categories could be specified. Interviews were conducted in Marathi and Hindi in separate, quiet rooms where confidentiality could be maintained. Interviews were always conducted by two ANMs - one asked questions while the other recorded the responses. This procedure allowed one ANM to give full and sympathetic attention to the women while ensuring a careful recording of the answers.

The in-depth interviews were conducted by pairs of trained ANMs at the homes of the women. Most interviews were spread over two meetings. At the homes, too, attempts were made to ensure privacy and confidentiality. The group discussions were conducted in rooms of the municipal health facilities, a few meetings were conducted in common community spaces.

The data from the in-depth interviews was coded and analysed using the ZYINDEX qualitative research package.

Findings

Analysis of the data around sexuality issues and relationships with their husbands revealed that at one level women experienced the feeling of being supported and cared for by their husbands; they described the concern exhibited by their husbands towards their illnesses. At another level, women spoke about how men exerted control and power over them.

Support and concern—Most of the women felt that their husbands were really concerned about their ill health. The concern was reflected in many of the husbands helping out with the 'harder' domestic work, e.g., fetching water, looking after the children, cooking for them, and feeding them. Gouri mentioned that her husband was very worried during her second pregnancy. She was admitted to a hospital after the delivery, and he did all the housework, took care of the children, etc. She felt that her husband was unlike other husbands because if she ever felt a little sick he would promptly do all the household work - right from filling water to cooking, and taking her to the doctor.

A woman with infertility spoke about how her husband especially bought her to Mumbai from the village for treatment. For the last 18 months, they were undergoing treatment at a hospital. Another mentioned that "he forces me to take medicines and he himself takes me for a check up (even) if I (only) have fever." Yet another mentioned that her husband restrained from having intercourse with her (even though he had the desire) because he feared that her symptoms would get further aggravated.

Against the perception of a high degree of concern and support mentioned by these women, there were others who thought that while their partners were supportive, they could be more so. Take for instance, Shanti, who had secondary infertility. She stated that while her husband supported her against the abuse of her mother-in-law and said that one child was enough, he did not accompany her for treatment. In her frame of reference, it appears that accompanying her for treatment is a sign of support and concern.

On the other side of the spectrum are husbands like Kanta's:

"... He is very shakki *(suspicious). When I got* safed paani ki taklif *(white discharge) he was very angry and said that I must be 'going out' with someone else."*

The following story is typical of the pattern of many women's lives. The group discussions also repeatedly brought out the themes of the husbands' irresponsibility and physical abuse.

Sumitra lives with her husband and children in a single room. Her husband refuses to work and demands money and food from her. "He drinks, smokes, chew tobacco, does everything…quarrels…He says that the wife should earn and the husband eat. He drinks and beats me every day. Just now he has gone out after beating me." Sumitra feels that she does not have any support from either her parental home or her in-laws. She works as a domestic help but the income is not sufficient. She always feels pressurized about money and food for the children. Her husband has complete control over her, "I don't get to go out. If I go out without asking him, he will not let me enter the house. I have to take his consent before going out, even if he is a drunkard."

Sexual coercion—Sexual coercion is defined as "the act of forcing (or attempting to force) another individual through violence, threats, verbal insistence, deception, cultural expectations or economic circumstances to engage in sexual behavior against his/her will. The touchstone of coercion is an individual women's lack of choice to pursue other options without severe social, or physical consequences."(Heise, 1995)

An analysis of the 240 interviews revealed the following about women's responses to sexual intercourse with their husbands.

Table 1: Women's responses to sexual intercourse initiated by husbands (n = 240)

Don't want and can't speak out	026
Don't want and husband does not listen	024
Forced intercourse	003
Don't want and husband understands	054
No information	133

Some of the responses which illustrates the first category of "don't want sex and cannot speak out" are as follows:

"When my husband tells me he wants to have relations, I cannot say no to him. He has got me by marriage. When my parents have given me in marriage to him, how can I tell him not to have relations? I get scared to tell him", - Maya

Maya appears to have internalised the societal diktats about marriage. Marriage is a contract in which a woman passes from parental care to the custody of the husband. He is supposed to provide for her, and look after her, and she has to keep her side of the contract by servicing his needs.

Another example of internalisation of society's norms is reflected in Sheila's views: "Men have more sexual desires than women.... One sees this all the time in movies, that the man is forcing the woman.... A husband has a right to sex and to say 'no' to him is out of the question."

Infertile women are more vulnerable, as guilt of not having a child makes them think that they have no right to deny their husband sex, as having a child and sex are believed to be the only two purposes of marrying. Mamta, a woman with infertility, is tormented by the guilt of not giving her husband a child. Her husband appears to use her guilt as a weakness, and forces himself on her.

"Even if I do not wish and he wishes, then he does it (has sex). I say (no), but he doesn't listen. Sometimes I am in trouble, I don't feel like (it). If I refuse, he gets angry, and abuses me. Then I have to be ready. I always think that I eat what he gives, he has given whatever I wear, then how can I go against his will? I do not even have a child of my own. On what basis can I go against his wishes?"

Men appear to have several ways of getting women to submit to non-consensual sex. As Nisha said, "If we don't want and we say no, he will rooth jayega (sulk)." Sulking and making a scene is a common way of getting the wife to submit. Voicing doubts about a woman's sexual fidelity is yet another way of having a woman give in. Kanta has a prolapsed uterus and experiences pain during intercourse. Her response to our question, - "Why do you keep sambandh (have a intercourse) when you suffer so much" - was typical. She said:

"What could I do? He is a man, matlab (which means) will he listen? Even after telling him, he grudgingly gives in. But if this is what I have tell him every time, how long will he keep quiet? There were misunderstandings and quarrels in the house. He sometimes felt that I had some other relationship outside (of this marriage), ... If we have to stay in the family, we have to stay according to their rules and wishes, isn't it?"

Verbal and physical abuse were also ways by which men got their wives to submit to unwanted sex. Krishna says that her husband gets very annoyed when she says 'no'. "He beats me like a dog, kicks me with his feet and forces me." Madhavi said: "He doesn't listen. Sometimes he gets up to beat me. He has to keep quiet because of the children. But sometimes when I am alone, I cannot control him." Ganga said: "My husband wanted to have sex after a month and a quarter of my delivery. I refused, because I felt that my stitches were still tender. So he beat me up." There are situations, however, where women are able to assert themselves. One such illustration of strength and assertiveness is Kavita. She described how her husband would drink and then want to have sex. "I told him that if he stopped drinking, then we would have relations."

Sushma's way of getting out of unwanted sex is by saying, " 'I am not feeling well,' then he doesn't bother me." It appears as though 'I am not well' is a major protective strategy that women use when they do not want to have sex. This is something that they can get away with, perhaps because of their husband's concern for their health.

Sexual coercion and reproductive health symptoms—How do men and women negotiate sexual relations when the wife has reproductive health symptoms? The picture is quite mixed. In spite of having problems, most women cannot say 'no' to sex because they feel that when husbands have got them in marriage they have the right to use their bodies as and when they desire. Gita said, "When it pains, I don't (usually) tell him. But when I cannot bear it, I'm forced to tell him. He says, 'If it pains, what can I do.' He still has it!"

Pushpa has a prolapsed uterus. She feels that her uterus comes out when she coughs, and after intercourse. In spite of these problems, she feels that she cannot say 'no' to her husband.

In most cases, women do not tell their partners about the pain, or troublesome symptoms that they have. They said in their interviews that they definitely did not wish to have sex when such symptoms were present, not only because it was troublesome or painful but also because they feared that their husbands would get their infection. As Madhavi said:

Madhavi: "We have fights over keeping sexual relations."

Interviewer: "Well, do you then have intercourse or not?"

Madhavi: "Yes. I do not want to have intercourse with my husband because I fear that if I am suffering from anything he should also not get infected."

Interviewer: "Does he listen to you?"

Madhavi: "He does not…Sometimes he gets up to beat me…"

Kaushalaya, during one of the groups meetings, spoke about sexual relations during her health problems. There seems to be two fears linked to the refusal of having sex. One is the fear that the husband would go to another woman and desert her. This in turn appears to be directly related to the second fear of the economic control or power that the man has over his wife. Kaushalaya said:

"Man does not agree to keep away when the wife has health problems. The wife may have tension and go away to her mother's home. But he can't live (without sex). He will come after her like a dog, or if, the wife is not around, there's always the side bazaar. He'll go there and catch AIDS. We try and persuade them not to go here or there. We warn: 'If you go, you will die, not I.' But if he dies, we will have trouble. Our suhaag will ujro (we will become widows). What will I do with four children? Beg? So even if it (sex) is difficult for me, let it be. Take what you want from me, but stay the way I want you to."

A number of other women mentioned about the fear of their husbands 'going out' as a reason for submitting to their unwanted sexual advances.

"During white discharge, sambandh is regular. You can't say anything about it (sex). We never can say about gents…If we don't give (sex) to them, they may find it outside."

Some women also described instances when the men either stopped having sex or reduced the frequency when they told them about their pain or infection. Mamta described her situation as follows:

"I feel as if I have suj (inflammation, swelling) at the lagviche jagya… Then we do not have sambandh. My husband is good…He agrees."

Discussion

These narratives indicate that there are a significant number of women who are forced into having sex with their partners even when they have symptoms of reproductive health problems. The reason why they submit to unwanted sex appears to range from internalised societal values of a woman's subordinate position in the institution of marriage, and their perceived obligations in the marriage contract, to fear of physical violence if they resist, and discomfort at having the man sulk around the house and create scenes. The data from these in-depth interviews indicate that sexual coercion is a small slice of violence that these women experience in their marital relations. The narratives also include descriptions of other kinds of violence, beating, and physical and verbal abuse that the women face in these relationships.

One can expect women to under report sexual coercion and violence at the hands of their husbands. It is also known that women tend to under-report sexual violence, both because forced sex by husbands or intimate partners is not perceived as violence, and because the element of shame and other factors inhibit them from admitting it (Jejeebhoy, 1997). As we had mentioned earlier, this data is drawn from a limited sample of those who sought services from the BMC's health care facilities. Data from community-based studies (which would include users and non-users) would possibly reveal that the problem of gender violence is much larger than what we see through a small section of our data.

What then are the implications for action? Strategies to combat violence must address not only the immediate health needs of battered women, but also the root causes of violence— unequal gender relations and the way these relations reinforce women's powerlessness. We know that many women contact health services only when they need assistance for a reproductive health concern, and there is evidence that abuse increases during and after pregnancy, or because of disputes over family planning. For these reasons, reproductive health services, such as antenatal clinics, maternity services and family planning services must be particularly alert to the possibilities of gender violence among their patients. Gynaecology clinics and STD clinics must also address the issues of sexual practices, especially forced sex. Counselling of partners, where necessary, must become a routine practice. In our study several women mentioned how the doctors' talking to their husbands about restraining from sexual intercourse, strengthened their own position in negotiating unwanted sex.

At the same time community education efforts directed towards adolescents, women, men, and family elders, must forcefully convey the need for gender equity and respect for women's rights - generally including their right to be free from violence. People also need to be made aware of the various means - legal, social supports and health care - available to women for protecting themselves against violence.

There is also a need to highlight the likely consequences of domestic violence on women's lives and health, and on the lives of the infants that they bear. The aim should be to reverse the social attitudes and beliefs that legitimise male violence, and the promotion of responsible sexual and gender attitudes among men. Efforts must promote women's understanding of their strategic needs and empower them to resist abuse.

Including violence against women as a health agenda has various implications on the roles of health care providers. The community health worker, who is closest to the women in the community, will have as her task, (a) organizing women around the issue of violence, (b) identifying legal and social support agencies in the neighbourhood where women could be referred. The community health worker, as a link person between the woman and the health care system, can also provide valuable information to the doctors and nurses about the violence inflicted on the client. Since the community health volunteer (CHV) lives in the community and understands the cultural mores, she can be a credible vehicle for the educational efforts directed at adolescents and men on the reconstruction of masculinity and femininity.

Male health workers are the second level health functionaries who have a key role to play in addressing men on the issues of violence against women, and transforming the notions of masculinity and male sexuality from the currently accepted social norms to the more gender-equitable constructions. The role of the male health worker has not been given much importance till now, it is time that this role is recognized, and thought be given to how male health workers can be prepared and equipped to become role models for men in the community.

And finally, doctors and nurses need to address violence during their consultations. Assessment of all forms of violence against women should take place for all women entering the health care system. A thorough assessment gathers information on physical, emotional and sexual trauma from violence, risk for further abuse, cultural background and beliefs, perceptions of woman's relationships with others, and the woman's stated needs. Women should be asked directly if they have been, or are currently in an abusive relationship, either as a child or as an adult. They should also be asked if they have ever been forced into sex that they did not wish to participate in. Shame and fear often make disclosures difficult. Verbal acknowledgement of the seriousness of the situation, and emotional and physical support; assist women in talking about past or current circumstances. After the assessment, the interventions should be decided on the principle of helping the woman to make decisions and take control of her life.

To conclude, guidelines and protocols should be developed to assist physicians and other health staff to address the issue of partner violence. Gender-based violence should be included in the basic and postgraduate training of health practitioners.

22

Hearing the Unsaid : Sexuality and Violence

Shalini

Whether one is intrigued about how menstrual periods happen, or worried about the effects of masturbation on health, or else furious about a stranger having flashed in public—people need assurance and knowledge in certain things. People need to be heard, want someone to listen to and validate their feelings, need accurate information, and need help to explore various options that are available in a specific situation. So very often people find themselves unable to get all these at the same time; one need is sacrificed at the cost of another. A determination to change this for the better is what has led to the birth of TARSHI.

TARSHI is an NGO that runs a telephone helpline to give information, counselling and referrals on reproductive and sexual health services. TARSHI attempts to help women and men live lives of dignity and freedom from fear, infection, and reproductive and sexual ill health. The helpline services are confidential and preserve the anonymity of the callers so they feel comfortable enough to ask questions of personal concern. The helpline is operated by trained counsellors and supervised by a qualified clinical psychologist. In less than three years of TARSHI's existence, we have received more than 28,000 calls from women, men, and children in the age range of 10 to 70+ years. The helpline is advertised as being especially for women, but is available to men also. Queries are answered, concerns aired, complicated feelings discussed and worked through, on the phone.

Most of the people who call on the helpline want to get some basic information about their bodies and/or the normal processes thereof. A number of times, however, the caller starts by asking for facts, but then as the call proceeds, the conversation unravels the caller's deeper concerns. These concerns are about the caller's emotional relationships with significant others, or about the appropriateness of one's feelings, attitudes or behaviours. Some callers question the prevailing social system and its basis. Often these concerns are related to violence and abuse.

Sexuality is an arena where the imbalance of power is manifest. Any such manifestation that is to the detriment of another person is violent and oppressive, regardless of the form it takes. The forms, of course, as we all know, are many, ranging from a leering look to a poke in a bus, to the most gruesome forms of battering and sexual assault.

A woman's consent is often either assumed or considered unimportant. For example, some men think that while travelling in a bus if they get an erection against a woman co-passenger, it is all right for them to indulge themselves and engage in what technically is termed 'frotteurism'. Some men, in this sort of a situation may even believe that the woman is also enjoying the act, and unless she raises an alarm, he presumes she does not object to his behaviour. At times, when she protests, it is considered pretence on her part in order to appear socially 'modest'.

Similarly, a lot of premarital sex ends up as date rape as the man assumes that if the woman has agreed to go out with him on a date or has kissed him, having sex with her is his prerogative. It seems as if it is difficult for some men to think that a woman can draw her own boundaries, and they may even think that if she has crossed the Laxman Rekha once, she had better be prepared for abduction, assault, a test by fire, and exile. Popular beliefs like "a woman actually means 'yes' when she says 'no'" also plays a crucial role in perpetuating violence against women. Other commonly held notions like "it is a man's job to initiate and perform sex and woman's duty is to provide him with her body" also contribute to women's abuse. These could be some of the reasons, again, for date-rape as well as marital-rape.

The question that arises is that if rape takes place in close relationships, then why is it happening? Who defines what is abuse? Who is abusing? Who is being abused? Why don't they stop it? Most abusers, perhaps do not label their actions as abusive, in fact, they often see what they do as their right, or else give some justification for it (she asked for it, she dressed provocatively, etc). One caller justified his abusing a child by saying that "Woh to barfi ka tukda hai, muh mein paani to aayega hi." (She is like a delectable sweet; of course one's mouth will water.)

Another man called to ask if it was safe for him to have sex with his wife when she was menstruating. After he got the information on safer sex, he went on to ask why his wife screamed and shouted while having sex during periods. On being asked what he thought could be the reason, he said that she never liked to have sex during periods and complained of pain and discomfort if they did have it on those days. But he added, "Since I have the urge to have sex I have to forcibly do it with her." It is evident that he thought it was his prerogative to have his "conjugal rights" fulfilled by his wife whether she wanted it or not.

Studies conducted across cultures show that most sexual abuse and violence are perpetrated by acquaintances, relatives, friends and others in position of power, and trusted by the survivor. It could be a 'doting' uncle, a 'caring' father, a 'trusted' neighbour, or a spouse—just to name a few. When we think of rape, what is it that comes to mind? Do we ever think that a commercial sex worker can be raped? Can a wife be raped? Can a girlfriend be molested? If penile penetration in the vagina is a requirement of rape, then what do we call the shoving of a bottle into a woman? A father placing his penis on his daughter's genitals every night without penetrating? A young boy going through forced anal sex?

Fear of rape is something that all women live with all their lives— no matter how old, how attractive, no matter where, or when. The numerous ways in which this fear is instilled in women's minds are insidious, and include their being expected to reach home before dark, to dress in a certain way and not dress in certain other ways, to not mix with boys, etc. How often do we hear things like, "She must have been raped because she dresses provocatively"; or "She was molested by her boyfriend's friend as she roams around with boys" All these words convey that if a woman goes through sexual abuse, it is because she asked for it. These also strengthen the myth that rape is a sexual act, whereas, in fact, it is an assertion/act of power.

Many women callers go through the dilemma of deciding on whether or not to have intercourse with their boyfriends before marriage. If it is the boyfriend who proposes or initiates sex and she refuses, she has to often go through the guilt of hurting his feelings, and of being blamed for not trusting him enough. On the other hand, if she decides to oblige him to pre-empt his sulking and/or emotional blackmail, she is often accused of being an easy lay in a half-joking manner, and is also quizzed on her virginity and her sexual history. If the woman wants to have sex with him she may not be able to initiate it, as she is scared of being perceived as "too fast". As far as sexual initiation is concerned, for men it is in the nature of an adventure, though, of course, accompanied by anxiety and peer pressure. Whereas for most women it is in the nature of an ordeal because of the stories (and in many cases the actuality) of pain and bleeding; that first-time intercourse carry.

Even married women complain about being called a "slut" on having initiated sex with their spouse. At the same time if the wife never initiates sex and/ or does not show enough interest, she is readily labelled "frigid". Husbands often threaten wives to be either more or less sexy, or else they would go astray.

The kind of sexual activities that people engage in also gives interesting insights into the power dynamics at play. Oral sex, as we all know, can be performed on both women and men. Fellatio, however, is practiced much more frequently than cunnilingus, as reported both by men and women callers. This difference is again not one of the first queries of the callers, and often comes across in the course of the conversation. The caller may start by asking about the possibilities of pregnancy or physical harm with fellatio. Having answered their queries, if we probe further and ask them whether they also engage in cunnilingus, many are surprised that something like that was also possible. Some others express serious concern about their disgust with cunnilingus. A woman caller who started with asking about the possible reason for her lack of sexual satisfaction, put it very aptly, "Madam, ye husband log mukh maithun karne main vishwas nahin rakhte, sirf karvane main vishwas rakhte hain" (These husbands don't believe in performing oral sex on their wives, but believe in having it performed on themselves) please check the translation.

What constitutes a "real sexual act" is conceptualised in male-centred terms and revolves around the penis. No wonder so many of our callers find it unbelievable that women too can masturbate and enjoy it even though they do not have a penis. The same phallo-centric thinking is what makes it easier for many people to believe that men can have sex with men, but find it rather difficult to accept that two women too can have sex with each other. It comes as a shock to them that for some people the penis might be redundant.

Another woman wanted to know about the possibility of tightening her vagina by washing it with alum water on the wedding night, as she did not want her husband to know that she was not a virgin. The premium that is placed on a woman's virginity also implies that she is seen as some sort of a commodity that can be legitimately used by only the owner of that property. Having had sex with a boyfriend before marriage, a woman often goes to extreme limits to keep even a seemingly meaningless relationship going, as she believes that she has to spend her whole life with the man to whom she has 'lost her virginity'. Some men, who have themselves had sex before marriage, call us up to ask how they could find out their wife's virginity status. Some even go to the extent of taking the wife to a doctor for a virginity test if she does not bleed on the first night. Men's premarital sex is excused, or is even eulogized as necessary for experience; their extramarital liaisons too are excused, as "he is a man after all."

The impending pressure to marry, that a woman almost invariably faces as soon as she reaches a "marriageable age", makes her go through various conflicts. She has to strive to be a perfect-looking, well-educated, modern, and yet a tradition-bound woman. Each of these eligibility criteria, however, has a catch. Let us take just looks as an example. We see that, surprisingly, almost all women are made to feel uncomfortable about their bodies—whether it is their breasts being too big or too small, or their complexion not being right, or their being too fat or too thin, or else their facial features not being perfect.

The culture that always makes it the woman's responsibility to adjust in order to keep the marriage happy (for everyone else) prevents her form sharing her agony and anger with anyone. Men are never called upon to adjust. The custom of kanyadaan contributes to this. Kanyadaan is more a way of thinking than a ritual. It always keeps a woman aware that her parents' role in her life ended with their having 'donated' her to this man, and that if she cannot keep her marriage, there is no place for her in her parental home.

Violence against women begins, as we all know, even before a girl is born (in the form of female foeticide). Language has an interesting role to play in nurturing the patriarchal psyche. One of the typical queries we get is that "Abhi tak ladka nahin hua" (We do not have a son as yet), when they in fact meant that they did not have a child as yet. It then should not come as a surprise if a daughter's birth is not celebrated, if her health and education are not attended to as thoroughly as that of the son's. Is it not only too obvious that a woman's self-esteem and sense of worth are hampered? Due to years, decades, centuries and generations of violence against her dignity as a human being, she also starts seeing this degradation of her as being her due.

It is not with much ease that a woman can share the anger and agony that she experiences because of the numerous ways she is abused by the 'culture' - taken in the broadest sense of the term. As a young girl she is given caring jobs, like taking care of her younger siblings. Her interpersonal behaviour is frequently under observation. She is always made aware that she has to go to a house where she will be responsible for everyone else's happiness, and her worth will depend upon their happiness. If she then finds herself in an abusive marriage as an adult, she typically feels that she either doesn't cook well enough, or look good enough, or is not good-natured enough, and so on. Only rarely is it possible for her to see that what is happening is wrong and is not her fault. She either does not comprehend it as violence, or is unable to articulate it, or has no one to listen to her and understand her, without blaming her. There is no way in which violence can satisfactorily be explained away. For many women, this insidious and subtle violence results in making them feel hopeless and grey about things; nothing excites them, including sex.

The most common responses to a woman's complaints of violence are to either disbelieve her account, or refuse to take cognisance of the seriousness of the problem, or to find out what she has done to bring on the violence, or ask to modify her behaviour by "adjusting", in short, to explain away what happened. Violence can never be explained away. What an abused person needs is an attentive ear, someone to help her sort out and validate her feelings, and to help her think of the options she has in her specific situation.

Very often we hear that there are laws in this country that deal with gender violence but for various reasons the problem lies in their implementation. One of them is said to be that a woman does not even report violence. But when we say that, are we not putting the responsibility of stopping the violence on the abused person herself? If she does report to the law or the police, are her requirements of being heard, being treated with respect, being understood… met? What we at TARSHI try to do is help her with these needs, as we feel that these are more primary and immediate than legal justice. She is also so used to not being heard that she often does not even speak. It then becomes a difficult, and yet important task, to listen to what she feels but is not able to articulate, to hear what has not yet been said.

For example, an English-speaking professional, says that her husband beats her up brutally, but actually he is a nice person, so even when she goes away to her parents' place, she says, "I miss him and want to go back." On being asked if she felt comfortable at her parents' place, she said she did not. On occasions she had to go to her parents' place after being abused by him, but has always gone back to him. Taking the conversation further, the caller and the counsellor both discovered that it was not so much a matter of going back to him as of having nowhere else to go. Even when there may be another safe place to go to, an abused person needs to discover this as a viable option for herself. She cannot be bullied or coaxed into this. She has first to be heard, and only then can she hear what the 'helper' is saying.

At TARSHI, abuse is not the primary focus but is a thread that runs through our work. Anything that lowers a person's dignity is abuse, whether it is shame around one's sexuality or restriction of individual freedom, or rape. By our efforts to provide information and counselling, we hope to enhance people's abilities to make choices. Through counselling, we help individuals express, articulate and thereby get in touch with their feelings, at the pace they are comfortable with. Once they know what they are feeling, the decisions they take will come from within them, and will be clearer. A listening ear begins to give them a sense of autonomy and dignity, and enables them to develop a sense of identity, which is the first step towards a violence-free and abuse-free life. The goal of attaining a life free of violence and abuse may seem closer for some than for others, but one wonders if there is anyone who has actually reached there.

23

The Role of the Examining Doctor in Sexual Assault : A Critique of the Management of Rape and Sexual Assault in Women and Girl Childern

Lalitha D'Souza

On September 21, 1997, an employee of the Observation Home for Children, in Umerkhadi, Mumbai, allegedly raped an unnamed deaf-mute 13-year-old girl with the label Billa Number 31.. A fact-finding team appointed by the Forum Against Child Sexual Exploitation investigated aspects of the case, including the medical procedure followed immediately after the crime was discovered (Kulkarni, Jesani, D'Souza, 1997).

Following an order by the superintendent of the Observation Home the honorary doctor examined the victim and recorded the clinical findings in four lines. This medical record was inconclusive, simply because it was incomplete. To start with, there was neither a record of a history taken by the doctor, nor was a call sent out for an expert interpreter, considering that the girl was not only deaf-mute, she had no sign language. Other than sealing the clothes she was wearing, no forensic specimens were taken, nor were any investigations ordered. Records showed that there was no attempt to re-examine the girl for developing signs of injuries and infection after an interval of a few days. The doctor failed to offer first-contact counselling, or treatment for the psycho-social trauma caused to the confused child. There was no record of whether she had been offered the prophylaxis for pregnancy and STD. Lastly, and most importantly, the doctor did not examine the assailant, who was on the premises at the time.

The case of Billa Number 31, a case of custodial sexual intercourse, and clearly a cognisable criminal offence, will probably be lost for lack of methodical and lucid initial medical examination of the survivor and of the accused.

A middle-aged resident of a slum in Mumbai was gang raped and physically assaulted late one night by a group of young men. When she reported to the casualty department of the nearest municipal general hospital with physical injuries. She was given a cursory examination by the resident doctor and prescribed painkillers. For lack of alertness and awareness the doctor failed even to elicit the history of sexual assault, let alone proceed with a detailed examination and collection of specimens. Although she told her story to the nurse, this was not conveyed to the doctor. As a result, precious evidence was lost.

A tribal girl in a remote village was raped by a police constable at the police station where she had been called along with her husband for interrogation (Mathura Rape Case, Supreme Court, 1979). The medical examination, made 20 hours after the incident, revealed no injury on her person, only an old tear of the hymen. Based on the medical findings, the Supreme Court held that sexual intercourse in this case did not amount to rape. Later, after much public protest, the case was reviewed and it was recognised that this was a case of criminal custodial sexual intercourse.

In another case of a young tribal girl from Gujarat, the medical examination was conducted and recorded in such a way that the doctors shielded the policemen and issued false certificates (Amnesty International, 1988).

We have examined the records of a number of cases and found that besides recording obvious signs of injuries and opining on the state of the hymen and the laxity of the vaginal walls, there are no detailed notes available. Examinations are at best cursory, and only a limited number of specimens are collected for forensic analysis. Doctors take on the duty of forensic examination, neglecting the psychosocial and physical impact on the woman or girl. The doctor-patient relationship is ignored, and sadly, ethics are forgotten.

When forensic specialists are available the examination is likely to be more detailed and the notes comprehensive. But how many women in India, who are violated in this manner, have the benefit of a doctor trained in the methods of examination of sexual assault, collection of specimens, production of neatly written records and expert appearances in court? It is true that in our country specialists are available in the cities. But we have seen ((Kulkarni, Jesani, D'Souza, 1997) that even in a city, which has a fair share of forensic scientists and gynaecologists, women may be examined by doctors with no training or apprenticeship in the methods to be followed in these difficult cases. Further, what of the hundreds of sexually assaulted women and girl children in remote rural areas who are dependent for their examination and treatment on doctors with no specialisation whatsoever?

What is the level of training of fresh medical graduates? More than merely a criminal justice issue, rape and sexual assault are now being recognised as an issue of health and human rights (Koss, Heise and Russo, 1994). Women who have been sexually assaulted experience "the threat of physical injury and death, threats to their sexual integrity, their personal control, their worthiness as human beings and to their confidence and trust in others" (Sohlberg, 1993). More often than not the first person that the violated women and girls meet is the doctor, therefore the doctor's management of the case is crucial to the way they recover, and the course that the case takes in court.

The Scale of the Problem

In 1995 there were 13,754 cases of rape reported from all over India. Almost one-third of these numbers were minor girls, 747 of them being below the age of 10 years. In the same year 28,475 cases of molestation were reported (National Crime Research Bureau, 1997).

But the reported cases are only the tip of the iceberg. In a country like ours where great value is placed on virginity, the reporting of cases is speculated to be much lower than actual incidence. Statistics show that the conviction rates of completed trials for rape are 30.5 per cent. Although no study has been conducted into the conviction rates of sexual offences, a high value is placed on a thorough and lucid report of the medical examination conducted soon after the crime. Initial medical examination and collection of forensic evidence is important because of the ethereal nature of evidences. Medical evidence is the most important component of evidentiary material that is considered in a prosecution for rape (Bakshi P. M. 1994).

Often, due to incomplete records and unnecessary comments, medical information is misused by law enforcing agencies, and in the courts. This leads to secondary victimisation of the woman, compounding the psycho-social impact of the event.

The Textbook Attitudes

We will now proceed to highlight the attitudes and discrepancies reflected in the standard textbooks of forensic medicine (Reddy. 1997; Nandy, 1995; Franklin, 1988; Knight, 1997) from which the undergraduate learns, and to which the novice refers.

There is a preoccupation with virginity. One forensic textbook shows sketches of no less than 15 different types of hymen. There is no doubt that in the examination of a sexually abused girl child, or a woman with no previous sexual experience, findings in relation to the hymen are important. But these are never isolated findings and they must be corroborated with other clinical findings of the genitalia. Specialists are inclined to use measuring cones or hymenoscopes to judge the size of the hymeneal opening. The result is that in every case of rape and sexual assault, a description of the hymen is recorded, even in the case of women who have borne several children. This seems to have been interpreted as the key to examination. In many instances, not much else is mentioned, as in the case of Billa Number 31. Only one textbook states that with regard to sexual intercourse, full penetration is not necessary and rupture of the hymen is irrelevant. Definite findings in the hymen should be recorded, such as signs of recent injury to the hymen - which could be bleeding, tearing and oedema.

The text usually goes on to advise the 'finger test' to distinguish between virgins and sexually habituated women. Some even urge the examiner to mention the findings in women who masturbate. "It is absolutely necessary to note the distensibility of the vaginal orifice in the number of fingers passing through the vagina without any difficulty," one author advises.

We argue that virginity, or the lack of it, need have no bearing on the case of a sexually assaulted woman. In fact these findings are misinterpreted in the courts and invariably used to humiliate the woman and discredit her evidence. Some textbooks warn against false allegations of sexual assault. Others assume that every charge made by a woman should be treated with suspicion. Secondary victimisation originating from such attitudes and comments is one of the reasons why women are reluctant to report cases of rape and abuse.

Another problem with the procedure lies in the matter of consent and willingness. It has been written that it is necessary to prove that the resistance offered by the woman was up to her utmost capability, and that every means, such as shouting, crying, biting and beating had been tried to prevent successful completion of the act. The majority of cases of sexual abuse are perpetrated by relatives and persons known to minor girls within their homes. A study of rape cases in New Delhi in 1996 showed that 89 per cent of the assailants were relatives, friends or neighbours (Deol, 1996).

In a section on medico-legal questions, one author poses the question: Can a healthy female be violated against her will? The assumption is that a working-class woman will succeed in frustrating the attempts at violation while a woman belonging to the middle or rich class will be rendered powerless from fright or exhaustion. No matter what socio-economic class a woman belongs to, she is not conditioned to react in an aggressive or loud manner, especially when the attack takes place inside the home by men who are powerful in the household or community. How, then, can one expect to prove, in a medico-legal record, that she did her utmost to resist an attempt at assault?

Further, there appears to be a misunderstanding with terms defined in textbooks and the same interpreted in the courts. Penetration, it is explained, is sufficient to constitute the offence of rape. The text goes on to clarify that the slightest penetration of the penis with the vulva, such as minimal passage of the glans between the labia, is sufficient to constitute sexual intercourse. One author writes that full erection, intermission (sic) and ejaculation are not essential. However, experience in our courts shows that this definition is not accepted as evidence of sexual intercourse. There is insistence on proof of complete penile penetration to charge for the crime of rape. Anything less is termed indecent assault.

There are records of cases where minor girls have been penetrated with fingers or objects, which have resulted in severe injuries to the internal genitalia. The examination of a girl child is a delicate task, beginning with eliciting the history to the examination of the genitalia. Only one author mentions the necessity of application of local anaesthetic and the need to take a decision of examining the child under light anaesthesia.

Contradictory statements regarding potency of the assailant have been noted in the text. Whereas authors of all the textbooks state that erection, penetration and ejaculation are not necessary to prove sexual intercourse, there is an emphasis on the potency of the assailant. Is the accused physically capable to perform the act? While questioning the usefulness of this test, it is pointed out that none of the textbooks guide the doctor on how to go about establishing the man's potency.

Lastly, let us consider the welfare of the patient as the over-riding consideration for the doctor. In certain circumstances, medical evidence may go against a case. In this situation it is preferable to depend on the statement of the woman and the circumstantial evidence. Nowhere is it mentioned in textbooks published in this country that the examining doctor should make an assessment of the case and advise the woman or the guardian of the girl child whether to take up and follow through with legal action.

Only a brief mention is made of the need to recognise the psycho-social impact of sexual assault, and the need to treat the immediate and long-term medical and psychological needs of the woman.

The Role of the Doctor

Considering the human rights and health aspects there is a need to clearly define the role of the doctor in a case of sexual assault. As we have pointed out earlier, the doctor is the first safe contact in most cases. Experts in forensic medicine have argued that in cases of criminal offences, in examining the victim and the offender the doctor acts on behalf of the state (CEHAT 1998). There is a need to emphasise here that the doctor is primarily a carer. The doctor-patient relationship, medical ethics experts point out, overrules all else and must be maintained in the best interests of the patient.

There are three well-defined roles a doctor must perform. First, and most importantly, the doctor must offer medical curative treatment, primary level counselling and referral for physical and psychological sequelae of the assault. For the traumatised woman it is most important for the doctor to believe her story and to offer comfort. Second, doctors can provide important evidence of the crime and help judges understand the physical and mental condition of the woman. Last, reports produced by doctors can serve to corroborate the woman's story and enhance her credibility (Physicians for Human Rights, 1991).

While a doctor has a special role in collecting forensic evidence and later being able to give that evidence in court, he/she is expected to treat the victim with kindness. Until everyone who works with victims can relate to the deep emotional pain and vulnerability and fear that results from rape, we won't have victims well cared for (The Lancet, 1998, MFC et. al., 1990).

The Patient Must Come First

It is true that in the preparation of medico-legal reports doctors have a public duty to perform. However, in carrying out this duty, medical ethics suggest that the mental and physical health of the patient should be the over-riding consideration. The doctor patient relationship dominates and informs every decision the doctor takes in regard to the survivor. Forensic scientists claim that in a situation where a doctor is completing a medico-legal investigation the woman is not regarded as a patient. We differ from this view, holding that the woman remains a patient just as the doctor remains a carer. A doctor ought to act only in the patient's best interests when proceeding with the investigation. Any information, such as, irrelevant past sexual history, or physical findings suggestive of active sexual activity, should be given with utmost caution.

Besides the more obvious sexually transmitted disease and fear of pregnancy as a result of rape, it is now well recognised that there is acute and long-term psycho-social trauma inflicted on the woman. A doctor may not abandon the patient after the medico-legal investigation without ensuring that medical care of these conditions is handed over to someone competent. Long term care of the psycho-social impact of the incident must be ensured.

A doctor must act independently or in collaboration with other doctors, and not be dictated to or influenced by political or administrative doctrines or pressures.

The Declaration of Geneva, amended by the World Medical Association in 1983, clearly states, "The health of my patients will be my first consideration. I will not permit considerations of religion, nationality, race, politics or social standing to intervene between my duty and my patients."

Conclusion

The examination of a survivor of sexual assault, is, at the best of times, a difficult and thankless task for the doctor. Experience and training is often inadequate and the conditions for examination are difficult. Textbooks on forensic medicine appear to be an inadequate guide for the novice. In remote rural and tribal areas there may be no proper examination table, no gloves, no female attendant and no vaginal speculum—let alone a sterile one.

23

Health Professionals in the Reporting on Domestic Violence : Legislation and Guidelines in the USA

Helen E. Sheehan

Introduction

In the United States, by the late 1980s, violence of all types was identified not just as a matter of concern for law enforcement, but also as a public health issue - "an epidemic of violence". As a result, studies of the causes and effects of violence, reporting and tracking of violent incidents by legal agencies and hospitals, and statements on violence by health professional organisations have increased during the past 10 years. In this paper, I intend to focus on one aspect of violent behaviour in the US - family and domestic violence. This paper will define family and domestic violence, identify the persons affected by it, and highlight some issues in legislation with respect to reporting on domestic violence. The guidelines that health professionals follow in identifying victims of domestic/family violence incidents will be outlined.

History in the US

In American society, with social, religious and legal traditions that value independence, individualism, privacy, and property holding, the arenas in which domestic violence take place - the marital relationship, the family, and the home - have been viewed as places where the state did not have the right to intervene. In traditional Christian marriage vows, the wife agrees "to obey" her husband, the wife was viewed as property; in child rearing, "children were to be seen and not heard", and parents were told "spare the rod and spoil the child"; in terms of privacy "a man's home is his castle". Wives and children were viewed as dependents, bound to obey the father and head of the household. With such sentiments and traditions, justification for physical means of punishment to insure proper behaviour and obedience, was easily found.

The concept of family and domestic violence in the US, as presently defined and interpreted, has reached public and professional recognition only during the last 25 years. Early efforts to cope with domestic violence included opening of shelters/homes for battered women, developing profiles of characteristics of batters, and dispelling of myths about family violence (husbands don't do such things to their wives, if he did, "she deserved it" etc.)

Prior to the 1960s and 1970s, reluctance to intrude into family life, had resulted in limited and inconsistent use of laws and remedies against violence that applied in other, non-family situations.

Definitions and Types

Domestic and family violence "is defined as a systematic pattern of abusive behaviours occurring over a period of time, which may become more frequent and severe and are done for the purpose of control, domination, and/or coercion."

Three types of domestic and family violence have been identified in the US - spousal/partner abuse, child abuse (physical and sexual), and elder abuse. In the US, certain distinctions have developed with respect to reporting of abuse by health organisations and health professionals. These distinctions fall into the categories of mandatory (required) reporting versus non-mandatory reporting.

For cases of child abuse and elder abuse, reporting of injuries by health professionals and agencies is mandatory. The rationale in these cases is that the child, who is underage, is not competent to understand what has happened, or to make the decision to report; hence, it is the responsibility of the professional individuals who first encounter and identify the abuse to report it. For the elderly, assumption of incompetence is also made, usually based on identification of physical and mental infirmities. In the case of spousal abuse, assumptions of competence on the part of the adult (usually the wife, since women are more likely to be victims of abuse than men) lead to interpretations in law that the adult victim should make the decision to report the abuse. The health professional is not penalised for not reporting the abuse. On the contrary he/she can be penalised for not reporting child and elder abuse cases.

Problems in Identifying Cases of Abuse

In the US, there are now guidelines available for identifying cases of abuse based on physical and psychological evidence. However, the complexity of factors involved in abuse, the location and manner in which cases may come to the attention of health care professionals, the intricacies of treating the victim, the ethical questions in sorting out problems of competency of the victim, and the requirements of legal reports and possible court appearances demand extraordinary commitment from medical personnel to become involved in these cases. For example, victims may arrive in an emergency room suffering from severe trauma from a beating or may visit a doctor's clinic with a minor bruise or burn, yet both may be victims of violence. The victim may deny the abuse, especially if the perpetrator brings them for treatment and denies harming the individual. In the case of an elderly person, their dependence on their son or daughter for day-to-day care may make them fearful to acknowledge abuse. Middle and upper class victims of violence may deny their victimisation to the family physician, who may also be a family friend. Cases of child abuse often prove complicated to document since the child may be too young to speak on to accurately describe what happened. Legal reports require added paperwork; court appearances to testify about abuse cases require time.

Guidelines for Identifying Victims of Family and Domestic Violence

Efforts to standardise guidelines to identify abuse victims have taken place over the past 25 years leading to protocols utilised by individual health practitioners, clinics, and hospitals. Speciality professional organisations (such as those of paediatricians and geriatricians), national medical organisations (such as the American Medical Association) and health administrative bodies (such as the Joint Commission on Accreditation of Health care Organisation (JCAHO), as well as state-level departments of health and family services have all developed guidelines for spousal, child, and elderly abuse identification and reporting. The emphasis in the recommendations is on the health care organisation providing a multi-disciplinary approach to the identification, treatment and follow-up of suspected abuse cases. Everyone in the health care organisation, from the admitting clerk to the treating physician and nurse to the social worker, are viewed as key players in the complex process. (See the guidelines for identifying physical and other signs of abuse of the adult victim and the elderly victim given at the end of the paper).

While advances have been made in identifying and verifying signs of spousal and child abuse, experts argue that agreement on and understanding about elder abuse is just developing - "Granny-bashing", as it is often called, is hard to identify because the elderly, often in a frail physical state and a confused mental state, may well be expected to fall and fracture a leg or hip; yet, the fall and fracture could also be the outcome of physical abuse. Likewise, claims of money or valuables being stolen could be attributed to mental confusion rather than to exploitative behaviour of a caregiver. Hence, the need to question both the elderly person and his/her caregivers to determine the context of the incident is emphasised.

Legislation Regarding Domestic and Family Violence

In the US, requirements by states for injury reporting originated in the need to identify suspected criminals who might be at a health care facility for treatment of an injury suffered in connection with a criminal act, such as, a robbery, or someone injured by a specific type of weapon—a knife or a gun, for example. As the social pressure for appropriate treatment and referral of domestic violence grew, these injury-reporting laws became the umbrella for domestic violence cases as well. However, concerns about the differing needs of domestic violence victims from those of persons suffering from injuries from other causes have led to re-evaluation of reporting requirements.

In domestic violence cases, there is concern for privacy and protection of the victim; in the US as well there is concern for privacy of medical information for all patients. The US Congress, therefore, drew up model legislation (the Uniform Healthcare Information Act) "to provide uniform laws, rules, and procedures governing the use and disclosure of health care information." Disclosure of patient information may be made to federal, state, or local law enforcement authorities if required by law (injury-reporting laws require such disclosure). In order to overcome the multiple concerns about the adult victim of domestic violence (including need for privacy and protection from fear of reprisal from the perpetrator) health care professionals are advised to obtain the victim's/patient's consent for disclosure. In this way legal requirements are met, but the confidence of the patient/victim in health care and legal procedures can be maintained.

Conclusion

As with many issues in modern society, the handling and resolution of these issues often falls under the purview of professionals, especially those in medicine and law. Cases of violence in the family once viewed as a private family concern in the US; are now regularly monitored by health care providers. Over the past 25 years, with growing awareness of the serious physical and psychological consequences of abuse for families, the need for effective and compassionate medical treatment, and legal resolution, has grown. It is clear that the health care professional, although perhaps reluctant to take on the role, is most frequently the first and most trustworthy individual the victim may encounter. Hence, clear comprehension and development of the medical, legal, and ethical requirements of the health care professional's role in family and domestic violence is called for. Each society will have to develop the regulatory framework in which medical care for these victims can be provided. In this paper, selected highlights in these developments in the US have been presented.

Guidelines

Domestic Violence: A Guide for Health Care Professionals, March 1990

(Source: State of New Jersey, Department of Community Affairs, Division on Women, Domestic Violence Prevention Programme)

1. Guidelines for Identifying Adult Victims of Domestic Violence

(a) Patient admits to physical abuse.

(b) Patient presents with unexplained bruises, lacerations, fractures or multiple injuries in various stages of healing. Common sites of injury for domestic violence victims are face, head, chest, breasts, abdomen and genitalia. Pregnant victims typically show injuries to the breasts, abdomen, and genitalia.

(c) Extent or type of injury is inconsistent with the explanation the patient gives.

(d) Substantial delay occurs between time of injury and presentation for treatment.

(e) Patient describes in a "hesitant, embarrassed or evasive manner the circumstances surrounding the alleged "accident".

(f) Patient repeatedly uses emergency room or other medical

services. Medical history reveals many—accidents," or contains remarks by nurse or physician indicating that previous injuries were of suspicious origin. Note that victims beaten at regular intervals may come to a hospital with psychosomatic or emotional complaints just before they expect another beating.

(g) No substantiating physical evidence supports complaints.

(h) Family member or friend accompanies patient and insists on staying close to the patient, appears to be under the influence of alcohol, or drugs, or otherwise exhibits suspicious behaviour.

(i) Untreated old injuries.

(j) A history of prior physical abuse, either as victim or witness.

(k) Injuries on area of body normally covered by clothing.

(l) Injuries consistent with burns, whip-like bruises, etc.

(m) Complaints of chronic pain.

(n) Psychiatric, alcohol or drug abuse history in patient or spouse.

(o) Depression regarding family situation, e.g. not wanting to return home, fear for safety of children.

(p) Previous suicide gestures or attempts.

2.Guidelines for Identifying Victims of Elderly Abuse

(a) Physical abuse, which includes beating, burning, rough physical handling and sexual abuse.

(b) Neglect, which includes wilful and unwilful neglect, abandonment, confinement, malnutrition, starvation, over and under-medication, and withholding of personal medical care. This type of abuse is the most common but is often difficult to detect.

(c) Psychological abuse, which includes verbal harassment, threats, enforced physical and emotional isolation, and any behaviour that causes fear in the elderly. This often occurs simultaneously with physical abuse and neglect.

(d) Financial abuse, which includes withholding or stealing funds, and the exploitation of personal property.

Part-VI
Violence Against Women : Women in Protitution

25

Combating Violence on Women in Prostitution : The Sangram Experience

Meena Sheshu

Women in prostitution constitute a community that bears, and will continue to bear, the greatest impact of the HIV epidemic in India. Communities of women in prostitution continue to suffer high levels of infection and re-infection; the children born to them may be infected by HIV. Apart from the stigma already attached to their work, society has further marginalised them by erroneously labelling them as core transmitters of HIV infection. Women in prostitution are but links in the broad network of HIV transmission.

HIV and Women

In 1990, the World Health Organisation estimated that out of the 8 to 10 million people infected with HIV in the world, over 3 million were women. And the rate of infection is increasing rapidly. It is also estimated that the number of infected women will equal, and overtake the number of men. Women are being infected at a younger age than men—on an average almost 10-15 years earlier than men.

There is no doubt that women are more susceptible to HIV infection and that they are more likely to be infected by a single act of intercourse with a partner who is infected by a sexually transmitted infection. Women's social vulnerability to HIV-the fact that women are likely to have male partners who do not protect themselves from the virus - is heightened by a range of physiological factors, which make it easier for a man to transmit HIV to a woman than vice versa. There is now scientific evidence that the reproductive tract of younger women is a poor barrier to the virus. This further increases the vulnerability of girls compared either with that of boys or older women.

The Myth of Women in Prostitution as Vectors of Spread of HIV

There is little doubt that women in general, and specifically women in prostitution, are more vulnerable to HIV infection rather than being core transmitters of the virus. Yet, as explained in the 1995-96 document titled, "Societal violence on women and children in prostitution," by the National Commission on Women, the most common depiction of women in prostitution in India today is as "pool of HIV/AIDS carriers". There has been a systematic promotion of this myth. The past actions since 1986 in HIV-related response in India are a reflection of this.

Unfortunately, despite all the arguments in favour of shifting the emphasis from a targeted approach, the Phase II AIDS Control Project Implementation Plan, 1999-2004, of the Maharashtra State AIDS Control Society (pp. 18-20) states emphatically that "commercial sex workers form a high transmitter core group for transmission of HIV infection to others. The truckers, migrant workers, STD clinic attendees, and street children constitute the bridge population for spreading this infection to the general community."

Using Anderson's formula for the spread of any infectious disease, the estimates of HIV transmission to the general community have been made. However, only brothel-based sex workers in Maharashtra have been used in this model as the data on the number of non-brothel-based sex workers, the number of their clients per day, and the rate of HIV prevalence among them is not available. According to available information there are at least 90,000 brothel-based sex workers (excluding Mumbai) of which 45,000 (50 per cent) are presumed to be HIV infected. It is also presumed that these sex workers entertain three clients everyday for about 250 days in a year. The transmission efficiency of the HIV infection ranges between 0.1 per cent and 0.01 per cent. The model does not account for STD-prevalence rates and condom-use rates among sex workers, as they are not available. It also does not consider repeat visits by a client.

Whether such models, or the calculation made through them, are applicable or not is the immediate concern of this paper. There seems to be a systematic and single-minded attempt to prove that women in prostitution are core transmitters of the HIV virus, and to project them as irresponsible members of society who "spread infections".

In fact, Nina Lopez argues in her article, "Resisting the virus of repression: Prostitute women and AIDS" (edited by her for the English Collective of Prostitutes), "Prostitute women have traditionally insisted on clients wearing condom, and so may well be less at risk then other women. Contrary to popular stereotype, we also have regular health checks for sexually transmitted diseases, again more often than other people whose livelihoods may not be so dependent on being free of venereal disease and who are less aware that their lover/partners/husband may be passing on illnesses gathered while wandering. Although clients are usually not keen on wearing condoms, most proposals for compulsory testing have targeted workingwomen rather than clients. Men go to prostitute women out of choice. If they really believe that workingwomen are 'spreading AIDS', they should insist on wearing condoms or abstain."

Framework

Several non-governmental organisations (NGOs) had, for years maintained that "it was not possible to work with women in prostitution and only a client-directed strategy would be effective in preventing the spread of the epidemic." But recent experiences from India and other countries has shown that women in prostitution are, in fact, very reliable enforcers of condom usage, for their own self-protection. Self-protection through self-organisation could ensure that an effective HIV and STD prevention programme be implemented with relatively less expense and sophistication than that required in several other HIV prevention programmes. Central to the programme would be the inclusion of women as effective educators of their clients. Thus, with marginal increases of both costs and efforts, a large proportion of the 'at risk' male population could be reached.

The project was designed with three underlying assumptions. First, that a sustained response to the epidemic was required. Second, that the community of women in prostitution would have to be able to build in the capacity to respond. And third, that for sustainability to be achieved, the women would need to organise themselves. Consequently, SANGRAM was formed with the primary objective of working exclusively with women. The organisation is committed to the feminist approach and its women-centred intervention is geared towards the benefit of women and children. SANGRAM has been working with the understanding that women in prostitution are most vulnerable to the HIV epidemic, and they will bear the greatest impact of the epidemic. They will suffer high levels of infection and re-infection, bear HIV-infected children, and be further alienated due to lack of counselling and care. SANGRAM also rejects the perception that women in prostitution are vectors of the spread of the virus. They are but links in the broad network of heterosexual transmission. Yet, they are destined to suffer from a harsh societal backlash that stems from the erroneous belief that these women are the core transmitters of the HIV infection.

Major Strategies used

Condom enforcement by women in prostitution— Women in prostitution are emerging as the best educators of their male clients. Using skills developed over hundreds of years to deal with men of all hues, they have evolved unparalleled negotiation strategies to enforce condom use in their unrelenting battle against HIV.

Commitment to the peer process— SANGRAM is committed to the peer model and has tried to develop this process in the communities of women in prostitution. This has emanated from the belief that 'outsiders' cannot hope to reach out effectively to all the members of the community. SANGRAM, while working with women in prostitution, has evolved certain norms in selecting peers. These are: (a) peer should necessarily be 'women in business', not brothel owners; (b) geographical basis is ideal for selection because proximity of the peer helps in condom distribution as well as to help the peer become friendly with the girls under her jurisdiction. The role of the peer includes: (1) distribution of condoms, (2) training and counseling of women who are unable to enforce condom use, (3) identification of STDs, and of women who are sick and in need of medical treatment and other services, and (4) liaison between the NGO and the community, and in some cases, with the brothel owner/pimp/malak (long-term lover).

Collectivisation— A sustained response to the epidemic is possible only if the women in the communities are united and organised. Empowerment through self-organisation is one of the primary objectives of SANGRAM. This has been followed by the formation of registered prostitute collectives, which would then take over the programme from SANGRAM. Thus the goals of the project were establishing contact with local communities of women, aiding the self-organization of women in prostitution, developing peer education STDs and HIV, providing condoms and accessing STD services.

The Policy which Shaped the Process

Participatory planning— The experience of the past has proved the invalidity of traditional organisation systems with their hierarchy of health care workers, centralised planning and a mode of authoritarian control over recipient communities. Thus, the SANGRAM project made the target community's participation and self-direction essential towards the efficacy of the programme. Action is based on community responses to problems wherein the community seeks the best possible solution. For example, the Nirodh Project Staff do not distribute the condom, Nirodh, directly to the women. Each community has evolved various techniques with the help of the peers to ensure the sustained supply of condoms and its distribution.

Core-group building—Small groups are formed within the community, which then seek a representative voice, and which develop negotiating skills to deal with existing power structures. These core groups are well informed and trained about the epidemic and are able to assess the impact of the virus on the entire community. A conscious attempt to mobilise control structures (for example, criminals, petty politicians, brothel owners, pimps, traffickers), to garner community support for an effective and sustained response to the epidemic, has been a priority in the services provided by the staff.

Self-organisation—In order to maintain a sustained response to the epidemic, the community of women is helped to be self-reliant by organising themselves in a collective. Self-organisation through collectivisation is a primary objective of the programme staff. Training programmes were undertaken to enable the withdrawal of the NGO from the community, except in roles of advocacy, after completion of the project and the formation of the collective. The formation of two prostitute collectives called VAMP (Veshya AIDS Muquabala Parishad) in Sangli and Solapur has been one of the major achievements.

Participatory evaluation—A process of reflection, coupled with a participatory process of systematic data collection, analysis and feedback, has been undertaken. Its primary objective is to empower the community, and fortify its ability to face challenges through joint efforts.

Networking— Women in prostitution have a very strong network of their own. We, at SANGRAM, have found these networks very effective to pass on messages of condom-enforcement and client-negotiation strategies. Nonetheless, the project has tried to reach out to NGOs working in the field of women in prostitution to promote safer sex as a necessity.

Information dissemination—The major information sharing system used by the project staff is the network that exists within communities of women in prostitution. Since these women are constantly on the move within the various communities, for professional and personal reasons, the dissemination of knowledge about the programme, and its very expansion, is made possible. This traditional, indigenous network proves to be more effective than information systems like mainstream media and professional educators from outside the communities.

Documentation—Publications about women in prostitution often lack ethical consent contracts. As a group/organisation, every attempt and care is exerted to provide a climate that is humane and compassionate. Infinite care is taken not to pass moral and value judgements that reduce the self-esteem of the members of the community. Thus, elaborate care is taken, and mechanisms evolved, to ensure an ethical climate.

The informed consent of women in prostitution who are being subjected to collection of data of any kind is ensured. The anonymity of individual members is at all times maintained. Stringent consent procedures are undertaken, when details regarding women are referred to in any forum. The nature of information requested, purpose of collection, use of this data, and option of not responding, is explained before consent is obtained. Thus, as a policy, publication of any kind is avoided as much as possible.

STD treatment/service provision—Women in prostitution are unlikely to attend government-run hospitals due to a history of discrimination and ill treatment. But increasing HIV-related illness has now forced them to explore the services provided by the government. SANGRAM has tried to bridge the gap between services provided by the government and those needed by the women in the community. The effort has been to try and minimise the trauma of being diagnosed HIV positive, and help affected women and their families to access such services.

Liaison with official institutions—Since the government has the largest infrastructure and health care system, every effort is made to ensure efficient provision of available services. A sustained campaign is being undertaken to try and provide equitable, accessible, and affordable treatment and care for HIV-positive women. This is, as yet, a distant dream.

Advocacy with control structures— Control structures within the community have to be dealt with for the success of any programme. With HIV, it has been relatively easy because the effect of the virus on the community is clearly visible. Besides, the persons 'in control' have close relatives who are ill, or they themselves are ill. Consequently, there is relatively less sense of isolation from their families or other women who work alongside them. Over the years, this factor has made it very easy to negotiate with such persons and smoothen out the process of intervention.

Impact of the Programme

The participatory approach has been a major strength of the programme. Planning and decision-making are done in a participatory manner and the focus, throughout, has been a major strength of the programme implementation.

As outsiders to the community, SANGRAM faced many ethical and critical issues ranging from discrimination and stigmatisation to consent procedures, values of the mainstream, personal convictions which would sometimes be at variance with community beliefs (for instance, the issue of superstition within the Devadasi system). However, the community and SANGRAM have together been able to transcend these conflicts. This was made possible because of the commitment of the peer workers and SANGRAM to each other, and to the policies of the programme within which all interventions were planned.

The 'peer-based programme' has had a definite impact on the community. For one, it has succeeded in creating a strong sense of loyalty to and 'ownership' of the programme. SANGRAM's policy, all along, has been to boost leadership from within the community, and to achieve this end it has intentionally played a passive role to facilitate effective and sustainable solutions.

This is not to imply that there is no conflict between SANGRAM and the community, and that everything always goes according to plan. There have been major conflicts between (a) the community and SANGRAM, (b) within SANGRAM, and (c) within the community. But these have been brought out into the open and discussed, however painful the process may be.

The space for such discussion could be created due to the participatory approach and has helped to sharpen the focus on several issues. For instance, we began working with the idea that the epidemic posed a grave danger to women from the mainstream, and the possibility of HIV infection to them through their husbands—the 'clients' of women in prostitution—was a major concern. However, as the work began, it became very clear that this 'hidden agenda' was violating a basic right that SANGRAM's major concern should be for them, not so much through them to other sections of the population.

This issue threw up a lot of painful truths regarding SANGRAM itself, its impetus to undertake the programme, and the short-sightedness and immaturity with which the programme was initially conceived. It was this change in our perception that influenced and shaped the entire programme. Women in prostitution became the focus—that was the community most vulnerable to the virus, not core transmitters of HIV. The use of the peer programme with a participatory approach thus achieved a new direction.

Women in prostitution have evolved new methods of dealing with individual clients, very often in a unique manner. They are able to gauge the different ways clients resist condom use and circumvent it in effective ways. They have developed different strategies for adolescents, young and old men, further dividing them into rural and urban categories ('Prem se' with love).

The women became the best educators of their male clients, for instance picking up, from the NGO, the most gruesome pictorial images of sexually transmitted infections (STIs) to show to their clients. They not only effectively disseminated information regarding STIs and HIV to their male clients, but also used immense intelligence to fight the virus that was threatening to take over their lives. However, the women have consistently rejected traditional information, education and communication material.

In most cases the women used condoms, except in instances where they were dis-empowered. Even then, they never gave up without putting up a fight. They also shied away from health camps as they found the mainstream methods useless and intimidating, as far as tackling their health problems were concerned. Besides, they rarely attended mobile clinics as these clinics associate most of their medical problems with STDs, and therefore preferred to go to private medical practitioners. Also, this became a legitimate 'time out' for the women.

Major Accomplishments

- The distribution and enforcement of condoms 3,50,000 pieces every month among 4,000 women over a radius of 250 kms among women in prostitution who work from brothels, are on the highways, from lodges, from regular truck stops, are on the street and occasionally, from the folk theatre.
- Drop in STD's and the number of abortions—this is anecdotal information. The peers claim that women who routinely took a

penicillin shot on the fifth day of the menstrual period, have stopped this practice completely due to the drop in STIs.

- Peers called 'arogya sevikas' have been trained to take over the programme from the NGO and to offer counseling, access to effective STD services, care for HIV-positive women, ensure 100 per cent condom use with paying clients, and help the community to cope with crisis situations.
- Counsellors among the women were trained for a year and the training included simplified pre- and post-test counselling techniques, home-based and community-based care, accessing medical care from the civil/government-run hospitals; women and health, and STD/AIDS symptoms and medical treatment.
- The formation of two collectives called VAMP in Sangli and Solapur. These collectives will continue the process of condom distribution and enforcement in the communities, run prevention and care programmes, awareness programmes of new entrants, and interact with control and official structures.
- In Solapur the collective has also decided that they will not allow child prostitution in their brothels.

Constraints and Problems

- The enforcement of 100 per cent condom usage in all sexual encounters is still a far-off goal. Lovers, pimps, male brothel owners, and the police, still have the power to refuse the use of condoms. These women fight an unrelenting battle every night to enforce condom use..
- Another drawback is the poor quality of condoms supplied. Some of the companies, e.g., LARCOM and TTK Biomed, used to supply sub-standard condoms. This became a bone of contention between SANGRAM and the Government of Maharashtra. SANGRAM wrote to the union and state-level ministries of health, sent out letters of protests to all the authorities concerned, and even enclosed two defective condoms per letter to prove its point. Yet, the condom quality has not greatly improved.
- No professional counselling services are available to women and their families.

- HIV positive women suffer immense discrimination in public hospitals. They are very often denied treatment, and families are asked to 'allow' the women to die because they have tested positive. This is a tough and ongoing battle with the medical establishment.
- Medical and paramedical staff at government hospitals have; a callous, indifferent and often humiliating attitude towards these women. They are often asked about sexual positions, whether the client had enjoyed himself, and other such irrelevant questions, which are embarrassing for them.
- The timings of the health services are highly unsuitable.
- Primary health centres (PHCs) are ill equipped for STD treatment, and services are available only at district headquarters. There are usually no provisions for the supply of drugs prescribed by doctors.
- The practice of uninformed testing for HIV/AIDS is commonly directed against these sex workers.
- They are usually infected by a male-customer who refuses to use a condom (Nirodh) but no one questions the men.
- Doctors, and sometimes social workers, force these women to have free sex with them.
- In some places after frequent meetings and NGO intervention, health services have improved considerably.
- The staff at health centre are irregular in their attendance with long periods of absence.
- Free supplies of Nirodh are not available in Goa, and in some places supplies have been discontinued.
- In some places they are forced to pay 'donations' to employer benefit schemes, ranging from Rs. 2 to Rs. 5, before the case paper or the outpatient slips are handed over to them.
- Doctors often refuse to treat and admit these women because they say they are carriers of HIV, and this has scared many of them.
- In many centres doctors make the peons and attendants carry out the physical examination and even the treatment of these women.

- Going to public health centers and hospitals is like a big disease for them.
- If services cannot be kept open in the afternoon the present timing should be extended to 1 p.m.

Conclusion

"As people who experience violence as part of our daily life, we are being increasingly penalised in a society that is trying to order and control our lifestyles. As women in prostitution, we protest against a society that forces on us the violence of a judgmental attitude." (A statement of women prostitution, from VAMP and SANGRAM, Sangli).

Creating a myth that women in prostitution are core transmitters of HIV serves the purpose of 'prostitution bashers' who revel in the moral and judgmental attitude that perpetuates the myth that AIDS is an 'impure disease' that afflicts immoral and evil persons. The net result is to further target the women which increases public and police violence against them, decreases their ability to assert themselves; allows customers to demand and force unsafe sex upon them; and increases the rate of HIV infection among women, customers and the families of the customers.

Responses by women in prostitution to this epidemic encapsulate this menace that is more threatening than HIV itself. Firstly, the suggestion by some policemen and politicians that legalised brothels and/or mandatory AIDS testing may be a solution to AIDS is little short of a proposal for concentration camps where 'contaminated' prostitute women will be locked away from the rest of the community to be visited sporadically by 'clean citizens' whom they will service. This will also set a dangerous precedent as any section of the population, which may be labelled 'high risk', could be interned. Secondly, the singling out of gays/ prostitutes/ junkies has created a new climate of hostility against prostitute women. It has lent legitimacy and credibility to anyone who wants to commit violence against prostitutes, whether they are from the police, the courts, the clients, social workers, counsellors, and even relatives. They all feel justified in their actions against prostitutes, as they are under the notion that they are contributing to a good cause. Ironically, despite this 'do-good' attitude there have been more rapes, more robberies, more blackmail, more neighbourhood spying and harassment. This anti-prostitute and anti-gay epidemic has been equally dangerous to our health as AIDS itself.

The perception of sex workers as 'vectors' of HIV transmission results in: (a) ignoring the fact that any population that has penetrative sex is at risk, unless a barrier like Nirodh (condom) is used during sex, (b) creating a false sense of security, and the failure to adopt safer sex practices by other groups, (c) increasing discrimination and violence against these women, causing further failure in their efforts to protect themselves from sex-related infectious and diseases, (d) failure to plan for appropriate services and responses to the HIV cpidemic.

26

Promoting Violence in the Name of Protecion

Smarajit Jana
Suparna Ghosh

Sex work as an occupation puts the sex workers at significant risk of personal violence from clients, from persons in economic control of the trade, and at times, from the police and persons in authority on grounds of enforcement of law. Children of sex workers and minors in the sex industry, also run the risk of physical and emotional abuse, because of the environment in which they are brought up and because of the stigma attached to the community. Systematic attempts to protect sex workers from police violence, from those in authority, by NGOs, researchers, etc., have proved futile in most of the cases. On the contrary, it seems that their efforts to protect sex workers from violence ends up in promoting violence. Three categories of such efforts are discussed in this paper.

(1) Preventing Minors from Entering into the Trade

With the apparent intention of preventing minors from entering the sex trade, police officials conduct raids in red light areas, pick up both adults and minors, and put them in the lock up. Once a woman, be she an adult or a minor, enters this profession or somehow gets involved in the sex trade, then she is neither accepted back by her relatives nor by the society; norms of which have been laid by the upper echelons of society. Since these women generally belong to the lower socio-economic strata, their relatives do not have the economic, political or moral strength to fight society. And the social taboos and stigma attached to this profession creates an environment that miserably fails to unite these girls with their families again.

Investigations were made in several cases (about a dozen) in the recent past where the police, after arresting minors, put them in custody, and through judicial proceedings they landed up in designated remand homes, where the living conditions were even worse than those in the red light areas. Ultimately these minors had no other alternative but to resettle back in the red light areas which they had left, thereby completing a full circle. The amount of humiliation, mistreatment and torture they receive in the process is unbelievable. In fact, the "exercise of violence" on them (social, familial or otherwise) forces them to enter this profession, and this is a result of a mindset, which gets strengthened by the same societal process in the name of "rescue and rehabilitation." These concepts have been designed by another category of "actors" through state patronage, who probably share common societal values, which, in fact, disrespect and derecognise the rights of individuals as a result of the awful power and position they hold in society. In the process it is not only the minors, but also the majors who are treated in the same manner, just to remind them that they have no moral right to enjoy basic human rights and dignity. Several NGOs have evinced keen interest or have got involved in this "rescuing" operation in collaboration with the police, having little or no knowledge about the structure and function of the sex trade scenario and its inner contradictions.

But in the process they serve the interest of another group of exploiters, and their actions strengthen state-mediated violence, which in turn justifies the social contradictions and the rule of a patriarchal society. However, in the recent past, sex workers' efforts to organise themselves, their struggle against the oppressors and exploiters, their demands for a self regulatory board, the repealment of that offensive act—the Immoral Traffic Prevention Act, and recognition of sex trade as a profession, etc, has percolated into the society. This was observed in the opinion poll conducted during the Calcutta Book Fair -98 where visitors to the book fair were found to be aware of sex workers' plight.

The opinion poll was conducted among 525 persons, out of which 78.7 per cent were males and 21.3 per cent females. 66.10 per cent of the male respondents belonged to the age group of 20-40 years, followed by the above 40 years age group. A similar trend in the age groups was observed among the female respondents. Regarding educational status, it was found that 39.62 per cent of the respondents were graduates and 26.7 per cent were technically qualified persons. Regarding the occupational status, a majority of them were service holders (31.4 per cent), followed by professionals like doctors, lawyers, engineers, journalists (21.9 per cent), who in turn were followed by students (18.1 per cent) and businessmen (15.8 per cent).

When asked if they had any idea about the nature of torture that sex workers had to face, only 54.7 per cent of the respondents said they knew about it. However, at the same time, about 77 per cent of the respondents expressed their eagerness to know more about sex workers. Regarding the reasons behind clients going to sex workers, 60.38 per cent of the respondents believed that physical urge was the main reason, 42.85 per cent said that both mental and physical urge was the reason, and 40.38 per cent said that it was curiosity about sex that brought men to the sex workers.

On the query about the reasons behind police raids, 72.76 per cent of respondents said that the police conducted raids primarily to earn money, and only 17.7 per cent believed that police conducted raids to nab goondas and anti-social elements.

When asked if they had heard about sex workers' organisation, 74.7 per cent of the respondents said they knew about it; 70.72 per cent had a positive attitude towards sex workers, and 57.21 per cent expressed their willingness to help them.

(2) Preventing HIV transmission through Research

In early 1996, an NGO in Central Kolkata experimented with an untested AIDS vaccine on hapless sex workers without prior permission from the government, thus diluting any demarcation between experimental animals kept in the laboratory and sex workers. This may be an extreme case, but as a rule rather than an exception, researchers carry out studies on HIV sero-surveillance and behavioural practices of sex workers without fulfilling ethical guidelines, and at times use force and even resort to physical coercion with the "objective to contain the spread of STDs and HIV/ AIDS" among sex workers. Researchers, in their zeal, hardly take cognisance of the basic rights of an individual and established policies of ethical review process. Sex workers, in their eyes, do not qualify as human beings with rights and dignity. In most cases, the media and the academia either prefer to keep silent or support the process overtly or covertly.

(3) Evicting Sex Workers to Prevent Growth of Sex Trade

Some segment of the society view sex work from the moral point of view and believe in the abolition of red light areas, and rehabilitation of sex workers as effective measures to prevent the growth of sex trade. During the era of AIDS control, it has become the endeavour of some vested interests, who in collusion with powerful lobbies and real estate agents, and with the tacit support of government authorities, try to manipulate people's sentiment and exploit the moral stance of the society to throw sex workers out of their homes and clear localities of red light areas, thus depriving sex workers of their livelihood. In all these instances, it has been observed that government policies and written codes of conduct have hardly helped in protecting the rights and livelihood of these under-privileged sections of the society.

Lessons Learnt

The perpetual violence within the sex trade cannot be altered, or the individual sex worker cannot be protected from its onslaught unless her social and legal status, and her working environment is transformed. Her vulnerability as defined by her powerlessness within and outside the trade, the stigma attached to the profession, and the historical bondage, which predetermines her status and position, makes her susceptible to social exploitation. It is also true of any newly designed programme meant to support sex workers, since the planners decide and chalk out plans based on their social values and concepts without taking into consideration the sex workers' perception of their profession.

Once in the profession, a sex worker continues to remain in it for various reasons. The most prominent of these being social ostracism, which does not allow her to live with dignity wherever she chooses to live and opt for some other occupation for her survival. A sex worker, then, cannot be truly "rescued and rehabilitated", and forcing her to take up some other profession which she does not want to, will be a violation of her human rights and her right to self-determination.

It can only be done through the empowerment of sex workers, not only at the individual level but also at the community level, and through the active participation of their community.

This issue has neither been addressed by social workers or by human rights activists. It is more likely that the "social exclusion process" that prevents sex workers from taking part in the social and political arena, also blinds human rights groups from looking into their issues. This exclusion process also holds back the sex workers, the most marginalised group of women in society, from raising their voices against violence and decide their own destiny.

27

Violence as Experienced by Sex Workers in Thiruvanathapuram

A. K. Jayasree

Women engaged in sex trade rarely enter the mainstream of society, including the health care system. They were excluded from feminist discourses also. Now there is space for them to interact with people in the mainstream, as a result of AIDS prevention activities. Their voice is much more audible to health care providers and social workers. But the existing medical care system and its analytical devices, are not sensitive enough to address the complex issues related to them.

Violence against sex workers must be considered as a form of gender-related violence. Domestic violence experienced by housewives, and all forms of violence towards sex workers, are different manifestations of a common etiopathology of a patriarchal society. But the nature, extent and severity vary from group to group. The present diagnostic tools used in medical care are not sensitive and specific enough to diagnose, cure, and prevent these problems. They are not properly addressed by the existing welfare system too. The complexities of gender violence in general, and sex worker's problems in particular, are to be approached in culture-specific contexts and a gender-sensitive manner. For this, the present outlook of the health care profession and health care services has to be changed. In this paper, an attempt is made to understand the complexities of the violence experienced by sex workers. This understanding is a prerequisite to evolve strategies to sensitise the system.

Interaction with the Community

A systematic data collection from the community of sex workers is difficult and unethical when they are left amidst the miseries of life. Hence, a study of the community has to be integrated with intervention. Intervention includes opening up a dialogue with them, creating a conducive environment for sharing their thoughts and problems, providing medical aid, providing legal aid, facilitating the process of organising themselves, etc. As a first step, rapport building was initiated through informal talks. That was difficult, because most of these women did not have their own houses. They could be met at pick-up points where they were busy searching clients. Building trust with them was also difficult. In such circumstances, the maximum effort was put to collect as much information as possible along with an intervention programme. The sampling followed the snowball technique. 37 women gave very short interviews during which questions were asked about violence. Content analysis of the notes, prepared after each interview and informal talk, was done. Detailed case histories of a few women were taken. The period of this interaction lasted from June to October 1998.

From informal talks and short interviews the following observations were made.

Almost all women (sex workers) have experienced some form of violence in the last one-month. (Prevalence of domestic violence among housewives varies from 13 to 70 per cent in different communities in India) The prevalence is more among sex workers.

- The form of violence produces injuries varying from mild to severe.
- Violence is inflicted by state agencies like police, clients, pimps; agents involved in legal action, caretakers, family members, co-workers, and life partners
- About 40 per cent of women engage in deliberate self-harm.
- The forms of violence include beating, kicking, throttling, and cutting with sharp weapons, rape, and so on.
- Most of the women who attempt self-harm cut their wrists or neck with a blade or swallow blades.
- Sometimes this violence ends in death.
- Accidents occurring at the time of running away from the police are very common. Sometimes they deliberately harm themselves to escape from police arrest.

The following case histories reveal the complex situation under which women experience violence, and how it is reinforced through different institutions and individuals so that the value system, favourable to the privileged gender and communities, is maintained in society.

Case History 1

Syama was encouraged to talk about her history at a drop-in centre through free association. She was under the effect of alcohol, but was coherent in speech and oriented to time and space. She was very co-operative in sharing her past. She was well known for repeated suicide attempts. Two days before the interview, she was admitted to the hospital after she bled severely from the wound inflicted on herself in the forearm. The very next day, she absconded from the hospital and was out on the street. Social workers at the centre say that she often came to the centre with bleeding wounds. She never took her medicines, but asked for a tonic from the visiting doctor. Talking with the centre's doctor for a few minutes made her happy.

With all these facts in mind, I spoke to her. She said that she had married 8 years ago and was 20 then. Her husband was a daily-wage labourer. She spent the initial months with him without many problems. Gradually, he started beating her, even for minor reasons. Her in-laws were staying with her, and they too contributed to this. Years passed by. She bore two sons.

She was often asked by her husband to get money from her house. Since her parents were very poor and she failed obey this diktat his brutality increased. At the same time she noticed that he had begun having a relationship with another woman. She could not bear this and started quarrelling with him. This made him more aggressive and the degree of violence increased. She was losing her moral strength and started thinking about suicide. One day after being severely beaten, she jumped into a well. Somebody saved her. This incident had no effect on her husband or other relatives. Their attitudes did not change.

Gradually, her husband stopped giving her money. And as if that was not enough, her in-laws harassed her too. She couldn't leave them because she didn't have any other means of looking after the children. During this period, she was craving for love. She wanted to be loved by someone. Helplessness and hopelessness led her to further suicide attempts. During this period she confided in some women of the village. One of them told her that there was someone who loved her and wanted to talk to her. They went to the city one day, and her friend introduced her to this man. They spent some time in a lodge. Later she came to know that her friend had received money from this man to bring her to him. She was trapped. She could not go back to her house. She started living with the 'friend' and entered the sex trade.

Even now she hopes that someone would love her. However, at times she gets into severe depression and attempts suicide. Occasionally, she visits her children. Sometimes she falls in love with a client, but that finally ends up in a bitter experience. This is her side of her story, and this is what the others had to say. Her co-workers said, "Oh she is worthless. It is because of her that police take us into custody. Damn her!". Welfare officers in the prison said, " Syama can be managed only if she is severely punished. Otherwise it is very difficult. She harms herself". Police officers said, "She cannot be changed. She repeatedly attempts suicide, and often gets beaten by clients."

A few days after the interview, she was severely injured by a co-worker at the drop-in centre. The wounds were very deep and she screamed so loudly that people in the neighbourhood gathered around her and finally called the police. They tried to take her to the hospital, but she was uncooperative. This angered many of the people. Finally, she was taken to the casualty department of a tertiary hospital. All the wounds were stitched without local anaesthesia. Nobody was there to stay with her. As soon as the stitching was done, she left the hospital. The following day, she consumed some poisonous fruits and directly approached the police. She was arrested and sent to the prison.

The violence experienced by Syama can be approached in different ways. The conventional approaches are based on bio-medical, psychopathological, subcultural or motive-attribution theories. The victim may be blamed or the assailant will be justified. This case exemplifies the complexities and intricacies of violence and self-harm as constructed and propagated in patriarchal societies through various agencies, like the family, the state, the group and the individual.

It also shows that domestic violence is related to other forms of violence experienced by sex workers outside the family. The problem of dowry and wife beating are characteristics of the patriarchal Indian society. In Syama's case domestic violence has contributed to the construction of a negative self-image and a realisation of her helplessness which has resulted in this behaviour: easy susceptibility to violence, self-harm, provoking others, and harm even from her co-workers. The police and prison officers think that she can be controlled only by punishment. They warn others not to be with her. It is an indirect message to these women to obey social rules. Since she does not compromise, she becomes susceptible to more violence from others who think that she is a problem-creating woman.

This case shows how different agencies work to maintain the status quo of a male-dominated society. Neither the status of the wife nor that of a sex worker was the choice of Syama. In her given situation she was in search of her identity, which ended in futility and helplessness. From the confinement of family, she was transferred to another arena where once again she developed craved for friendship and love, again leading to despair. She realized that those were false values, which added to her negative self-image. Her co-workers hated her because she became a threat to them, when they were struggling to cope with state violence through compromise, or by accepting themselves as immoral. Health care givers want to dispose her as early as possible so that she does not 'pollute' the hospital environment, or they do not have to spend time in the court unnecessarily. She herself accepts her doings as that of a victim and wants to die, even though her ambivalent state brings her glimmer of hope.

To summarise, different sections of society have contribute to women's oppression, and to maintain the state's ideology on morality. All these factors should be taken into consideration when strategies for violence against women are discussed.

Case History 2

Vanaja shared her life experience while we walked together one evening. She was under tension because of a cold war with her partner, another woman called Deepti. They started living together after a ritual, "thalikettu", and have an idealised concept of romance. Even though these two women started an ideal life, one of them has taken the dominant role of a man. Deepti looks after financial matters, and psychically hurts her counterpart. But Vanaja earns money through sex work and Deepti looks after her daughter. Here certain roles of a man-woman relationship have been swapped. Somehow, Vanaja 'the woman' has to undergo physical violence at the hands of her partner. Since they have a comparatively stable, emotional relationship, and have a better financial set up, she does not suffer from violence from her co-workers. But she had some traumatic experiences with the police, and in one of which her hand was broken. She entered the sex trade as a revenge against her family members as they wanted to protect her uncle who had raped her and made her pregnant. Hence, she undergoes severe mental torture whenever she visits her family members. She cannot stay in her family. She chooses a life with Deepti, even though she is subjected to physical torture. She showed the scars on her neck and hands. Deepti also used to undergo self-harm.

In this case, the dominant partner subjects the woman who has taken the submissive role in the relationship to torture. The dominant-submissive relationship internalised by these women is a reflection of the societal values, though the relationship was entered into as a rebellion against an oppressive and sexually discriminating society. Since there is no movement in society to support them emotionally, or morally, the whole responsibility of the relationship is ascribed to the partners themselves. They have got into this relationship as a survival strategy; to establish mutual support and resist harassment from the stakeholders of sex trade, and from social pressures for conformity - either to the hegemonic culture of the society or to the subculture of the sex workers. Hence, the violent behaviour is not only due to interpersonal conflicts, but also determined by outside pressure.

These two cases demonstrate the varied nature of the violence experienced by sex workers, and of gender violence in general. For any preventive measure to be successful we need to look into the complexities of these issues, and therefore social institutions must be sensitised to it.

Conclusion

Domestic violence and violence experienced by sex workers in a gendered society are varied manifestations of the same etiopathology of a male-dominated ideology. Violence against women is practised in all institutions and towards all categories of women.

The frequency, prevalence, and severity of violence is more experienced by sex workers than by housewives.

The nature of violence inflicted upon sex workers is specific. This includes a greater amount of sexual violence, murder, and self-harm.

Violence on sex workers operates through various agencies, such as the police, clients, caretakers, family members, and sex workers themselves. Violence on sex workers and domestic violence can be abolished together because both are inter-related.

Cases of violence against women should be managed by a speciality of the medical system, since it requires special attention and gender-sensitive diagnostic tools. There should be counselling facilities too.

Women of different categories must organise themselves to resist violence. Different groups should mutually support each other to resist male-dominated, moralistic values.

All social institutions must interact with women's movements to reconstruct a new value system and an equitable social order.

Part-VII
Human Right and the State of Health Sector

28

Threat to People's Right to Life : ICU-ICCU Hospitals in Mumbai

Herat R. Parmar

Introduction

Unless I took a stand and did something about the plight of 'Critically ill patients' admitted in private ICU-ICCU hospitals in Mumbai I would be compromising my moral beliefs and perceptions of my professional responsibility. My conscience told me that I could no longer stand by and do nothing. The pathetic plight of this vulnerable class, deceived in the name of critical care, provided the impetus to study, analyse and present the results to show how the most fundamental human right - the right to life - is totally violated by these hospitals.

The phenomenal mushrooming of private ICU-ICCU hospitals- critical care hospitals-in Mumbai parallels with the commercialisation of the medical profession, and is fast devouring the ethics and morals of the profession. They are, in fact, 'death-traps', and do enormous harm to unsuspecting, critically ill patients. There are no standards - even the minimum - in the setting up of critical care units, which form part of private nursing homes, and which are all unregulated, unchecked and cater to almost 85 per cent of Mumbai. The aim of this study was to evaluate the data collected on the basis of a questionnaire and site visits. The analysis given here is, as it exists in the name of 'critical care'. The glaring deficiencies found in each and every unit, which relate to infrastructure, equipment, services offered, manpower, monitoring facilities, emergency care, procedures followed, qualification of specialists, qualification of duty doctors and nurses, the protocol of critical care, if any, and other basic elements to call them critical care units, are studied, analysed and presented.

The Objectives and Methodology of the Study

- To study the infrastructure, equipment, staffing and overall functioning.
- To examine the existence and/or non-existence of regulation by various bodies and the role of these bodies.

- To study the feasibility of improvements on the basis of a questionnaire.

The questionnaire was prepared on the basis of the study of standard critical care books and other literature. Visits to municipal hospitals, discussions with experts who are ethically and morally concerned, and are knowledgeable as well, were made. The help of specialists was taken for site visits.

In Mumbai four categories of ICU/ICCU hospitals are functioning: (1) The free government and municipal hospitals, (2) the highly subsidised charitable trust hospitals, (3) private trust and corporate hospital with the most modern super speciality wings, and with facilities for ideal critical care, but prohibitively costly, (4) the totally private ventures, undertaken singly or in partnership, usually by doctors of various qualifications and from different streams, or by businessmen with doctors on call. and charge heavily for the poor services.

This is the study of 40 private ICU/ICCU hospitals, randomly selected and belong to the last category.

Findings

These hospitals admit cases for critical care referred by family physicians, specialist practising in the area, owner-doctors admitting their cases, and at times, patients who directly come for emergency admissions. The doctor on duty, who is a non-allopath, examines the case. The specialist may or may not come to visit the patient, and orders treatment on the telephone to the non-allopath duty doctor. The specialists visit their cases once or twice a day, but round the clock critical care, monitoring, and assessment are left to non-allopathic duty doctors and unqualified nurses. The in charge and the specialist are the only qualified doctors in the premises, but are not always available, and in emergency situations this is risky.

The various specialists at these units are also attached to some other private ICU/ICCU hospitals or to some charitable, municipal or government hospital. Obviously, emergencies in these critical care units during the day or night will result in certain death due to the non-availability of the specialist on time. Specialists owning or managing these units have no special knowledge or training in critical care. They have expertise in their own field but know little about other streams and the likelihood of an associated system that may crop up during the course of the illness. Except for specialist attached to teaching institutions, knowledge of the recent advances is poor among the staff. These specialists, running from one hospital to another, have neither the time nor the inclination to advance their knowledge, nor there is the compulsion to do so. Critical care needs a holistic approach, and in the absence of an exposure to recent advances, and the narrow-minded approach of presenting symptoms of one's speciality only, result in misdiagnosis and wrong treatment, and even death. Often cases are admitted as ICU/ICCU cases, simply because the bed was vacant. The fear created in the mind of the patient due to such admission, itself causes avoidable panic. Nowhere the names and qualifications of the resident medical officers are displayed. The unsuspecting public recognises these doctors by their white apron and dangling stethoscopes, and believes them to be allopaths. The public has no way to find out or question their qualification - their names are not on the display board or on the apron. These RMOs are non-allopaths, namely homoeopaths and ayurveds, not trained in allopathic medicines. They have acquired practical training by the hit and miss method.

These non-allopath RMOs even start the treatment on their own. They give D.C. shocks in the event of an emergency, and in the absence of a specialist who invariably is never present in the premises most of the time. The specialist is subsequently informed if the patient survives, and visits at his convenience. In all the 40 hospitals surveyed, the doctors on duty were either homoeopaths or ayurveds, with an occasional allopath or specialist present for a short duration.

The availability of a qualified doctor round the clock, is the most basic requirement of any critical care unit. Critical care needs to be closely watched and monitored by qualified specialist. Hence, at least three specialists on an eight-hour duty should be available at any unit for it to be called a 'critical care unit'. The owner or specialist or administrator in-charge violates the basic right of the critically-ill patient by delegating duty to non-allopath doctors for round-the-clock management, and himself visits various other hospitals, at times travelling 10-20 km from his place. In the case of an emergency he can never make it to the hospital, because of thc distance. The most common indication for an emergency admission is heart failure. In fact, most of the ICU/ICCU hospitals were put up for prompt attention to such cases, but in the present scenario distance has become a deterrent for prompt treatment.

Medico-legal cases were refused admission in most units. The main reason for refusal was monetary, rather than the need for such admission. Medically, the average stay for ICCU care is 2-3 days, and for ICU care three or more days. However, in most ICU/ICCUs the criterion for stay was monetary. Even when there was no need to occupy ICU/ICCU beds, patients continued to be kept there and were transferred out when new cases arrived, in order to keep these beds occupied and thus be earners all the time. The charges for ICU/ICCU care vary from area to area and from hospital to hospital. The minimum charges varied from Rs. 600 to Rs. 800 per day, and the maximum charges varied from Rs. 1,200 to Rs. 1,500 per day. The above charges include charges for the cot and and for the use of the cardiac monitor only. Extra charges are levied for the use of oxygen, defibrillator, ECG, laboratory tests, medicine charges, use of respirator and other gadgets as per the need. All catheters, syringes and disposables are charged extra, or replaced.

A specialist's fee depends on his whims or on the time of the visit. It could be somewhere between Rs. 400 and Rs. 1,000 per day. Each follow-up visit is charged at the rate of half the first visit. The minimum total expense per day could range anywhere between Rs. 2,000 and Rs. 3,000. With 85 per cent deficiency in every aspect of their services, the charges levied by the private ICU/ICCU units are very high, even by Indian standards. Except for some practical experience these nurses have no formal training, but pose as being knowledgeable. Moreover, they know nothing of critical care.

Such nurses and non-allopathic doctors form the backbone of these units and offer round-the-clock services. They learn by trial and error at the cost of the life of the patients, and are mechanical in their approach, and devoid of critical care concepts. The monthly salary of these nurses and RMOs could range from Rs. 1,500 to Rs. 2,000. Thus, the savings on salaries is substantial. The expected salary of a qualified nurse could range from Rs. 6,000 to Rs. 7,000 a month, and of a specialist on duty from Rs. 15,000 to Rs. 20,000 a month.

The data on mortality could not be obtained as no separate record was maintained specifying the number of ICU/ICCU deaths. In private nursing homes no system of medical auditing exists. Most of the deaths are accepted as recorded in death certificates.

The most effective outcome of an ICU/ICCU admission is when it is done for observation and monitoring and for timely diagnosis of life threatening situations, which may come up any time during the night or day. However, this concept of admission as a precautionary measure for high-risk cases is glaringly absent not only among the public but also among family physicians, specialists, and doctors running these set-ups. However, a reality check of these units tells us that the unqualified staff does not have the knowledge and the expertise for the diagnosis and treatment of these critically-ill patients, and obvious the outcome is death. In fact, the services of relatives is solicited for such jobs like sponging, giving medicines, giving bed-pans, feeding, and making beds. But the most deplorable part is that relatives are asked to take on the task of observing the monitor, and report changes in the cardiac rhythm or a deterioration in the condition of the patient and awaken the sleeping RMO and nurses and alert them.

All the 40 hospitals under study offered commission for referral. The percentage varied, the specialist also got a commission from the owner of the ICU/ICCU for a referral. The specialists in turn gave a commission for a referral to the family physician. Some family physicians had to be paid deposits ranging from Rs. 1,000 to Rs. 25,000 by the specialist and hospital. The accounts were settled subsequently, as per the total monthly receipts. The prevalént commission rate in Mumbai is 30 to 40 per cent in the eastern suburbs and 40 to 60 per cent in the western suburbs.

This commission put a heavy burden on the finances of these ICU/ ICCU units. This results in substandard services at highly inflated rates. The ethics of the doctors take a walk and the tendency is to extract more and more, very often wrongly. In all the 40 hospitals under study, the equipments available at the ICU/ICCU were mainly cardiac monitors, defibrillators, ECG machines, suction machines, oxygen cylinders and Ambu bags.

Table: 1: Analysis of equipments or gadgets (n = 40)

Equipment	Avail able	Not avail able	Equipment	Avail able	Not avail able
Central monitor	21	19	Holter monitor	02	38
Ventilator/ respirator	12	28	Generator	23	17
Central oxygen	08	32	Fire extinguisher	03	37
Pacing	16	24	Image intensifier (fluroscent)	-	40
Pulse oximeter	10	30	Central suction	03	37
2-d echo-cardiography	10	30	Arterial blood gas analyser	-	40
Infusion pump	03	37			

Only 21 out of the 40 units under study had a central monitor. The unit with one to three cots did not keep a central monitor. In six units the central monitor was located in the consultant's room, it was kept in the ward of the ICU/ICCU cubicles in 4 units, it was at the ICU/ICCU reception in 11 units, and 19 of them had no central monitors at all. Respirators were not available in 28 units, and certain cardiologist-owners were of the view that it was not required in an ICU. This view was indeed shocking!

In the event of a respiratory failure, they intubated the case with an endotracheal tube and started ventilation with an Ambu bag and transferred the patient in that moribund state to another Trust or general hospital to be put on a ventilator. One can easily anticipate the outcome of transferring such dying patients.

The pace maker facility was available in 16 hospitals. But in the absence of expertise to operate the instrument, which a specialist can only do, and who is invariably not present at critical junctures, it spells sure death for the patient. Moreover, life saving gadgets and equipments need a standby generator.

The fire extinguisher, the fluorescent image intensifier and the arterial blood gas analyser were not available in 37 of the 40 units. The equipment and gadgets were not periodically checked and serviced, and their proper functioning in routine or emergency use was doubtful. Although oxygen cylinders were there in sufficient numbers for direct use, or for supply to the central oxygen system, very often there was no oxygen in the cylinder, and simply the catheter or mask was placed on the patient symbolically. The central suction was available in three units. The facility and expertise to carry out the various procedures are mandatory requirements in an ICU/ICCU unit. The need for 24-hour surveillance by qualified and trained personnel cannot be over-emphasised.

The central venous line was used selectively, and often avoided, due to practical difficulties and lack of expertise; hence, in spite of the avability of special catheters in the units, it was often avoided. The most invasive procedures are avoided in the units, as it needs proper infrastructure, knowledge and qualification.

The facility of intubation by endotracheal tube was available in all units. However, when the need arose for intubation, it was neither available then nor in the correct size and number. Moreover, the specialist who could perform this endotracheal intubation--a life saving procedure—was not always available. Intercostal drainage facility was available and made use of but none of the other invasive and specialised procedures, such as intra-cranial pressure monitoring, was possible in these units.

Table: 2

Name of the procedures

Name of the procedures	**Available**	**Name of procedures**	**Available**
Central venous lines	4	Intercostal drainage	30
Swann ganz cathether	No	Intracranial pressure	No
Total parenteral nutrition	No	Bed side cardiac pacing	16
Invasive arterial blood pressure	No	Ventilatory support	7
Endotracheal intubation	36	Bedside bronchoscopy	No
Tracheostomy	16	Bedside dialysis	No

The specialists were of the opinion that fluroscopic facility and image intensifier were not needed and pacing was done under cardiac monitor control.

Other Facilities in ICU/ICCU units

Some units do not have a laboratory back up and therefore have to depend on laboratories outside their unit. Cardiac monitoring and minimum mandatory tests, such as frequent ECGs were not carried out as a matter of routine. No standard protocol or format for critical care in hospitals was followed. Each individual worked according to his own whims, and followed his own methods, which varied from admission to admission. Each specialist had his own visit schedules - the time of visits and number of visits - and fixed his own fee. One also observed that there was no uniformity of management, that no common platform of discussion and teamwork existed even when more than one specialist was involved in the management of cases.

It was also observed that in the middle of the night and at odd hours relatives had to run near and far to get drugs like streptokinase, t-PA, nitro-glycerine, urokinase, and they were often made to pay fancy prices by chemists who were also in league with these units. The facilities of cathlab for angiography and angioplasty were not available in any of these units.

Table: 3

Items	Not available	Available
Drugs of routine use	18	22
Drugs of emergency use	25	15
Streptokinase on premises	32	8
T-pa	40	Nil
Nitroglycerine	32	8
Heparin	32	8
Laboratory in premises for routine test for special test and blood enzymes	38	2
Recuscitation equipment and drugs on trolley properly stocked and checked	38	2
Blood bank on premises	39	1

The discussion with cardiologists, physicians, surgeons, anaesthetists and others who run such set ups agreed that these units could not be called ICU/ICCU at all. As stated earlier, there was a total absence of even the minimum standards required for general and critical care management in all the units, as also the absence of a set protocol, and of data recordings in a proper format. Originally put up for cardiac emergency, these set-ups are not suitable for the critical care of other categories of patients. The area for a single cot in an ICU unit is 50 to 70 square feet, which is extremely insufficient for emergency management in critical care. The available manpower for critical care management was inadequate for the number of cots that are there in the ICU. It was distressing to note that critical care had been delegated to unqualified nurses and non-allopathic (homoeopathic and ayuevedic) medical persons, projected as expert 'doctors' to the public, and thus cheating the public.

Doctors did not update their knowledge. No care was taken to provide facilities essential for patients, such as, telephone, refreshment, clean drinking water, clean linen, dust-proof adequate space, toilet, and washbasin, and a place for relatives to rest. In fact, dust and cobwebs were noticed in many units. Essential equipments, drugs and services, which were absolutely necessary, were not available. Ventilator, pacing intubation, essential life-saving drugs, laboratory for routine and specialised blood tests, and blood enzyme studies were not available in the premises at critical junctures. Visiting specialists did not attend to the cases as and when needed for such care, although they were aware that medical care was under the supervision of unqualified staff. The specialists totally lacked a holistic approach, needed in critical care, and were oblivious to the fact that a human being was not just an assembly of organs. There was no auditing of mortality by any agency. 2D echocardiography, pulse oximeter, image intensifier, portable sonography, central lines, Swan-Ganz catheter, blood gas analyser facilities, tracheotomy, prompt availability of routine and emergency drugs on trolley not available in most of the set-ups. In all the units no checking was undertaken for nosocomial infection.

Ambulance and heart-brigade facility from outside may or may not be available in time, causing risk to the life of the patients. Cuts and commissions existed in all the units. The minimum parameters to be monitored regularly are temperature, pulse, respiration and blood pressure, and even that was not done as routine, or as often as necessary. So was the case with routine investigations such as blood count, X-ray, chest, blood electrolytes, blood chemistry, and blood sugar. Moreover, detailed serum enzyme tests, CT-scan, MRI study were often postponed due to the lack of a holistic approach in the management.

The facility for invasive procedures was not available in most hospitals, though these patients could require it any time during their illness. This facility got inevitably avoided as it was not available or was delayed, and often the patient was transferred by ambulance in moribund conditions.

Discussion

The "Saving of Life" is the purpose of critical care admission. However, this very purpose was not served, as there was 'nothing' at all in any of these private ICU/ICCU units to project them as 'critical care units'. That "India is a poor and developing country" was merely an alibi to cover up all that was offered in the name of critical care. There was no justification whatsoever in offering such poor, substandard services to critically ill patients and charge them heavily for that. Whether due to design or ignorance, commercialisation or lack of respect for human life, the setting up of such 'Death Traps' in the name of private ICU/ICCU in its present form was deplorable, and be forthwith banned by one and all, be it by individual activism, medical council, various medical associations, and most effectively, by learned specialists and "intensivists" themselves. Legal action in its present form cannot be an effective remedy

In fact, the data presented and analysed clearly indicates the miserable health care provided by private ICU/ICCU hospitals, and that too at a tremendous cost. Economically, it is impossible to set up and run private ICU/ICCU hospital with 'maximally' minimum standards. The infrastructure and equipments needed even for that low standard will cost Rs one crore at least, besides monthly expenses of at least Rs one lakh. The reading of medical journals, attending medical conferences and workshops - both national and international, visiting medical stalls in conferences and holding high tech discussions are all meaningless when in reality these very medical experts themselves run private, substandard ICU/ICCU units.

For every hospital and nursing home a minimum standard should be laid down and which should be legally binding. Otherwise the lure of money will continue to allow the mushrooming of so-called intensive care units.

The present ICU/ICCU hospitals in Mumbai must recognise and adapt to the realities of available resources rather than permitting inadequate or inappropriate care, detrimental to the health and life of the public.

There is everything in a 'name'. When you name it ICU / ICCU hospital – CRITICAL CARE HOSPITAL – it should give that care. The very life of these unsuspecting unfortunates cannot and should not be allowed to be extinguished; by anyone at any time.

"What skill is there in deceiving those who put faith in us"

"What manliness is there in killing one who is sleeping in our lap?"

29

Violation of Citizen's Right in the Care of Tuberculosis Patients in India

Thelma Narayan

Introduction

Tuberculosis was recognised by the new government of independent India in 1947 as one of the country's biggest public health problems. Interventions were introduced in 1948. This formed part of the government's constitutional mandate and pledge to protect and promote the health and well being of its citizens. BCG vaccination within a vertical programme was the main strategy, with a focus on urban areas and children, among whom TB was then considered to be the major problem. With limited finances, it was felt that prevention was the best approach. Fortunately, indigenous research was initiated and supported by the government through the establishment of new institutional bodies, in order to understand the problem better.

Over the years, research findings challenged the then current assumptions and gave shape to the National TB Programme (NTP) in 1962. By this time, effective chemotherapy was available at low cost. Better drug regimens were developed by the 1970s. The functional unit of the NTP was the District TB Programme (DTP). BCG, early case detection, domiciliary chemotherapy, integrated with general health services, supported by district and state TB centres were conceptualised as the key strategic components. The NTP idea influenced TB control programmes globally through the World Health Organisation. Later, the world's largest controlled BCG trial in Chinglepet, India, found that the vaccine did not prevent adult pulmonary TB, and that it played no role in controlling disease transmission.

Infrastructure for the NTP at state and district levels began to be established, and training of DTP teams was undertaken. Major problems in implementation became recognised and reported by the government and other research institutions and bodies from the early 1970s. However, these findings and evaluation reports resulted in little change in action and performance.

Poor implementation has resulted in more than half a million deaths annually. Thus, from 1947, about 25 million people have died of a disease that has been curable at low cost from the 1960s. Many more millions suffer needlessly. The poor, at greatest risk, are most affected, having limited access to effective care. A proportion get functionally disabled due to advanced disease and a substantial proportion also become indebted due to the disease.

Understanding and Defining the Problem of Tuberculosis

Policy makers and planners conventionally define, and therefore understand the problem of tuberculosis within epidemiological, bio-medical, public health and programmatic parameters. This is necessary and important and these dimensions are outlined in the next paragraph. However, they are insufficient to bring about a change in practice or in implementation of the programme. Hence, they are unable to produce an impact on the preventable disease among the population.

Epidemiological dimensions of isease burden— Tuberculosis has been known and named in India as Rajya Roga, the king of diseases, since many centuries. The disease and its high rate of infection has been noted from the early 20th century. Before that it was reported to be more rare or infrequent.

A large proportion, about 30-52 per cent of the population gets infected. Only a small proportion of those infected succumb to the disease at some point of time. The disease in all its forms (lung and extra-pulmonary disease where other organs are affected) currently affects 1.6-2.2 per cent of the population. This is the disease prevalence. It is inclusive of 0.3-0.4 per cent of people suffering from sputum positive TB of the lungs who can infect others. Public health planners focus on diagnosis and treatment of this smaller sub-group of patients, with the hypothesis that the chain of transmission would be cut and the disease would be controlled. Patients with sputum smear negative, active pulmonary TB or with childhood or extra-pulmonary TB, being non-infectious and consequently not threatening society, receive cheaper, less effective drug regimens, though physically suffering as much or more. Justified by resource constraints, this policy is discriminatory and represents societal relations and state priorities.

The disease and infection prevalence rates increase with age and TB is largely an adult problem, with 8 per cent occurring in children. While disease prevalence is higher among poorer socio-economic groups, this fact does not receive any particular policy attention. Disease prevalence is lower among women than men. But women have less access to general health care, and hence, possibly to TB care. More young women in the reproductive age die of TB than of other causes.

Though declining, the mortality from this preventable and curable disease is still unacceptably high at 50-84/100,000.

Currently India has approximately 13.5-17 million TB patients of whom 3.6 million are infectious. In absolute numbers, more persons are affected now than in 1947. While this is due to demographic or population growth, it also indicates that control strategies and interventions have been ineffective.

TB is equally prevalent in rural and urban areas. With a predominantly rural population of 74 per cent, the TB problem is thus largely rural based. Patients are widely dispersed with roughly 10-12 patients in each village. This requires widespread basic health care services in order to make TB care available and accessible.

These epidemiological understandings and other findings are derived from several good quality research studies undertaken by government research institutions such as the National Tuberculosis Institute, Bangalore, the Tuberculosis Research Centre, Chennai, and the Indian Council for Medical Research. They countered the current thinking, which perceived TB as an urban problem and one of children, etc.

Public health and programming parameters— These include rates concerning case-finding, case-holding, default, relapse and treatment failure. The research bodies mentioned above and others have repeatedly and consistently reported gaps between expected performance and outcome (ICMR, 1975, ICORCT, 1988, GOI/WHO/SIDA, 1992). After 40 years of intervention into what was termed India's most important public health programme, only approximately 8-16 per cent of expected cases of TB receive complete treatment from the public health services annually (Radhakrishna, 1988). Case detection in 1987 was 1/4th the annual incidence of TB (ICORCI, 1998). This was too low for any significant impact on the problem. Only 27 per cent of those starting treatment made 12 or more monthly drug collections from 1982-86. Furthermore, poor functioning of the programme among those registered/treated is indicated by high fatality rates - 25 per cent in a district using short course chemotherapy (Datta et al, 1993), high ratios of prevalence to incidence, increasing proportions of chronic execrators and increasing drug resistance. Since the mid 1980s this scenario has been further compounded by IIIV-TB co-infection, rates of which are increasing. A review in 1992 stated that "the program is not having a measurable impact on transmission and appears to function far below its potential." (GOI/WHO/SIDA, 1992)

Policy process perspectives—The technical indices mentioned in 1.1 and 1.2, though crucially important, do not explore or reveal the reasons for the dismal scenario, or for the disparities and discrimination that exists within those affected by TB. It has been observed that techno-managerial approaches to TB control policies are insufficient to grasp important socio-political and policy process factors that influence and determine implementation (Narayan, 1998). Underlying epidemiological and public health indices are conflictual societal relations and interests, which surface in sectoral action and non-action. These include inadequate manufacture of TB drugs by pharmaceuticals despite indigenous availability of technology and expertise. Production meets market demands but not epidemiological need (ICSSR/ICMR, 1981), and government primary health centres and district TB centres chronically report inadequate and irregular drug supplies, preventing good chemotherapeutic practice. There has been a lack of research into newer TB drugs until the re-emergence of TB in 'developed' countries. Another factor has been the promotion of the growth of the private medical care sector, which dominates TB care with little regulation or standardization of diagnostic and treatment practices. Irrational prescribing practices for TB by private practitioners (Uplekar and Shepard, 1991), overmedication and over diagnosis of X-ray positive suspects, benefits the industry and providers. The poor are financially unable to complete treatment with the private sector.

Distressingly high rates of indebtedness have been reported among this impoverished group of patients (Uplekar and Rangan, 1996, Narayan, 1998). This pushes their families further into the cycle of poverty, which with the associated under nutrition and poor housing, is itself a breeding ground for TB.

Governmental neglect of the NTP is evident in the under-financing of the programme, which received only about 1.5 per cent of the Central health budget until a few years ago. Budgets below critical levels, with most of the expenditure on salaries and maintenance, rather than on effective services, are wasteful and counterproductive. Drug resistance in TB due to low funding, and the consequent irregular, poor quality of drug supplies is harmful as well as costly, besides violating the human rights of the patients and society.

In the absence of effective public sector services, 80 per cent of health care utilization occurs in the private sector for profit. Rough estimates suggest considerable national spending on TB, with gains accruing to the diagnostic and drug industries, and to medical professionals whose macro interests differ from those of the patients and that of public health (Narayan, 1998).

Weakness in state intervention is further evident in infrastructural gaps in the public health care system. For instance, the large proportion of vacancies in microscopists/laboratory technician's posts at primary health centres (PHC) makes diagnosis difficult. Frequent staff absentism, including those of doctors, and the rude behaviour towards patients, particularly the poor, also aggravates the situation. It has been found that the programme is the weakest at the PHC level, which was conceptualised as being the main interface between the majority rural population and the general health service with which TB care was integrated. This was the point closest to peoples' homes. The district TB centres, supposedly the technical backbone of the programme, are reduced to being curative centres for those living nearby. In the absence of adequate trained staff and vehicles, their more essential role of providing professional leadership and support through training, supervision, analysis of records and research is not performed. Poorly functioning and weak peripheral institutions serving the majority of the rural population reflect power relations in society, and comprise an important reason for poor implementation. Even here, better-off patients can access the private sector or the services of the government sector for a fee, exemplifying the stratification of the Indian society and the lack of entitlement of the poorest to essential health care.

This stands in sharp contrast to the Family Welfare programme, with its population control undertones, which received Rs. 65,000 million or 1.5 per cent of the total Ninth Plan Outlay (1992-97) as against the entire Health budget, which received 1.7 per cent of the total plan outlay. Another contemporary comparison is with the national AIDS programme, which in the early 1990s received 25 per cent of the central health budget though its epidemiological magnitude is much smaller than TB. The use of conditionalities and aid as leverage for policy change by multilateral and bilateral agencies is one of the factors responsible for this.

More broadly, support to the growth of an unregulated private sector for profit, including the pharmaceutical sector, has undermined the NTP and the public sector. Direct and indirect policies, such as, subsidies to medical education producing graduates for the private sector, support to capitation-fee medical colleges, allowing or turning a blind eye to private practice by government medical officers and others, have promoted the private sector. Thus, TB services were made available in the market. More powerful sections of the society, with the ability to pay, accessed these private services, reducing pressure on the public sector to perform.

Implications of Problem Definition on Strategies

It has been hypothesised that the way one understands the problem of TB influences the choice of intervention strategies (Narayan, 1998). This is illustrated in the table below.

TB and Society: Levels of Analysis and Strategies

Levels of Analysis of TB	Causal Understanding	Control Strategies
Surface phenomenon (medical & public health problem)	Infections disease/germ theory	BCG, case finding and chemotheraphy
Underlying cause (symptom of inequitable relations)	Poverty deprivation, unequal access to resources	Land reforms, social movements towards an egalitarian society
Basic cause (inter and intra-national relations)	Contradictions and inequalities in socio-economic and political systems at international, national and local levels	More just inter and intra- national trade, finance and political relations.

These are not either/or approaches. One needs to recognise that groups working at different levels are in solidarity with one another, and better linkages and alliances across sectors would be beneficial.

Another illustration is about the employment of strategies depending on the way in which an issue such as default gets understood. In one approach, patient-related failures and factors get stressed with an element of victim blaming, without adequately addressing health system failures, or the circumstances of deprivation and difficulty in which the person lives. This approach then focuses on patient-education and on supervised therapy to ensure compliance. This is justified on technical grounds of preventing transmission and development of drug resistance. Other approaches see default as also resulting from poor TB-case management, deriving from the systematic failures of health and related services. This approach would stress the need for increased funding, improved infrastructural functioning (with microscopes, microscopists, doctors, uninterrupted drug supplies, follow-up by health workers, management of concurrent illnesses/drug side effects/complications, etc), supportive supervision and humane attitudes and behaviour of health personnel towards patients. While theoretically an integrated approach is used, in practice, the second approach has been greatly neglected by the state sector in India. The experience of NGOs who have adopted these approaches shows much better success in terms of cure rates and patient satisfaction.

Impact of Implementation Gaps on Patients, Families and Society

Loss of life, often in young adulthood, disablement and indebtedness comprise the heavy price paid by patients and their families. This situation is particularly true for the poor. While the middle class and rich also get TB, they have access to early care and cure, and hence do not suffer these consequences.

The economic loss to patients, families and the nation is significant, while suffering is immeasurable. The economic costs of TB have been estimated at Rs 20,000 million a year through person hours of work lost (Ram Kumar, 1993). Indirect costs of treatment to affected families are high, including transport, food, costs of accompanying person, loss of economic productivity of the patient, and at least one other member of the family. These are larger than the direct cost of diagnosis and treatment (Narayan, 1998).

It is a reflection on the structure and priorities of our society that we spend millions obtaining the latest medical technology, even in government institutions, to diagnose relatively untreatable conditions, while resource constraint arguments are put forward to fund killer diseases like TB, which can be diagnosed relatively easily and cured. When one considers the amounts spent for sports extravaganzas and the defence of borders, the disparities become more stark and obscene. Somehow, the loss of half a million lives is not considered a national security problem calling for the best and urgent social defence. Some lives perhaps are more important than others.

Preventing Violence, Caring for Victims/Sufferers, and those Disabled by it

The magnitude of the human problem caused by TB, especially with its current co-infection status with HIV, is such that it is ethically imperative for all to respond in some measure. If morals do not convince, at least from a point of self-preservation, it is important. The spectre of drug resistant TB may touch anyone. The government sector has to be pressurised to perform with a sense of accountability. This is because the major source of funding of the government health services is from the taxpayer who is largely the common person, as indirect taxes form the major source of its income. Also, the government has now taken a large loan from the World Bank for the TB programme on which interest will be paid, also by the taxpayer. Besides, it is a Constitutional mandate. For NGOs, critical collaboration needs to be established with the government in which one's watchdog role and issue-raising capacity as citizens of the country need to be acknowledged. This should not be swamped over by playing the alternative service provider role, which is what may often be looked for. Government expertise, personnel and services need to be specifically focussed on the poor. While the role of the private sector is recognised, regulation of standards of care in maintaining accepted norms in diagnosis and treatment needs to be ensured. The public sector will have to be a major actor in what is still a major public health problem. It has to take the responsibility of ensuring implementation of its own strategy of early diagnosis and provision, and completion of effective treatment and supportive care for all forms of TB in partnership with the major stakeholders of the programme, namely the patients. This requires the strengthening and non-fragmentation of basic health care services through primary health centres in rural areas, and municipal corporation dispensaries and hospitals in urban areas. Additionally, social security and rehabilitation measures for advanced cases are required. More flexible, area-specific, community-based, humane approaches are required. These have proven to work in India and elsewhere. In spite of adverse economic conditions, countries like Cuba have achieved success in their TB control programmes.

We need to be alert regarding the functioning of the NTP, and supportive of TB work in whatever way we can. TB is also, in a way, a case study, and, much of what is said would be applicable to infectious diseases, and more importantly, to general health care services.

30

Family Welfare for Population Control : The State Sponsored Violence Against Women

Malini Karkal

The planet is getting polarised in demographic and economic terms. Developing countries experience problems with their population growth along with pervasive poverty. Demographic projections of population raise questions on the ability of the earth's carrying capacity to maintain people at an adequate standard of living. In spite of the overall improvement, there are wide variations in the quality of life of the people. High rates of population growth therefore certainly need to be contained. Thomas Malthus in 1798, exactly two centuries ago, had warned about maintaining the balance between population and food-supply. The population in these two centuries has grown sixfold—from one billion to six billion. Food available in the market is enough to feed all, and on this count, Malthus has been proved wrong. If people still go hungry, it is because of the absence of distributive justice in the prevailing social system. A similar situation prevails with respect to other resources.

The problem of having adequate resources is not necessarily a problem of the future. Many non-renewable and renewable resources are already being used in an unsustainable manner, and consumption is more than the earth can regenerate. Available information indicates that the economic inequity among people is very rapidly growing. A fraction of the world's people consumes disproportionate amounts of natural resources.

During the pre-independence period, national leaders active in movements for improving the life of the people in general, and those working for the welfare of women, such as the All India Women's Conference, had discussed the health problems faced by women and children. Some of the elite, who were exposed to Malthusian thesis on population, set up Neo-Malthusian Leagues on the lines of those functioning in England and Europe to warn people of the dangers of a large population. First, such League was established in 1929, in Chennai City. Similar leagues were established in Pune and Mumbai. However, the data available from the censuses has shown that the rate of growth of population was low. During 1911 and 1921 the population had actually declined from 252.1 million to 251.3 million because of high mortality. Health of the people was a major problem.

Professor R.D. Karve, who was the main motivator for the work of the League in Pune, was convinced that to improve the health conditions of the people, the conditions of women needed to be improved. He also realised that the poor conditions of women were both products of their neglect, and results of the problems such as high morbidity/mortality in society. To improve the conditions of women, among the issues he dealt with were, child marriages, widow remarriages, access to knowledge on sexual health, and availability of contraceptives to regulate child bearing. Dr Karve started a magazine named *Samaj Swasthya* that discussed issues of social well being. It advised men and women to use contraceptives so as to make men see reason in taking their share of responsibilities in parenting a child, and prevent unwanted pregnancies, thereby reducing incidence of induced abortions.

The Bhore Committee set up in 1943 to asses the health situation in the country, submitted its report in 1946. The Committee recommended the setting up of a health infrastructure that would promote preventive health through primary health centres (PHCs) spread to cover the entire population. Incidentally, the WHO Assembly held in Alma Ata in Russia, which suggested health for all, had the same principles for designing health services. The Bhore Committee had also suggested the need to control population. In the First Five-Year Plan (1951-56) provision was therefore made for a family planning programme. It is to be noted that similar work of guiding couples to regulate fertility, in order to liberate women from the cycle of pregnancies and deliveries, carried out in England by the Planned Parenthood Federation, was called Birth Control. The Indian programme, which aimed to improve the health of mothers and their children, was named Family Planning.

The programme came in operation in 1952. India became the first country to accept fertility regulation in the national programme. A sum of Rs 6.5 million was provided in the First Plan. The Programme was to provide services for care during pregnancies and during the post-natal period, and motivate couples for regulating fertility in the interest of the health of the mothers and their children. Advice and services for contraceptives, as well as research, was also included in the programme. Since family planning was a part of the health programme a cell was created in the office of the Director General of Health Services.

The number of family planning clinics rose from 50 in 1951 to 156 in 1956 at the end of the First Plan, and to 4,134 by the end of the Second Plan (1956-61). To assure that services were available to all the couples, the clinics were spread through the rural as well as the urban areas.

"Based on a mathematical model, Coale and Hoover showed that with the rate of growth of population experienced by India, in 30 years the per capita income would be lower by 40 per cent. Coale and Hoover's work stimulated interest in economic-demographic relationships of populations. A large number of Western writers highlighted the public sector costs in Third World countries of supporting rapidly multiplying numbers of people. Among the areas that were to be affected were education, health, job opportunities, income distribution, food, other resources, and effects on environment. Leff analysed data from 74 developed and developing countries, and concluded that higher fertility increases dependency burden and adversely affects saving rates." (Karkal Malini, 1989, pp. 24-25)

"In the light of the growing concern about the growth rates of populations, the General Assembly of the United Nations carried a resolution in December 1962 asserting the relationship between population growth and economic development. The Assembly authorised United Nations to take steps designed to provide assistance in population problem. Simultaneously, the Government of the United States of America issued a Statement of United States Policy. The Statement expressed concern about the population trends and offered to help other nations." (Karkal, 1989, ibid, p. 25)

The year 1965 saw famine in the country. There was shortage of rain the following year too. India experienced a food crisis, and the United States government discussed the food shortage and population situation in India. The U.S. government sent Dr Jack Lippes with the new method—Intra Uterine Device (IUD)—for females that he had developed. The method was promoted saying that it was simple, inexpensive, easy-to-use and 'one-time-motivation' method that could remain in situ for a long time.

In 1962 the Indian family planning programme set for itself a demographic goal. To achieve the goal the target was set at achieving a birth rate of 25 by 1972. K. Srinivasan says, "With the setting of the demographic goals for the programme, and achievements of these goals being made the responsibility of the health departments, the programme became entrenched in a HITTS model, i.e., health-department operated, incentive-based, target-oriented, time-bound and sterilisation-focused programme. In my view, 1962 was the beginning of the HITTS approach, which lasted until 1972 with varying degrees of emphasis on each of its components of involvement of health functionaries, change of incentives, targets, and the time-frame for the achievement of targets, leading to the 'coercive approach' during 1976-77." (Srinivasan K., 1998, p. 6)

"During the Third Plan (1961-66) the programme expenditure increased to Rs 248.6 million, 11 times more than the Second Plan. It was again raised to Rs 704.6 million, almost three times the expenditure during the five years of the Third Plan. Expansion of personnel at the PHCs and urban family planning centres occurred rapidly to pursue the HITTS model." (Srinivasan, 1998, ibid, p.6) The budget provision for family planning during the Fourth Plan was Rs 3150 million. "The infrastructure was considerably expanded and there was a strong desire on the part of the Government of India to resolve the population problem once and for all by intensifying on the HITTS model by organising vasectomy camps on a mass scale." (Srinivasan, 1998, ibid, p. 6)

In the camp-approach the staff of the local clinic motivated couples who gathered at a nearby place on an assigned date. The services of city doctors, who were perceived as professionals were made available at these camps. The financial incentives at the camps were larger than the normal ones. Group pressure and mass motivation worked at these camps to bring in a large number of individuals. The success of the camp depended on the ability of the organisers to collect people. The largest camp was organised in Ernakulam, in Kerala, in July 1971, where 6,26,913 men underwent vasectomy. (Krishnakumar S., 1974, 58-61)

"The law on abortion was liberalised to further reduce the birth rate. However, in spite of the promotion of terminal methods such as sterilisation, and making abortions easily available, the birth rate at the beginning of the Fifth Plan (1974-79) was 33 per 1000 population. It was therefore decided that the programme should be carried out more vigorously. The demographers who were responsible for estimating the number of couples that had to be 'protected' (from pregnancy), decided that the target for achievement during the Plan period should be 40 to 42 million couples. The number of couples who had been 'protected' during the Fourth Plan was 15 million. Obviously, the pressure on the staff and other government officials to meet the targets increased." (Karkal Malini, 1998, p.169-70)

"Till 1970, female sterilisation could be performed only during the post-partum period. However, to decrease the number of childbirths, a terminal method that ensured that the couple would have no more children was needed. This was vasectomy or the sterilisation of the male. In patriarchal societies it is never easy to get men to take the responsibility to ensure that family is not burdened and the health of women is not strained. Under these conditions, the men who could be operated upon were poor, especially from the rural and tribal areas." (Karkal Malini, 1998, ibid, p.168)

The then Prime Minister, Indira Gandhi, believed that there was a desperate need to control the size of the population. In her address to paediatricians, she said, "To bring down the birth rate speedily, to prevent the doubling of our population in a mere 28 years, we shall not hesitate to take steps which might be described as drastic." (Goverment of India, 1976)

"The family planning programme in India went through a traumatic phase during 1976-77. With the declaration of a state of Emergency in the country; a national target of 4.3 million sterilisation for the period from April 1976 to March 1977 was announced. The sterilisation programme was implemented with coercion, especially in the northern states where the achievements in earlier years were relatively poor. The brunt of this was borne by the poor, illiterate, lower castes, scheduled castes, and Muslims. Since the programme had become target-oriented, the staff was threatened with punishments, such as, stopping of their increment or cutting their salaries if they did not meet the targets given to them. During the Emergency, the abuse of clients and the implementers was widespread" (Karkal Malini, 1998, ibid, p.170). The number of sterilisation done during April 1976 and March 1977 was 8.26 million, more than the number done in the previous five years, and more than the number done at any time in any other country in the world. In spite of the excesses, the target of reaching the birth rate of 30 by the end of the Fifth Plan was not achieved.

Demographers supported the achievements of the sterilisation programme conducted during the Emergency. The means used to achieve the targets for reducing birth rate, and the impact on the lives of the common people, was none of their concerns. In spite of the strong evidence that mere reductions in birth rate could not assure better life for substantial proportions of the population, demographers argued for a demographic transition as an objective to be achieved at any cost. K. Srinivasan, a well-known demographer and ex-director of a World Bank project, ex-director of UN-GOI Institute for Population, and now the executive director of Population Foundation of India, praised the achievements of the coercive programme during the Emergency. Commenting on the slowing down of that programme due to strong national and international criticism, he said, "From a retrospective analysis it seems that India made a sacrifice in terms of delayed demographic transition, and possibly socio-economic development to safeguard her people's democratic rights. It is doubtful whether a compulsion in family planning programme can ever be implemented in India within the present political structure, or that centrally specified demographic goals can be imposed on the states" (Srinivasan K., 1995).

Srinivasan is not alone in providing moral support to coercive family planning programmes. There are other demographers who hold similar views. Among them is Ashis Bose, Founder Member of the Indian Association for the Study of Population. Bose says, "The main reason for the success of the Indonesian model is the excellent military-style logistic in running the programme. In India we have an overdose of democracy." (Bose Ashis, 1994) It is therefore not surprising that the population policy drafted by the committee chaired by the agricultural scientist, M.S. Swaminathan, and of which Bose was a member, had suggested the use of the army for implementing the Indian family planning programme.

The target of the programme so far was the birth rate. Seeing that in spite of implementing the HITTS model under the guidance of the demographers, the birth rate had not shown a reduction to the desired level the Sixth Plan aimed to reduce the family size to 2.3 with a net reproductive rate (NRR) of one, i.e., limitations on the number of daughters a mother was to have, and which was to be achieved by 1996. Obviously, the underlying logic of the goal of the Plan was to reduce the number of women - the child-bearers in the population. During the Sixth Plan (1980-85) an allocation of Rs. 10,780 million was made in the sector of family welfare, while the actual expenditure was Rs. 14,480 million.

Since the voluntary response to the programme was poor, and infant and child mortality continued to be high, and it was believed that acceptance of family planning depended on the survival of children, a programme of Child Survival and Safe Motherhood (CSSM) was started with funding from the UNICEF. All along, mothers and their children were considered together under the Mother and Child Health (MCH) programme in operation as a part of the normally provided health services. The new programme separated the mothers from their children, when the fact is that the health and well being of the children was dependent on the health and well being of the mothers.

Thus, the programme that was started with the objective of welfare of women and children became a population control programme with demographic goals, and its targets became the women. The mainstay of family planning now is sterilisation, and that largely of women. And to have a larger impact on the birth rate, interests are to sterilise women at young ages. The National Family Health Survey (NFHS) (International Institute for Population Sciences, 1995, National Family Health Survey 1992-93), which collected data from 99 per cent of the Indian population, reports that the TFR (average number of children a woman is estimated to bear) has declined from 5.1 in 1971 to 3.39 in 1992-93. This has been achieved by increasing the proportion of couples using contraceptives from 10 per cent in 1971 to 44 per cent in 1992. More significant is the fact that 84 per cent of the total users are using terminal methods such as sterilisation, and 88 per cent of the sterilised are females. The average age of the women among the sterilised is 26 years, and in Andhra Pradesh, Maharashtra and Karnataka it is as low as 24 years. It is also important to note that the majority of the sterilised have never used any temporary method before going for a terminal method, such as sterilisation. Thus raising doubts about women's role in the decision to accept the terminal method, and the methods used to promote population control.

The states of Bihar, Madhya Pradesh, Rajasthan and Uttar Pradesh are known as BIMARU states because of their lower acceptance of family planning and higher TFR. The NFHS however shows that irrespective of differences in TFRs, the number of children aged five is about 2.6 in all the states, including the BIMARU states. Further, the Registrar General of India reports that 37.3 per cent of the total deaths are of children under the age of 15. This percentage for Bihar is 41.5, for Madhya Pradesh it is 45.3, for Rajasthan it is 45.4, and for Uttar Pradesh it is 47.7. There is evidence that high mortality among the young is closely linked with the health of the mother and their status in society.

The NFHS also shows that every third child born in India is handicapped at birth as it is born with a weight of 2500 grams or less, and has not had opportunities for the full expression of the innate genetic potential for mental and physical development. The data also shows that order of birth does not make much difference to being born low-birth-weight, indicating that limiting number of births is not a solution to the problem of quality of the health of the children born. Such inequality is the cruellest form of social inequity.

Among the reasons for the high incidence of low-birth-weight babies, high infant and child mortality, as well as high maternal mortality is child bearing at a young age. Though there is a law prohibiting marriage of girls until the age of 18, NFHS data show that about 5 per cent of the girls in the age group of 10 to 14 are married. This percentage for the age group 15 to 19 is 36 (for rural areas it is 41 per cent). (The data is provided by C.P. Prakasam of the International Institute of Population Sciences, Mumbai).

The maternal mortality rate (MMR) in India is one of the highest compared to several other countries. The NFHS reports 437 deaths for rural and 397 deaths for urban areas per 100,000 mothers. This implies that 100,000 women die each year for causes related to pregnancy and childbirth. Other studies show that for loss of a mother due to death there are about 16 who suffer serious damage to their health. Post-mortems of mothers in a hospital in Mumbai, had shown that even when the death certificates showed that the mothers had died due to direct obstetric causes, a majority of them were diseased and had poor health. It is to be noted that 73 per cent of the deliveries take place at home and are conducted by traditional birth attendants (35.2 per cent), and by relatives or friends (29.5 per cent), and counting even the minimum ante-natal care only 68 per cent of the mothers received ante-natal care. (IIPS, 1995 pp. 239-240)

Analysing NFHS data, Raju (1997, p. 417) reports, "The analysis indicates that MCH services are probably reaching often to mothers who are potential cases for sterilisation. The reason seems to be that there is a lot more emphasis on achieving family planning targets, and MCH services have become a means to achieve the targets as these services form a part of the overall family planning programme."

Despite cuts in most areas of public expenditure, including health, the government's budget for family planning has increased from Rs 3,200 crore for the five-year period 1985-1990 to Rs. 1,000 crore for the one-year period 1992-1993. The UNFPA has increased its assistance from $52 million for 1985-90 to $90 million for 1991-95. By 1995, the population growth rate is to be reduced from 2.1 per cent to 1.76 per cent and the crude birth rates from 30.5 to 26.7 per 1,000 people. The use of contraceptives is to be increased from 43.3 per cent to 53 per cent. The USAID has given a financial assistance of $325 million for decreasing the total fertility and mortality levels, from 5.4 to less than 4, and increasing couple protection rates from about 35 per cent to 50 per cent by the year 2000. This is the largest foreign assistance for a programme on reducing population growth rates that the country has ever embarked upon.

Women's movement has gained considerable clout. The United Nations has now accepted an NGO forum as a part of its major conferences. At the 1992 Rio de Janerio conference on environment, and at the 1993 human rights conference in Vienna, women vehemently opposed the move to blame the problems on rate of population growth on them. Before the International Conference on Population and Development (ICPD), scheduled for 1994, women organised strong international networks that argued that the population control programmes were anti-poor and anti-women. They pointed out that the consumerist lifestyle of the 20 per cent of the world's population was not only creating shortages of resources but was causing irreparable damage to the environment.

The Program of Action (POA) of the International Conference on Population and Development (ICPD) officially condemned the practice of quotas and targets, and other ways of measuring the success of family planning programmes by the number of users of so-called "modern" contraceptive methods. POA stated, "Government goals for family planning should be defined in terms of unmet needs of information and services. Demographic goals, while legitimately the subject of government development strategies, should not be imposed on family planning providers in the form of targets or quotas for the recruitment of clients." India is a party to the decision. But the condemnation on paper has not brought about a change in behaviour.

There is a growing feminisation of poverty in India. Gender equity and free and informed choice for women are critical for the empowerment of women. There is a need to shift the burden of family planning from women and aim to foster a "culture of joint responsibility of the couple." There is also a need to emphasise the problem of women's status as such in the family, the dynamics of control, domination and violence against women that characterise the working of the family, and the lack of access to an independent income that most women suffer. Coercion and consent, economic power, and cultural authority within the family are used to secure and perpetuate the subordination of women. It is clear that unless a working model of the various types of families and their dynamics is posited, notions of 'joint responsibility' cannot simply be realised in practice, nor can policies and programmes be sufficiently sensitive to the needs and rights of women and children.

"The major focus of most human rights institutions that deal with procreation and reproduction is on family planning, which is equated to limiting births. The broader issues of health care, economic resources and social security, to say nothing of freedom from sexual abuse and discrimination, remain unaddressed, though these conditions are directly related to women's lack of reproductive self-determination. The policies that demand maternal and child health have essentially emphasised the child, while the women remain an unspoken word. The starting point of reproductive rights has to be health, well-being and empowerment of women. The approach to reproductive rights has to be women-centred and social change oriented, with an emphasis on health issues. This means top priority to reducing women's morbidity and mortality related to reproduction and sex, as well as maximising the conditions that make authentic choice—whether to have a child or not—possible. Under the present situation, such demands mean women walking a thin line between women's need for services and their need not to be controlled or coerced by them. A woman's self-determination is an intrinsic part of her dignity as a human being. Whether anti-natalist or pro-natalist, population policies tend to treat women's bodies as the instruments of male-dominated populationist ends." (Karkal, 1998, ibid, p.177)

Part-VIII
References and Notes

References and Notes

Abbott Jean, Robin Johnson, Koziol-McLain, Jean,. Lowenstein, Steven R (1995). "Domestic violence against women: incidence and prevalence in an emergency department population". Journal of the American Medical Association. 273, 22, pp.1763-1767.

Achutananadan V.S. (1991). "Prabandhavathranam" (Speech While Presenting a Paper) in Sudhakaran G. (ed) "Keralathile Karshaka Thozhilali Prasthanam, Varshikakosha Smaranika, 1990-91", Alappuzha: KERALA agriculture Workers Movement Golden Jubilee Celebration Committee.

Agnes, Flavia (1990). "Journey to Justice: Procedures to be followed in a Rape Case", Mumbai:Majlis, pp. 68.

Agnes, Flavia (1992). "Give us this day Our daily bread: Procedures and case laws on maintenance", Mumbai: Majlis, 1992, p. 170.

AKN Sinha Institute. "Home study course in training family physicians as counsellers for torture surviors" (Manual) by A.K.N. Sinha Institute of continuing medical and health Education and Research with support of United Nations Voluntary Fund for Victims of Torture and Endorsement of International Rehabilitation Council for Torture Victims and National Human Rights Commission, India.

Alexander K.C. (1968). "Changing Status of Pulaya Harijans of Kerala". Economic and Political Weekly, Vol. 2, Nos. 26-28.

Amnesty International (AI) (1988). "India: Allegations of Rape by Police: The Case of a Tribal Woman in Gujarat, Guntaben", London: AI, March (AI Index: ASA 20/04/88).

Amnesty International (AI) (1992). "Torture, Rape and Deaths in Police Custody," London: AI, 1992, p. 73.

Anonymous (staff reporter) (1991). "State has one lockup death every month" in The Independent, Mumbai, December 16.

Asian Age (1998). "Demolition sends infants to Cama". May 23,1998: 1&11.

Bakshi, P. M. (1994). "The Offense of Rape and Certain Medico-Legal Aspects". A study for the National Commission for Women.

Basu, S. K. (1990). "Health of the Underprivileged". New Delhi: WHO Regional Committee on South East Asia, 43rd Session, September18-24.

Bates, L., Redman S., Brown W., and Hancock L. (1995). "Domestic Violence Experienced by Women Attending an Accident and Emergency Department". Australian Journal of Public Heath, *19, 3, (June), pp. 293-299.*

Bewley, S., Friend, J., Mezey, G. (ed.) (1997). Violence Against Women. *London: RCOG Press.*

Bhatti, Ranbir Singh, "Sociocultural Dynamics of Family Violence," Bangalore: NIMHANS, (Mimeo, undated and unpublished).

Bhatti-Sinclair, K. (1994). "Asian Women and Violence From Male Partners", in Lupton, C., Gillespie, T. (ed.) Working With Violence. *London: Macmillan/British Association of Social Workers.*

Biennia, V., Harked, G., Nikon, J. (1981). "Leaving Violent Men". Bristol: Women's Aid Federation, 1981.

Biswas, Bipasa, Das, Sujit Kumar, et el. (1990). "Post Torture State of Mental Health: Report of a medical study on the delayed effects of torture on Nagas in Manipur". Kolkata: Drug Action Forum, West Bengal, July.

Bose, Ashis (1994). "Tamil Nadu's Successful Demographic Transition". Financial Express, *January 4.*

British Medical Association (BMA) (1998). Domestic Violence: A Health Care Issue? *London: British Medical Association.*

Buchanan, Francis (1807). A Journey From Madras Through the Countries of Mysore, Canara and Malabar. *Vol.2, London: T. Cadwell & W. Davis. p. 370.*

CEHAT (1998). "Notes on a Workshop on Sexual Assault of Women and Girl Children: Collection of Medical and Forensic Evidence". Mumbai: CEHAT. Unpublished.

Census of India 1991 (1992). "Final Population Totals". Serious 1, Paper 1 of 1992, Vol. 1. p. 15.

Central Bureau of Health Intelligence. Health Information India, 1992. *Government of India, New Delhi.*

Chentarassery, T.H.P. (1979). "Ayyankali". Thiruvananthapuram: Prabhatham Printing & Publishing Co. p.15, p. 82. (Qtd from Travancore Legislature Assembly Proceeding) and pp. 31-32, pp. 46-51, p.63.

Corbett, J. (1988). "Famine and Household Coping Strategies". World Development, *16(9): 1099-1112.*

CPDR (Committee for the Protection of Democratic Rights) (1990), "Another Lock Up Death : An Investigation". Mumbai: July.

D'Souza, Lalita (1998). "Manual and Kit for Collection of Medical and Forensic Evidence in Cases of Sexual Assault on Women," Mumbai: CEHAT.

Das, Arvind. "High Living and Low Thinking: Mandalisation of the Metropolitan Mind". The Times of India, *Mumbai.*

Das,. D. Jayadeva (1983). "Working Class Political in Kerala: A Study of Coir Workers". Thiruvanauthapuram: T. C Lilly Grace. p. 208.

Deepika *(Malayalam Daily) Kottayam, 1942.*

Deol, K.S. (1996). IPS, Unpublished study New Delhi.

Department of Health (DoH) (1997). On the State of the Public Health: The Annual Report of the Chief Medical Officer of the Department of Health for the Year 1996. *London: HMSO.*

Department of Health and Social Services (DHSS) (1997). Well into 2000: A Positive Agenda for Health and Well Being. *Belfast: Department of Health and Social Services.*

Department of Health and Social Services (DHSS) (1998). "Fit for the Future: A Consultation Document on the Government's proposals for the Future of the Health and Personal Social Services in Northern Ireland". Belfast: Department of Health and Social Services.

Dobash, R, Dobash, R.E. (1992). Women, Violence and Social Change. *London: Routledge.*

Dobash, R.E. and Dobash, R. (1979). Violence Against Wives: A Case against the Patriarchy. *New York: Free Press.*

Domestic Abuse Intervention Project (DAIP). Duluth, Minnesota (Undated).

Edleson, J, Tolman, R. (1992). Intervention for Men Who Batter. *London: Sage.*

Foucault, Michel (1977), Discipline and Punish, *Penguin Books, pg. 276.*

Foucault, Michel (1997). Il faut defendre la societe. Cours du Collège de France, 1976, *Gallimard, Paris.*

Franklin, C. A. (ed.) (1988). Modi's Medical Jurisprudence and Toxicology. *Twenty First edition. Bombay: N. M. Tripathi Private Ltd.*

Ganapathy, R. S. (1985). "On Methodologies for Policy Analysis," in Ganapathy, R. S. et al. (ed.). Public Policy and Policy Analysis in India. *New Delhi: Sage Publications.*

Geetha, S. and Swaminathan, M. (1986). "Nutritional Status of Slum Children of Mumbai: A Socio-economic Survey". Economic and Political Weekly *19(14): 896-900.*

Gelles, R., Pedrick – Cornell, C. (1990). Intimate Violence in Families. *London: Sage.*

George, Alex (1986). "Subjective Consciousness of Pulayas of Travancore". Unpublished. Ph. D. Dissertation, University of Bombay.

George, Alex (1987). "Social and Economic Aspects of Attached Labour in Kuttananad Agriculture". Economic and Political Weekly, *Mumbai, December 26.*

George, Alex (1990). "The Militant Phase of Pulaya Movement of South Travancore: 1884–1914", Work Document No.22. Amsterdam: Center for Asian Studies.

George, Alex (1997). "Issues in Equity of Access to Health Care in India", WHO. Workshop: Towards Equity-Health Sector Reform and Basic Health Services, Oslo, October 1-3, 1997.

Ghai, O.P. (1982). Essential Paediatrics, *New Delhi: Interprint.*

Gladstone, J.W. (1984). Protestant Christianity and People's Movements in Kerala; 1850–1936. *Thiruvananthapuram: Seminary Publications. p. 266.*

Glass, D (1997). All My fault: Why Women Don't Leave Abusive Men. *London: Virago.*

GOI/WHO/SIDA (1992). "Tuberculosis Programme Review: India 1992". Unpublished Report. GOI/WHO, New Delhi and Geneva.

Goverment of India (1976). "Background to the News. Mrs. Gandhi's Inaugral Address to the 31st Conference of the Association of

Paediatricians of India". New Delhi, Ministry of Information and Broadcasting, January 22.

Habib, Irfan (1963). Agrarian System of Moghul India (1556–1767), *Mumbai: Asia Publishing House. pp. 120–121.*

Heise, Lori L. (1994). Violence Against Women: The Hidden Health Burden, Washington DC, World Bank, pp.72.

Heise, Lori L., Raike, Alanagh, Watts, Charlotte H., Zwi, Anthony B. (1994). "Violence Against Women: A Neglected Public Health Issue in Less Developed Countries", Social Science Medicine, Vol. 39, No. 9, pp. 1165-1179.

Hester, M, Radford, L (1996). Domestic Violence and Child Contact Arrangements in England and Denmark. Bristol: Policy Press.

Home Office (1995). Don't Stand for It. Inter-Agency Co-ordination to Tackle Domestic Violence. *London: Home Office.*

Hoof, L. (1990). Battered Women as Survivors. *London: Routledge.*

ICMR (Indian Council of Medical Research) (1975). "A Review of the National Tuberculosis Programme". Report of the ICMR Expert Committee. New Delhi: ICMR.

ICORCI (Institute of Communication, Operations Research, and Community Involvement) (1988). "In-depth Study on National Tuberculosis Programme of India". Unpublished Report for GOI. ICORCI, Bangalore.

ICSSR/ICMR (Indian Council of Social Science Research and Indian Council of Medical Research) (1981). Health for All: An Alternative Strategy. Indian Institute of Education. Pune.

IIPS (International Institute of Population Sciences) (1995). "National Family Health Survey: India", pp.239-240.

Indian Medical Association (IMA) (1995). "Report on Knowledge, Attitude and Practice of Physicians in India Concerning Medical Aspects on Torture". New Delhi: IMA, 1995, Pg.24.

Iyer, Aditi, Jesani, Amar (1995). "Women in Health Care: Auxiliary Nurse Midwives", Mumbai: Foundation for Research in Community Health, pp. 159.

Jejeebhoy, Shireen (1998). "Wife-beating in Rural India: A Husband's Right?" Economic and Political Weekly. 33 (15). April 11. Pp. 855-62.

Jejeebhoy, Shireen and Rebecca, Cook (1997). "State Accountability for Wife-Beating: The Indian Challenge." The Lancet. Women's Health Supplement. (March).

Jesani, Amar (1995). "Violence and Ethical Responsibility of the Medical Profession." Medical Ethics, Vol. 3, No. 1, January-March, pp. *3 5.*

Jesani, Amar, Alyosius, D'Sa, Alphonse, Mary (1993). "Bombay Riots: January 1993". Mumbai: Solidarity for Justice, Pg. 180.

Jose, N. K. (1982). Pulaya Lahala. *(Malayalam). Kottayam: Prakasam Publications. p. 139.*

Joseph, Sherry. "Emerging Gay Movement in India: A Liberal-Conservative Movement" in Balachandran and Baalagaopal (ed): The Indian Closet: 'In' and 'Out*', University of Illinois Press, USA, (forthcoming).*

Judical Department Documents of Travancore (JDDT) (19909, 1914). English Records Section, Kerala Govt. Secretariat, Thiruvananthapuram.

Kabir, M., Krishnan, T. N. (1992). "Social Intermediation and Health Transition: Lessons from Kerala". Harvard University-NCAER Seminar, Health & Development in India, New Delhi, January 2 – 4, 1992, Qtd. from cover file No. 3181, 1894, Kerala State Archives, Thiruvananthapuram.

Kamalasanan, N. Kuttanadum (1993). "Karshaka Thozhilali Prasthanavum". (Kuttand and the Agricultural Labour Movement) Kottayam: D.C. Books. p.45.

Karkal, Malini (1985). "How the Other Half Dies in Bombay". Economic and Political Weekly, August 24.

Karkal, Malini (1989). "Can Family Planning Solve Population Problem?" Mumbai: Stree Uvach Publication, pp.24-25

Karka,l Malini (1998). "Family Planning and the Reproductive Rights of Women" in Lakshmi Lingam (ed.) Understanding Women's Health Issues: A Reader. New Delhi: Kali for Women.

Khanna, Shamona (1992). "Gay Rights". The Lawyers. June.

Knight, Bernard (ed.) (1997). Simpson's Forensic Medicine. *Eleventh edition. London: Arnold.*

Koss, M.P., Heise, L.L., Russo, N. (1994). "The Global Health Burden of Rape". Psychology of Women Quarterly. 18

Krishnakumar, S. (1974). "Ernakulam's Third Vasectomy Camp Using the Camp Approach". Studies in Family Planning, Vol. 5, No.2, February, pp.58-61.

Kruegar, R.A. (1994). "Focus Groups". Second Edition, New Delhi: Sage Publications.

Kulkarni, Sudha, Jesani, Amar, D'Souza, ///Lalitha(1998). "Investigation Report: Sexual Assault of a Deaf Mute Juvenile in Observation Home, Umerkhadi, on September 21, 1997" Mumbai: Forum Against Child Sexual Exploitation (FACSE), February 1998, pp 11.

Kumar, Dharma (1965). Land and Caste in South India. *London: Cambridge University Press, pp. 31–34.*

Logan, William (1981). The Malabar Manual. *Thiruvananthapuram: Charithram Publications (Reprint),. pp.180 –182.*

Mahajan, Madhurima A. (1995), Family Violence and Abuse in India, *New Delhi: Deep and Deep Publication, pp. 178.*

Malayala Manorama *(Malayalam Daily), Kottayam, 1901, 1909.12.*

Mama, A. (1989). "The Hidden Struggle: Statutory and Voluntary Sector Responses to Violence Against Black Women in the Home". London: London Race and Housing Unit.

Mann, J, Gruskin, S. (1997). The 2nd International Conference on Health and Human Rights: Bridge to the Future in Health Human Rights, Special Issue, 1997: 2 (3): 1-3.

Mateer, Samuel (1883). Native Life in Travancore. *W H Allen & Co. Pall Mall, South West. pp.41, 58.*

"Mathura Rape Case" (1979). SC 185. AIR

Mayhew, P., Aye, Maung N., Mirrless-Black, C. (1993). "The British Crime Survey of England and Wales 1992". Home Office Research Study 132. London: HMSO

Mayhew, P., Mirrless-Black, C., Percy, A. (1996). "The British Crime Survey England and Wales 1992". Home Office Statistical Bulletin, Issue 19/96. London: Home Office.

McLeer, Susan V., and Rebecca, Anwar (1989). "A study of Battered Women Presenting in an Emergency Department". American Journal of Public Health. *79, 1, pp. 65-66.*

McUlloch, Malcom, Chris, Jones, John, Nailey (1995). "Post Traumatic

Stress Disorder Turning the Tide Without Opening the Floodgates". Medical Science Law. *Vol. 35 No. 4 Pp 287-293*

MFC (Medico Friend Circle), YUVA, Women's Centre et el. (1990). "The Jogeshwari Rape Case- A Report". Mumbai: MFC.

Nandy, Apurba (1995). Priniciples of Forensic Medicine. *Kolkata: New Central Book Agency.*

Narayan, T. (1998). "A Study of Policy Process and Implementation of the National Tuberculosis Control Programme in India". Ph. D. thesis, London University

Nathan, Tobie (with Alain Blanchet, Serban Ionescu and Nathalie Zajde) (1998), "Psychothérapies", Paris, Odile Jacob, p. 96.

National Crime Research Bureau (1997). "Crime in India". New Delhi: Government of India, Ministry of Home Affairs.

Olson, L., Anctil C., Fullerton L., Brillman J., and others (1996). "Increasing Emergency Physician Recognition of Domestic Violence." Annals of Emergency Medicine. 27, 6 (June), pp. 741-746.

Ommen, T. K. (1978). Doctors and Nurse: A Study in Occupational Role Structures, Mumbai: MacMillan

Pahl, J. (1985). Private Violence and Public Policy. *London: Routledge.*

Patel, Vibhuti (1998). "Campaigns against Gender Violence (1977-1993)" in Kudchedkar, Shirin and Alissa, Sabina (1998) (ed.) Violence Against Women, Women Against Violence. *Delhi: Pencraft International.*

Patton, M.Q. (1990). Qualitative Evaluation Methods, *London: Sage Publication.*

Physicians for Human Rights (1991). "Medical Testimony in Victims of Torture". Boston: Physicians for Human Rights.

Prasad, Shally (1996). "The Medico-Llegal Response to Violence Against Women in India: Implications for Women's Citizenship". Paper presented at the international conference on Violence, Abuse and Women's Citizenship, Brighton, UK.

Radhakrishna, S. (1998). "Direct Impact of Treatment Programme on Totality of Tuberculosis Patients in the Community". Ind. J. Tub. 35, 110.

Raju, S. (1997). "Maternal and Child Health Services". The Indian Journal of Social Work, *Volume 58, Issue 3, July, p.417.*

Ram Kumar, E.R. (1993). June 5-11. The Illustrated Weekly of India, Mumbai.

Ramaseshan, Geeta (1998). "Treating Terrors of Torture". The Hindu, April 19, Sunday Magazine.

Ranjana, Kumari (1989). Brides are Not for Burning. Radiant Publishers. pp 29-30.

Rao, Sathyanarayana, Rao, Vasumathy, et al. (1994). "A Study of Domestic Violence in Urban Middle Class Families", Mysore: Department of Psychiatry, J. S. S. Medical College and Hospital, (mimeo, unpublished).

Reddy, K.S. Narayan (1997). The Essentials of Forensic Medicine and Toxicology. *Sixteenth edition. Hyderabad: K. Suguna Devi/Medical Book Company.*

Richardson, J. and Feder G. (1996). "Domestic Violence: A Hidden Problem for General Practice". British Journal of General Practice, *46, 405 (April), pp. 239-242.*

Rustamji, K. F. (1992). "Passion of the Fanatic: The Government's Response has been a Confused One" in The Afternoon Dispatch and Courier, *Mumbai, February 18.*

Saradamani, K. (1980). Emergence of a Slave Caste: The Pulayas of Kerala. *New Delhi: Peoples Publishing House. pp.93 – 94, 147 – 48.*

Schornstein, S. (1997). Domestic Violence and Health Care. *London: Sage.*

Scottish Office (SO) (1998). Working Together for a Healthier Scotland. *Edinburgh: Stationery Office.*

Secretary of State for Health (SSH) (1998a). The New NHS: Modern, Dependable. *London: Stationery Office.*

Secretary of State for Health (SSH) (1998b). Our Healthier Nation; A Contract for Health. *London: Stationery Office.*

Secretary of State for Scotland (SSS) (1998). Designed to Care: Renewing the National Health Service in Scotland. *Edinburgh: Stationery Office.*

Secretary of State for Wales (SSW) (1998). NHS Wales Putting Patients First. *Cardiff: Stationery Office.*

Sharma, Rajeev Lochan (1991). "The Communal Virus Among Doctors", in Health for the Millions, *June. Pg. 9-11.*

Shetty, Harish, Chhabria, Anjali (1997). "Bombay Riots: A Case Study with an Emphasis on Psychosocial Consequences" (rough draft), presented at the national workshop on "Psycho-Social Consequences of Disaster," December 4-6. NIMHANS, Bangalore (Organised jointly by NIMHANS, NCDM, SUPPORT and OXFAM).

Shivashankarappillai, Thakazhi (1985). "Randitangazhi" (Two Seers of Grain). Kottayam: National Book Stall. p.42.

Sidel, V. W. (1986). /// title of article????///Quoted in the new BMA book on human rights and originally published in The New Physician, *March*

Sofat, Rajesh, Saxena, D.K., Siddiqui, Md. Najeeb (1991). "When Falsehoods Breed Their Kind", in Health for the Millions, June. pp. 2-6. Also see, Sofat, Rajesh, Saxena, D.K., Siddiqui, Md. Najeeb (1991). "A Report: An Inquiry into the Causes and Forces Behind the Allegations of Massacre of Hindu Patients by Muslim Doctors in JNMC, Aligarh, which Flared up Aligarh Riots in December, 1990", New Delhi: Delhi Medicos' Front, January.

Sohlberg, D. (1993). "Care and Rehabilitation of Rape, Torture and Other Severe Traumas of War in the Republic of ex-Yugoslavia".

Solidarity for Justice (1991). "Human Rights Issues Emerging from Investigation into the Murder of Sr. Sylvia and Sr. Priya". Mumbai: Solidarity for Justice.

Sommer, A., Tarwotjo, I., Hussaini, G., and Susanto, D., (1983). "Increased Mortality in Children with Mild Vitamin A Deficiency". The Lancet, ii: 585-8.

Southball Black Sisters (SBS) (1993). "Domestic Violence and Immigration Law: An Urgent Need for Reform", in Home Affairs Select Committee Report on Domestic Violence. Volume 2: Appendix 9. London: HMSO.

Srinivasan, K. (1995). Regulating Reproduction in India's Population: Efforts, Results and Recommendations. New Delhi: Sage Publication.

Srinivasan, K. (1998). "Population Policies and Programmes Since Independence: A Saga of Great Expectations and Poor Performance". Demography India, Vol. 27, Number 1, January to June.

Stevens, KLH (1997). "The Role of the Accident and Emergency Department", in Bewley, S., Friend, J., Mezey, G. (ed.) Violence Against Women. London: RCOG Press.

Thadani, Giti (1991). "Giti Thadani – Independent Lesbian Researcher". Interview with Lesbia magazine reprinted in Shakti Khabar, Issue 14.

Thapar, Romila. "Social Mobility in Ancient India With Special Reference to Elite Groups". Ancient Indian Social History: Some Interpretations, Orient Longman, New Delhi, p. 180.

The Lancet *(1998). "Standardising the Approach to Rape in the EU".* The Lancet. *351 (9096)*

*Unni, Raman K. (1975). "Source of Agricultural Labour in Kerala: Some Social Perspectives" in Nair, Balakrishna N. (ed.) "*Culture and Society: A Festschrift to Dr. A. Aiyyaappan*", Delhi: Thompson Press (India) Ltd, Delhi. Pp.231.*

Uplekar, M.W., Shepard, D.S. (1991). "Treatment of Tuberculosis by Private General Practitioners in India". Tubercle. *72, pp. 284-290.*

Uplekar M.W., Rangan S. (1996). "Tackling TB: The Search For Solutions". Mumbai: Foundation for Research in Community Health.

Venkatratnam, R. (1979). "Medical Sociology in an Indian Setting," Mumbai: MacMillan.

Walker, I.E. (1979). The Battered Woman. *New York: Harpers and Row.*

Weller, Malcolm P.I. (1985). "Crowds, Mobs and Riots". Medical Science Law, *Vol. 25, No 4, pp. 295-303.*

Wilson M., Daly M. (1988). Homicide. *New York: Aldine de Gruyter.*

World Bank (1993). World Development Report, 1993: Investing in Health, *Oxford: Oxford University Press.*

World Medical Association (WMA) (1996). "Declaration on Family Violence". Adopted by the 48th General Assembly. South Africa: World Medical Association.

Index

E